"*A Hitchhiker's Guide to Jesus* is a wonderful travel guide for pilgrims perplexed by the multiple maps hawked by recent scholarship. But it is also an invitation for homebound believers to join a journey of discovery to the mysterious places where history meets hope. Bruce Fisk is a wise and imaginative tour guide, and this book will open new angles of vision for readers seeking to investigate the path of Jesus."

—**Richard B. Hays**, Duke University Divinity School

"Bruce Fisk has possibly written the most creative, fascinating, and informed book on the Gospels in a generation. My students will love this book. Think Gerd Theissen's *Shadow of the Galilean*, but in this case the narrator isn't a first-century grain merchant but a hookah-smoking college student named Norm. Norm is an honest inquirer who goes in search of the realities behind the Gospels and all along trades correspondence with his liberal professor. The crisp narrative and the theological points Fisk scores are delicately and effectively knit together. In countless cases, I found myself amused and impressed with how Fisk could illustrate things. 'Genius' could well describe many of the pages in the book. Fisk is a first-rate scholar as well as a brilliant communicator. Every New Testament teacher owes it to his or her students to consider this as a fresh new text on the Gospels."

—**Gary M. Burge**, Wheaton College

"With warmth, wit, and penetrating insight, Fisk writes for all who find themselves fascinated by the enigmatic prophet from Nazareth yet unwilling to settle either for the naive certainties of 'simple faith' or for the latest 'assured results' of biblical criticism. *A Hitchhiker's Guide to Jesus* provides no pat answers, but in the spirit of faith seeking understanding, it compellingly poses all the right questions, setting the quest for Jesus in its proper context—the search for meaning in a world of beauty and strife, love and loss."

—**Ross Wagner**, Princeton Theological Seminary

"This is really three books in one. It is a (very hip) college textbook written by an expert: an introduction to New Testament criticism, including the quest for the historical Jesus, the synoptic problem, and so on. It is also a kind of handbook to travel and politics in modern Israel. And finally, it is a novel with a protagonist on a personal quest for a faith that will hold up in the face of honest questions. I read an early draft of a few chapters of Fisk's book and was captivated, but I wondered if he could pull off all three of these books. He did, and what a satisfying read!"

—**Bruce Hindmarsh**, Regent College

"Students often find the academic study of the Gospels disorienting as they discover a previously unexplored world of literary, historical, and theological questions opening up before them. In *A Hitchhiker's Guide to Jesus*, Bruce Fisk proves himself a reliable guide—knowledgeable, candid, steady, and witty—through this territory. He takes no shortcuts or easy paths as he travels with his readers in the quest to discover faith in Jesus that takes intellectual questions seriously."

—**Marianne Meye Thompson**, Fuller Theological Seminary

"This volume introduces students to New Testament scholarship by telling them a story—a lively romp that combines travelogue with quest narrative, spun in a style sparkling with wit and replete with idioms of the Facebook generation. Along the way, we are introduced to the key issues that occupy modern scholars, and we discover why those issues would matter to people in the world today, including contemporary college students. This is definitely a creative way of granting students access to modern and postmodern fields of New Testament study."

—**Mark Allan Powell**, Trinity Lutheran Seminary

"I've never seen (nor imagined!) anything like this book. Following trails with many twists and turns, readers traverse the territories of biblical scholarship, Judaism, Greco-Roman religion, and the Christian tradition in a journey of personal and spiritual reflection. It's an expedition that takes us to a deeper understanding of Scripture and Jesus Christ. Fisk has inaugurated a new genre in biblical studies that deftly combines academic study with the human experience. Readers will love it; scholars will wish they'd written it."

—**Kenton L. Sparks**, Eastern University

A
Hitchhiker's
GUIDE
to Jesus

**Reading the Gospels
on the Ground**

Bruce N. Fisk

Baker Academic
a division of Baker Publishing Group
Grand Rapids, Michigan

Published by Baker Academic
a division of Baker Publishing Group
P.O. Box 6287, Grand Rapids, MI 49516-6287
www.bakeracademic.com

Printed in the United States of America

Library of Congress Cataloging-in-Publication Data

Fisk, Bruce N.
    A hitchhiker's guide to Jesus: reading the gospels on the ground/Bruce N. Fisk.
      p. cm.
    Includes bibliographical references.
    ISBN 978-0-8010-3606-4 (pbk.)
    1. Bible. N.T. Gospels—Criticism, interpretation, etc. I. Title.
  BS2555.52.F57 2011
  226′.06—dc22
                                                        2010051710

12   13   14   15   16   17   7   6   5   4   3   2

Contents

Author's Preface

This is the story of Norm, a precocious college graduate, who journeys to the Land called Holy to learn whether he can follow Jesus and study him at the same time, and whether curiosity will make him a better disciple, or no disciple at all. Norm is a figment but his predicament is real. Indeed, it's *norm*al—especially among students who have read their way into the world of religious studies, a world where faith is often suspect, where ancient texts are fodder, where final answers are elusive, and where scholars' portraits of Jesus hang audaciously in the gallery alongside those of the four evangelists. The tale of Norm's pursuit, over land and Gospel, does not presume to resolve the big questions about Jesus. It simply wonders whether asking them might be a sacred exercise in faithful following.

The thing about Norm is that he refuses to choose between curiosity and conviction. He feels no impulse to become the Christian intellectual who must suspend his faith when he goes to work. But neither can he be the unreflective enthusiast who must whistle in the dark when doubts assail. The course Norm charts lies between the two, toward something we might call *vigilant trust*, which turns out to be more compelling to him and more sustaining than either agnosticism or certitude.

Many of Norm's exploits are adapted from my own (mis)adventures in the Middle East. Others are made up. I leave it to the reader to decide when history stops and legend begins, though I predict that separating the two, like separating Jesus from the evangelists, will prove more challenging than one might expect. As for Norm's close encounters with modern scholars, they are, each one, entirely fabricated. I have shamelessly placed words in the mouths of contemporary figures like Dale Allison, John Crossan, James Dunn, Bart Ehrman, Scot McKnight, John Meier, Ben Meyer, Jonathan Reed, and Tom Wright. These remarks are, I suggest, the *sorts of things* they might have said under the circumstances. I will be disappointed if I have misrepresented their ideas and would urge readers to consult their works directly to see for themselves.

It is in the nature of story to be open, unfinished, even ragged.[1] Some readers may find the openness of this particular story unsatisfying. In one place Norm knows what he thinks. In another he is frustratingly indecisive. Here his convictions are clear. There he peers into mist. Even at the end, profound questions remain. The unevenness of Norm's quest is not, however, merely a function of literary genre; we all see through a glass darkly, and Norm is no exception.

I would be delighted if this book sparked an overdue conversation or two—between pastor and professor, parish and academy, congregation and classroom. Each side has words the other needs to hear. Academics need not sheathe the sword of biblical criticism if they will but acknowledge the dullness of the blade. Believers need not fear the historical quest for Jesus; they should join the hunt as an act of discipleship.[2] The church should not shun voices from the ivory tower; like John's from the river, they call us to repent of all efforts to fashion Jesus in our image. At the same time, interpreting Scripture is necessarily a communal, churchly activity; it is a collective act of theological imagination, not a solo exercise in discourse analysis.[3]

When a book takes too long to write, the list of people to thank runs long as well. I am rich with friends and colleagues whose lives have taught me so much of what it means to be at once relentlessly inquisitive and rigorously faithful. Those to whom I am particularly indebted include Charles Farhadian, Tom Fikes, Richard Hays, Bruce Hindmarsh, Wayne Iba, Rev. Don Johnson, Jon Lemmond, Marilyn McEntyre, Scot McKnight, Dwight Peterson, Rev. Allan Poole, Brian Schultz, Christopher Stanley, Marianne Meye Thompson, Isaac Villegas, J. Ross Wagner, Jonathan Wilson, Telford Work, and Bishop N. T. Wright.

A number of students have read drafts of this book or discussed its ideas while hiking with me across the Middle East. Deepest thanks to fellow trekkers Cory Anderson, Nick Baer, Tyler Baldridge, Andrew Corkill, Ryan Dalbey, Steven Denler, Stephen Dickson, Lauren DiSalvo, Susanna Douglas, Amanda Elliott, Katrina Falde, Jenna Fikes, Morgan Gillaspy, Darelle Good, Graham Hamner, Wesley Hargrove, Elliott Haught, Derek Jones, Dustin Jones, Rita Jones, Alex Kincaid, Matthew Kletzing, Daniel Lew, Elizabeth MacRae, Jesse Matthews, Travis McClain, Tim McInerney, Kristen Mezger, Peter Neuenschwander, Flavia Onufrei, Nicholas Pope, Kathryn Robison, Andrew Schwemmer, Taisiya Skovorodko, Cassie Strange, Brett Stuvland, Jay Visbal, Anne Walker, Jake Werley, Johanna Willis, and Jessica Zeuhlsdorf, and to my three children, Benjamin, Alison, and Donovan Fisk. Their companionship made my load lighter; their questions kept me up at night; their insights made the final draft better and (mercifully) shorter. Among them I must single out Rita Jones, who pressed me hardest to rewrite, to "show, not tell," to end each paragraph on "strong detail." Not only did she make me a better writer, but she has also penned all of Norm's doodles and sketches. Rita, thank you.

Westmont College, where I have been fortunate to teach as this book took shape, kindly underwrote several solo trips to the Middle East. Without their support Norm would scarcely know the Med from the Dead. Thanks also to David Neunuebel for his generous support and his passion to see a just peace come soon to the peoples of Israel and Palestine. Jim Kinney, editorial director of Baker Academic, has been unaccountably patient and encouraging to me over too many years. He would be most grateful if you would buy this book.

Photos, if not taken by me, are kind gifts from Cory Anderson, Nick Baer, Andrew Corkill, Wes Hargrove, and Tim McInerney. The bibliography was ably prepared by Julie Darcey.

I happily dedicate this book to my parents, Rodney and Alison (d. 2003), and to my wife Janice. The dinner table of my youth was a haven for struggling believers and emerging intellectuals. Mom and Dad listened well, withheld easy answers, and wisely released their kids to explore the edges of their faith. My wife Jan, herself a busy professional, generously read through multiple drafts, posing thoughtful questions, extending timely encouragement, and rescuing me from many an awkward phrase. Her sustained belief in this project was powerful incentive to get it right, but also to get it to the publisher. Mom, I miss you dearly. Dad and Jan, thanks for walking beside me all these years.

A Brief Word from Norm the Elder

So much has happened in the eight years since my first pilgrimage to the Middle East. I returned to watch my mother die and to enroll in graduate school, where I read my way to two degrees in religion. Along the way I got married, bought a motorcycle, and landed my first teaching job—a junior post at a small liberal arts college on the West Coast—which means I now get paid to guide students through the same "theological puberty" that once afflicted me.

You can thank my students for persuading me to publish the book in your hands. It's a chronicle of my audacious Jesus quest, my attempt to hitchhike simultaneously across Gospels and land in search of the truth about the Galilean. These students of mine seem to think others would enjoy following my trek. I hope they are right.

I tried to preserve the feel of the original journals as much as possible, though I did fix a few howlers and insert some headers. Okay, and I added an extra paragraph here or there when the remarks of Norm the Younger were cryptic or confusing. So if young Norm suddenly seems way too smart, it may be me. I've also added endnotes and a reading list so that if any of you should be as zealous now as I was then, you'll have resources to carry on.

My hope is that Norm's story will help other young hitchhikers, like you perhaps, to discover the wonder of humble faith, welcome the companionship of honest doubt, accept the limits of historical knowledge, and celebrate the holy chaos of the Christian tradition. If Norm's expedition inspires you to chart your own course toward Jesus, I wish you joy in the journey and great conversations along the way.

CHAPTER 1

Between Heaven and Earth

In which a German ghost and a Roman aristocrat inspire Norm to embark on a dangerous quest.

Anyone who doesn't know how to fasten a seat belt is either an idiot or an alien. After sprinting for the gate and scrambling up the jetway, I was in no mood for the perky flight attendant. Even though Guilder had warned that El Al security would take me aside, I was still annoyed when they emptied my pack, swiped each item for explosives, and made me drop my pants.

"Wine, beer, and cocktails are complimentary in first class."

The 32B on my boarding pass meant I was wedged into Economy with neither window nor aisle. In the window seat an underweight, olive-skinned kid in a yarmulke was nodding to his iPod. I decided he was returning home after year one at a boarding school. If he was returning to what he knew, I was venturing into what I didn't. On the aisle a hefty, scented lady was letting her left elbow and carry-ons encroach into my space. A Christian, I surmised, on a ten-day packaged pilgrimage to the Holy Land. The fact that she and I shared the same faith made me uncomfortable. She retreated into a hardback—familiar author, new title—as the plane queued up for takeoff. Trapped. Sixteen hours between a rich pubescent introvert and someone's suburban aunt.

I closed my eyes and replayed scenes from earlier in the day. There was my mother, teary, behind her Voyager on the departure ramp, compressing home baking into an already crammed pocket on my pack. Only a strong woman would release her only son to pursue his questions, armed only with a care package and curiosity. "Don't settle for *easy* answers," she would say, the downbeat on *easy*. Cuisine and cheerleading notwithstanding, she understood that *my* questions were not *hers*. She had never studied religion in a university. She had never waded into modern biblical scholarship. Her faith world had scarcely changed since youth group back in the seventies. For Mom it made no sense to distinguish between the Jesus *of the Gospels* and the Jesus *of history*. *Text* and *event* were two words for the same thing. Matthew, Mark, Luke, and John were God's impartial secretaries—inspired coauthors of a single, seamless, harmonious account of Jesus's life. Part of me envied her premodern, precritical world. Part of me longed to live there—back where every Bible story was taken at face value and where God's every word had me specifically in mind. But Mom had never read Rudolph Bultmann.

Bultmann's Specter

The day I sat down with Bultmann's *History of the Synoptic Tradition* was like the day Neo took the red pill. It yanked me out of my comfortable matrix and thrust me into the harsh world of biblical criticism from which, it seemed, there could be no return. Bultmann was thoroughly skeptical of much of what the New Testament had to say about the Jesus of history. He could take a straightforward episode in, say, the Gospel of Mark, pin it down, and dissect it into bits—shared memories and embellishments, shaped by the dominant mythical worldview. The Gospels are, Bultmann would say, products of a devout imagination. They catch Christian storytellers in the act of preaching. They reveal little about Jesus but lots about Jesus's followers and their faith.[1]

Unnerving stuff for a Sunday school graduate like me. Amazing thing is, Bultmann was more than an axe-wielding academic who thought Jesus's corpse was still in the grave. He was also a devoted churchman who wanted to preserve the pure kernel of Christianity now that modernity had cast off the old husk of miracles, demons, and resurrections. If

> "There is no historical-biographical interest in the Gospels, and that is why they have nothing to say about Jesus' human personality, his appearance and character, his origin, education and development. . . . The Gospels . . . do not tell of a much admired human personality, but of Jesus Christ, the Son of God, the Lord of the Church, and do so because they have grown out of Christian worship and remain tied to it."
>
> Rudolf Bultmann, *History of the Synoptic Tradition*, 372-73

Bultmann galloped in to slay the dragon of mythology, it was so he could liberate the Christ of faith.[2]

These days many of Bultmann's radical ideas look quaint—antique, even. Pure Bultmannians are an endangered species. Even his own students, sporting names like Ernst Käsemann and Günther Bornkamm, couldn't tolerate his straight-faced dismissal of so many of the Gospels' historical claims.

By the sixties everyone saw (finally) that when you stop questing for the "historical" Jesus, any number of nonhistorical, malleable, Silly Putty Jesuses fill the void. That, according to my religion professor, Randall Guilder, was exactly what had happened in the years before World War II and why it was so easy for many Christians to tolerate Hitler's anti-Semitism. Detach Jesus from his ancient Semitic roots, Guilder said, and you can bend him any way you like. Aryan. Marxist. Republican. Democrat. Hippy. CEO. So the historical quest continues. Scholars continue to study evidence—coins, scrolls, inscriptions, traditions—where it turns up. And they continue to debate whether the Gospels wove historical "facts" together with theology, myth, and imagination, and if so, how.

Should any of this matter for those who read the Bible as scripture? My freshman encounter with the German giant encouraged me to trade youth-group hype for something more sustaining, but it wasn't clear my faith would survive the transition. What if the only honest alternatives to naïveté were agnosticism and lifeless intellectualism? Could I be rigorously honest with the evidence *and* thoughtfully faithful to the tradition?

Two things happened in sophomore year. First, I discovered I was going through "theological puberty." The diagnosis comes from another German, Helmut Thielicke, whose quaintly titled book *A Little Exercise for Young Theologians* describes the "theological change of voice" that happens to people like me when they enter, for the first time, the world of biblical studies. Thielicke taught me that my theological anxieties were normal growing pains, that I should not presume to solve in a term paper problems

Dead Germans on Jesus

H. S. Reimarus (d. 1768): Jesus was a revolutionary who expected God would help him defeat the Romans. His disciples stole his body, invented the resurrection, and turned his failure into a religion that promised life after death through a suffering savior.

D. F. Strauss (d. 1874): Jesus stepped into the shoes of John the Baptist and only gradually came to see himself as the Messiah. His supernatural birth, miracles, resurrection, and ascension are myths—not frauds but "eternal truths" told by the early Christians to unpack Jesus's significance.

W. Wrede (d. 1906): We know very little about Jesus: he was a Galilean preacher who died a victim of the system. Mark's account (our earliest) of Jesus is largely pious fiction, revealing more about the imaginations of the early Christians than about the Jesus of history.

A. Schweitzer (d. 1965): Jesus was a misguided prophet who announced the end of the world and tried to force God's hand to bring it about. He failed tragically, but his noble death remains an inspiration.

that had baffled intellectual and spiritual giants for centuries, and that I shouldn't take myself too seriously. He also taught me to keep still. As he put it, "during the period when the voice is changing we do not sing, and during this formative period in the life of the theological student he does not preach."[3] So now at least I had a name for what I was going through. And I knew I wasn't alone.

The other thing that happened that year was that Bultmann's ghost (lurking under my bed) was joined by a chorus of other phantoms, all German, all older, and all eager to discount the historical reliability of the Gospels. Particularly noisy was the quartet of Hermann Reimarus, David Strauss, Wilhelm Wrede, and Albert Schweitzer. Some questers saw themselves, like Bultmann, as rescue workers plucking authentic faith from the floodwaters of modernity. Others hoped to see Christianity drown. Reimarus's answers were so radical they stayed secret until his body lay cold in its grave. Strauss's got him fired. Was I foolish to follow in their steps? Was it safe to peer behind the curtain of tradition? The plane surged forward under full throttle. I felt myself getting heavier.

By junior year I began to realize that my *historical* quest had to include a *literary* one. I needed to know what *kind* of books the Gospels were. Did the evangelists fact-check their sources? Did they ever embellish the story to enhance the reputation of their hero? I worried that if I posed these questions in church I'd feel like a traitor, an irreverent smart-ass. Mom must have said something because my pastor loaned me *The Challenge of Jesus* by N. T. Wright. Wright plants one foot in the academy and the other in the parish, and he is himself on a quest for Jesus. Like fellow academic Indiana Jones, he can't pass up an adventure. Unlike Jones, Wright doesn't like to work alone; he thinks everyone should mount a camel and join him.

If Wright is right, Jesus-questing isn't for sissies. And it certainly isn't just for scholars. Wright says he conducts his quest out of loyalty to Scripture. The goal is not to substitute his own reconstructed Jesus for the Jesus of the Gospels. On the contrary, he quests in order to read the Gospels more carefully and to notice details obscured by the haze of repetition and familiarity. In other words, he does so to avoid creating Jesus in his own image. I didn't know what sort of Jesus I would find, but I resolved to take up Wright's challenge.

Mom sensed my restlessness but wisely did not belittle what she did not understand. Instead, she offered to finance a graduation trip to the Holy Land. How can you be on a quest if you stay home? she asked. You're like Thomas, she reasoned. You need to see things before you can believe.

> Can I be used to help others find truth
> when I'm scared I'll find proof . . . it's a lie?
>
> I'm a doubting Thomas.
>
> Nickel Creek, "Doubting Thomas,"
> on *Why Should the Fire Die?*

That was months ago. Now, beside the van, she was crying and passing out zucchini bread. What I didn't know at the time was that days before my departure she had received news that her cancer had returned after five years in remission. She knew I would have canceled my trip, so she kept the news to herself.

Beside Mom stood Jake, my roommate, shifting awkwardly and reminding me to track down his uncle Jesse in Israel. Behind both of them, hanging out the window, was Gimli, my border collie, listening eagerly for an invitation to come along.

Pliny's Quest

Images of Gimli faded as the woman beside me shifted her weight. I drew from my pack one of the books that had made the final cut—a worn copy of *The Letters of the Younger Pliny*.[4] I was drawn to the mail of this Roman aristocrat, perhaps because my prof said Pliny's personal letters were our clearest window on the empire of his day. And because I admired a public figure who could thrive during turbulent times without becoming a tyrant. The back cover advertised his dates: 61 to 113 CE. A lad, I thought, when the apostle Paul met his death under Nero and when

Titus's troops stormed the Jerusalem temple. Seventeen the day Mount Vesuvius erupted to bury nearby towns under thirty feet of ash. A teenager, perhaps, or twenty-something, when the Gospels were published.

Images of Vesuvius took me back to my sixth-grade volcano project. Each of us had to research a real volcano and build a working model. My best friend picked Mount St. Helens. I opted for Vesuvius, which was how I discovered Pliny the Elder, whose curiosity drew him toward the eruption and then killed him. I thumbed the index and turned to Pliny the Younger's account of his uncle's demise.

My uncle was stationed at Misenum, in active command of the fleet. On 24 August, in the early afternoon, my mother drew his attention to a cloud of unusual size and appearance. He had been out in the sun, had taken a cold bath, and lunched while lying down, and was then working at his books. He called for his shoes and climbed up to a place which would give him the best view of the phenomenon. It was not clear at that distance from which mountain the cloud was rising (it was afterwards known to be <u>Vesuvius</u>); its general appearance can best be expressed as being like an umbrella pine, for it rose to a great height on a sort of trunk and then split off into branches, I imagine because it was thrust upwards by the first blast and then left unsupported as the pressure subsided, or else it was borne down by its own weight so that it spread out and gradually dispersed. In places it looked white, elsewhere blotched and dirty, according to the amount of soil and ash it carried with it.

I remembered my Vesuvius oozed baking soda. Less dramatic than the original blast, but a successful home brew nonetheless.

Volcano Recipe

1 cup vinegar
red or yellow food dye
2 drops of dish soap
2 tablespoons of baking soda

Build volcano using flour & water paste around a tall tin can or milk carton. Let dry. Combine vinegar, dye, and soap in the container. Add baking soda to produce red lava.

The beverage cart was creeping toward me at lava pace. I resumed reading.

> My uncle's scholarly acumen saw at once that it was important enough for a closer inspection, and he ordered a boat to be made ready, telling me I could come with him if I wished. I replied that I preferred to go on with my studies, and as it happened he had himself given me some writing to do.
>
> As he was leaving the house he was handed a letter from Rectina, wife of Tascus whose house was at the foot of the mountain, so that escape was impossible except by boat. She was terrified by the danger threatening her, and implored him to rescue her from her fate. He changed his plans, and what he had begun in a spirit of inquiry he completed as a hero. He gave orders for the warships to be launched and went on board himself with the intention of bringing help to many more people besides Rectina, for this lovely stretch of coast was thickly populated. He hurried to the place which everyone else was hastily leaving, steering his course straight for the danger zone. He was entirely fearless, describing each new movement and phase of the portent to be noted down exactly as he observed them.

I pictured Pliny's uncle, one hand on the tiller, taking notes with the other. How much of this story, I wondered, captured the "historical" Pliny and how much of it was poetic license, depicting how the author thought things "must have been" or how heroes "would have acted" under the circumstances? That prompted other questions: Were the Gospels any different? Could their stories boast an author as well connected to their champion as Pliny junior was to his? Pliny means to report what actually happened, and I was inclined to believe most of it, but his letter was also a eulogy—a narrative tribute to his fallen hero. His uncle's eventual collapse, like Jesus's crucifixion, was the story of one giving his life for many. Does admiration always lead to exaggeration? No beverage or mixed nuts yet, so I continued.

> Ashes were already falling, hotter and thicker as the ships drew near, followed by bits of pumice and blackened stones, charred and cracked by the flames: then suddenly they were in shallow water, and the shore was blocked by the debris from the mountain. For a moment my uncle wondered whether to turn back, but when the helmsman advised this, he refused, telling him that Fortune stood by the courageous and they must make for Pomponianus at Stabiae.

Pliny boldly comes ashore, exuding calm in the midst of chaos. Remarkably, he insists on going to the bath and having dinner.

> Meanwhile on Mount Vesuvius, broad sheets of fire and leaping flames blazed at several points, their bright glare emphasized by the darkness of night. My uncle tried to allay the fears of his companions by repeatedly declaring that these were nothing but bonfires left by the peasants in their terror, or else empty houses on fire in the districts they had abandoned.

At which point Pliny, like Jonah in the storm, decides to take a nap. Panicked pedestrians are baffled to hear his loud snoring.

> By this time, the courtyard giving access to his room was full of ashes mixed with pumice-stones, so that its level had risen, and if he stayed in the room any longer he would never have got out. He was wakened, came out and joined Pomponianus and the household who had sat up all night.

Together they debated whether to stay or flee. Earthquakes were making it unsafe indoors, but outside you had to dodge falling pumice.

> After comparing the risks they chose the latter. In my uncle's case one reason outweighed the other, but for the others it was a choice of fears. As a protection against falling objects they put pillows on their heads tied down with cloths.

"Something to drink?" The flight attendant put Vesuvius on pause. The coffee was lukewarm. Across the aisle an older man matched the profile of Pliny's uncle: stout, unconscious, and breathing heavily. Reading glasses askew, hair disheveled, his head was encased in a traveler's pillow.

> Elsewhere there was daylight by this time, but they were still in darkness, blacker and denser than any ordinary night, which they relieved by lighting torches and various kinds of lamp. My uncle decided to go down to the shore and investigate on the spot the possibility of any escape by sea, but he found the waves still wild and dangerous. A sheet was spread on the ground for him to lie down, and he repeatedly asked for cold water to drink. Then the flames and smell of sulfur which gave warning of the approaching fire drove the others to take flight and roused him to stand up. He stood leaning on two slaves and then suddenly collapsed, I imagine because the dense fumes choked his breathing by blocking his windpipe which was constitutionally weak and narrow and often inflamed.

As I watched the aging Pliny peering bravely into ominous darkness, I felt a sudden impulse toward self-protection. Wasn't my voyage almost as dangerous? His was a quest to get close to the source of a volcano in order to rescue friends from certain death. Mine was to get close to the sources of a religion and perhaps to rescue my own faith from the ashes of modernity. The analogy was weak, but somehow old Pliny's expedition seemed less foolish now than when I was twelve. I pressed on to the end of the letter.

> Meanwhile, my mother and I were at Misenum, but this is not of any historic interest, and you only wanted to hear about my uncle's death. I will say no more, except to add that I have described in detail every incident which I either witnessed myself or heard about immediately after the event, when reports were most likely to be accurate. It is for you to select what best suits your purpose, for there is a great difference between a letter to a friend and history written for all to read.

The final words caught my eye: "there is a great difference between a *letter to a friend* and *history written for all to read*." How easy is it to draw a line between private opinion and public fact? Can history, even Gospel history, ever be more than somebody's spin on the past? Neither my questions nor my seat offered much comfort.

Ex-Christians

"Whatcha readin'?" the hefty woman asked, her voice almost as perky as her hair.

"This?" I glanced up. "Some letters written by Pliny, a Roman aristocrat." My tone was polite but maybe a bit intimidating. The line between serious student and naïve tourist ran down the middle of our armrest.

"Roman aristocrat? Hmmm. When was this?"

"Pliny wrote between . . . um, around the turn of the second century."

"What does he write about?" she persisted. "Was he a Christian or a pagan?"

"Definitely not a Christian," I said. My hunch about her religious loyalties was holding up. Her world divided neatly into insies and outsies. "Christians puzzled him," I continued. "They made him nervous. There was no empirewide policy against Christianity so Pliny wrote the emperor for advice."[5]

"I thought emperors only gave orders." For an overweight, middle-aged, middle-class matron, you had to award her points for perseverance. I flipped to book 10, letter 96, where last term's pencil markings littered the page. She gladly accepted my offer to read to her.

96. Pliny to the Emperor Trajan

[handwritten: has punishing Christians become routine?]

[handwritten: suck up!]

[handwritten: evidence of Christian households?]

It is my custom to refer all my difficulties to you, Sir, for no one is better able to resolve my hesitation and to inform my ignorance.

I have never been present in an examination of Christians. Consequently, I do not know the nature of the extent of the <u>punishments usually meted out to them</u>, nor the ground for starting an investigation and how far it should be pressed. Nor am I at all sure whether any distinction should be made on the grounds of <u>age</u>, or if <u>young people</u> should be treated alike; whether a pardon ought to be granted to anyone rejecting his beliefs, or if he has <u>once professed Christianity</u>, he shall gain nothing by renouncing it; and whether it is the <u>mere name of Christian</u> which is punishable, even if innocent of crime, or rather the <u>crimes associated with the name</u>.

[handwritten: rumors of exotic crimes like cannibalism, ritual intercourse, infanticide??]

"Hasn't Pliny heard of the separation of church and state?" she interrupted.

"I think that was an American invention," I quipped. "Religion in the Roman Empire was always social and always political. People didn't so much believe in gods; they just had gods. A good governor would welcome emperor-friendly religions and banish the rest. Pliny's just doing his job."

"Why was Pliny so hard on Christians?"

> Those who attempt to distort our religion with strange rites you should abhor and punish, not merely for the sake of the gods, but such men by bringing in new divinities in place of the old, persuade many to adopt foreign practices, from which spring up conspiracies, factions and political clubs which are far from profitable to a monarchy. Do not therefore permit anyone to be an atheist or a sorcerer.[6]

"Hard to say. Christians seemed antisocial when they refused to worship the emperor and revere the state's gods. What could be more threatening to an empire and more certain to provoke hostility? Maybe the main problem with Christians (and Jews) was that they promoted foreign ideas and strange practices and stubbornly refused to give them up. Anything non-Roman was suspect." I took her nod as permission to continue.

For the moment this is the line I have taken with all persons brought before me on the charge of being Christians. I have asked them in person if they are Christians, and if they admit it, I repeat the question a second time and a third time, with a warning of the punishment awaiting them. If they persist, I order them to be led away for execution; for, whatever the nature of their admission, I am convinced that their stubbornness and unshakable obstinacy ought not to go unpunished. There have been others similarly fanatical who are <u>Roman citizens</u>. I have entered them on the list of persons to be sent to Rome for trial.

was Jesus executed for being "defiant"?

Paul's Roman citizenship saved him too (Acts 25-26).
See Pliny, 10.5-6, 104-107

"So the problem was not so much what they believed, but how?" she broke in again.

She was sharper than I thought.

"It was both, I think." I repeated something Guilder often said about Rome's obsession with public order and its preference for political stability over individual rights. "Trajan took stubbornness seriously.[7] He didn't even let Pliny train firemen because he thought their meetings might turn political and become divisive!"[8]

She told me her husband hated union busters.

Now that I have begun to deal with this problem, as so often happens, the charges are becoming more widespread and increasing in variety. An anonymous pamphlet has been circulated which contains the names of a number of accused persons. Amongst these I considered that I should <u>dismiss any who denied that they were or ever had been Christians</u> when they had repeated after me a formula of invocation to the gods and had made offerings of wine and incense to your statue (which I had ordered to be brought into court for this purpose along with the images of the gods), and furthermore had <u>reviled the name of Christ</u>: none of which things, I understand, any <u>genuine Christian can be induced to do</u>.

Others whose names were given to me by an informer, first admitted the charge and then denied it; they said that they had <u>ceased to be Christians</u> two or more years previously, and <u>some of them even 20 years ago</u>. They all did reverence to your statue and the images of the gods in the same way as the others, and reviled the name of Christ.

did Peter denied Christ, "swore an oath"

Mark 14:71 - when Peter denied Christ, he "cursed" and "swore an oath"

"Pliny wants to sound organized and level-headed," I remarked. "He doesn't want anyone to think he would condemn on false charges. If someone tried to dispatch an annoying neighbor by labeling him *Christian*, Pliny would let the accused defend himself. So he gets points for that. And the guy could walk if he'd say a prayer to the gods, nod toward the emperor—and curse Christ."

"Some of these folks had followed Jesus for quite a while."

"And it seems like there were a few *ex*-Christians as well."

"Interesting that they *reviled the name of Christ* to prove their loyalty to Roman gods. I guess it was one or the other." Her mind was churning. "Reminds me of Saint Peter's curse the night Jesus was arrested."

"And interesting that they could prosecute someone who had stopped believing decades earlier," I added.

"What made them lose their faith, I wonder?" Her voice was suddenly earnest.

"I don't know. Peer pressure maybe. Or troubles at home. Or persecution. Or perhaps some other cult offered a better deal."[9]

I couldn't read her quizzical expression.

"Maybe a better question," she offered slowly, "is why so many other people remained loyal to Jesus even when their lives were on the line."

Why indeed? Why did Christians keep on believing, in far-flung places like northern Turkey, eighty-plus years after Jesus had come and gone? What was it about Jesus that they found so compelling? Gentiles in Bithynia had no roots in Jewish tradition. No cultural reason to harbor an unwelcome, foreign religion. Yet cling to Jesus they did, many of them in the face of death. I looked out the window upon a sea of clouds.

"Please continue," she said.

She didn't need an answer so I offered none.

"Here's the part that everyone likes to quote."

They also declared that the sum total of their guilt or error amounted to no more than this: they had met regularly before dawn on a fixed day to chant verses alternately amongst themselves in honor of Christ as if to a god, and also to bind themselves by an oath, not for any criminal purpose, but to abstain from theft, robbery, and adultery, to commit no breach of trust, and not to deny a deposit when called upon to restore it. After this ceremony, it had been their custom to disperse and reassemble later to take food of an ordinary, harmless kind; but they had in fact given up this practice since my edict, given on your instructions, which banned all political societies. This made me decide it was all the more necessary to extract the truth by torture from two slave women, whom they call deaconesses. I found nothing but a degenerate sort of cult, carried to extravagant lengths.

Handwritten margin notes:

See Phil. 2:5-11, Col 1:15-20, Rev 5:11, 13

Trajan fears all local political associations

does "as if" imply that Christ was known to have been a man?

were there rumors of bizarre rites/feasts?

Compare how Jesus is addressed along with God in Rev 4-5

"Is Pliny torturing Christians to find out what they believe?"

"Yup. That was Rome's way of making slaves tell the truth."

"But those slaves were women! Deaconesses in the church!"

"I agree—this is nasty."

"What's that part you underlined?"

So she was reading over my shoulder.

"My professor says this is the oldest outsider's account of Christian worship, which makes this part important. They gathered early on Sunday mornings to sing and worship Jesus, and then later to share a meal and celebrate the Eucharist. He says it lines up nicely with what we find in the New Testament."[10]

> I have therefore postponed any further examination and hastened to consult you. The question seems to me to be worthy of your consideration, especially in view of the number of persons endangered; for a great many individuals of every age and class, both men and women, are being brought to trial, and this is likely to continue. It is not only the towns, but villages and rural districts too which are infected through contact with <u>this wretched cult</u>. I think though that it is still possible for it to be checked and directed to better ends, for there is no doubt that <u>people have begun to throng the temples which had been entirely deserted for a long time; the sacred rites which had been allowed to lapse, are being performed</u> again, and flesh of sacrificial victims is on sale everywhere, though up till recently scarcely anyone could be found to buy it. It is easy to infer from this that a great many people could be reformed if they were given an opportunity to repent.[11]

see Acts 16:19; 19:11-14

My seatmate was disturbed that Pliny had managed to turn Christians into pagans. I thought of several high school friends who attended church for a few years and then gave it up. Mercifully, the woman left me with my thoughts. I pushed back and closed my eyes.

Matter of Faith

The smell of curried chicken brought me back to life. The kid beside me surfaced long enough to eat and pee. The woman, whose name was Dorothy, asked me how I knew so much about ancient Rome.

"I just finished my BA in Religion," I said, peeling the lid off my juice. "I had to write a paper on Roman ideas about Christianity so I read Pliny junior and two other guys."

"Why would you study Christianity in a *university*?" Dorothy asked.

"My mom wonders the same thing."

"If you ask me," she began.

I hadn't.

"The Bible is a matter of faith. If we have the Spirit it makes sense. If we don't, it won't."

My mouth was full so I had time to think. If the Bible *belongs* anywhere, it is in church, not the academy. But that can't mean that it belongs only in the heart, not the head. That a wall separates belief and inquiry. Or is there no room at the inn for Christian scholars?

During one of my darker periods—the summer after sophomore year—I discovered the work of Lesslie Newbigin. Newbigin contends that both fundamentalists and liberals have embraced the Enlightenment lie that we must hold out for certainty. It's good to be confident about the things we've studied—the shape of the earth, say, or the facts of the past—but silly to hope for objectivity. Each of us views the world *from somewhere*, so all judgments are provisional. Newbigin said belief was foundational to doubt, not the other way round.

My reply to Dorothy was weak. Only time would tell, I said, whether my faith and studies would get along. I wanted to say more—that the unbelieving academy often asks great questions, and sometimes even provides the most persuasive answers. But I held back. Dorothy's Bible soared above history in a rare atmosphere ideally suited for spirits and saints but too thin for earthbound academics. Professor Guilder's Bible, on the contrary, belonged far below, where air hung thick and fields were dusty. Somehow I flew between the two—riding the hermeneutical equivalent of a le(a)d zeppelin, eager to inhabit both worlds, reluctant to choose between conviction and curiosity.

Notorious Depravity

"So who were the other two?"

"Excuse me?"

"Besides Pliny. You said you studied three Romans." Even though all that mattered was faith, Dorothy wanted to talk about history.

> "I have a lot of faith. But I am also afraid a lot, and have no real certainty about anything. I remembered something Father Tom had told me—that the opposite of faith is not doubt, but certainty. Certainty is missing the point entirely. Faith includes noticing the mess, the emptiness and discomfort, and letting it be there until some light returns. Faith also means reaching deeply within, for the sense one was born with, the sense, for example, to go for a walk."
>
> Anne Lamott, *Plan B*, 256-57

"Tacitus and Josephus."

"Who're they?"

"Let's see. Tacitus was a senator during the reign of Domitian. Then, under Trajan, he governed next door to Pliny. He's mostly famous for writing up Roman history. Many would say he was the greatest Roman historian ever."

More questions, now about whether Tacitus persecuted Christians like Pliny did. I didn't know, but I told her that Tacitus despised nontraditional religions, including Christianity, for corrupting Roman morals.

"Have you heard of the Great Fire of Rome?" I asked.

"Nero fiddled while Rome burned?"

"Yeah, that fire. Nero didn't fiddle—that's a legend—but he was emperor when the fire broke out, in July of 64. As Tacitus tells the story, Nero pinned the blame on the Christians." I dove into my pack and produced another ratty Penguin classic. The cover read *Tacitus: The Annals of Imperial Rome*. I flipped open to book 15.37 and read aloud, this time from Tacitus's description of Nero's decline.

> *Tacitus admits when he doesn't know* →
>
> Disaster followed. Whether it was accidental or caused by a criminal act on the part of the emperor is <u>uncertain</u>—both versions have supporters. Now started the most terrible and destructive fire which Rome had ever experienced. It began in the Circus, where it adjoins the Palatine and Caelian hills. Breaking out in shops selling inflammable goods, and fanned by the wind, the conflagration instantly grew and swept the whole length of the Circus. There were no walled mansions or temples, or any other obstructions, which could arrest it. First, the fire swept violently over the level spaces. Then it climbed the hills—but returned to ravage the lower ground again. It outstripped every counter-measure. The ancient city's narrow winding streets and irregular blocks encouraged its progress.
>
> Terrified, shrieking women, helpless old and young, people intent on their own safety, people unselfishly supporting invalids or waiting for them, fugitives and lingerers alike—all heightened the confusion. When people looked back, menacing flames sprang up before them or outflanked them. When they escaped to a neighbouring quarter, the fire followed.

I paused and looked up. "You get the idea. The fire rages. Gangs start looting. Certain ones claim they'd been ordered to keep the fire going!"

"Ordered! By whom?"

"By Nero. He didn't even return to Rome until the fire threatened his mansion! To his credit, he organized relief efforts, let fire victims camp on his land,

Guilder's Guiding Principles

(Taken from Ernst Troeltsch, 1865–1923.)

1. Methodological doubt: conclusions are always subject to revision; historical inquiry only offers degrees of probability.

2. Analogy: events past and present are fundamentally similar; nature's laws have not changed since biblical times.

3. Correlation: all events are connected; no event escapes the sequence of historical cause and effect.

and supplied the masses with cheap corn, but the word on the street was that he wanted to give the city a facelift." I scanned the page. "Listen to this."

> Yet these measures, for all their popular character, earned no gratitude. For a rumour had spread that, while the city was burning, Nero had gone on his private stage and, comparing modern calamities with ancient, had sung of the destruction of Troy.

"So he didn't fiddle. He sang."

The man across the aisle—Professor Pliny—adjusted his weight, screwed up his eyes in my direction, and promptly went back to sleep.

"Tacitus provides a damage report," I continued. "Ten of Rome's fourteen districts suffer in the blaze. Treasures go up in smoke along with shrines, temples, public buildings, shops, and countless ramshackle houses. When the smoke clears, Nero begins a massive building campaign: grander palace, wider streets, more stone, lower rooflines, better water supply. It's an economic stimulus plan Roman style."

"But why did he . . ."

"Blame Christians for the fire? Two words: survival politics."

Next came attempts to appease heaven. After consultation of the Sibylline books, prayers were addressed to Vulcan, Ceres, and Proserpina. Juno, too, was propitiated. . . . But neither human resources, nor imperial munificence, nor appeasement of the gods, eliminated sinister suspicions that the fire had been instigated. To suppress this rumour, Nero fabricated scapegoats—and punished with every refinement the notoriously depraved Christians (as they were popularly called). Their originator, Christ, had been executed in Tiberius' reign by the governor of Judaea, Pontius Pilatus. But in spite of this temporary setback the deadly superstition had broken out afresh, not only in Judaea (where the mischief had started) but even in Rome. All degraded and shameful practices collect and flourish in the capital.

"*Notoriously depraved Christians?*" Dorothy was not impressed. "It's amazing how Rome could be open to so much superstition yet be so suspicious of the truth."

"Actually, you've got it backward. The Romans *hated* superstition. They saw their religion as traditional, old-fashioned, and good for the Empire. Like oatmeal for breakfast. Christians, on the other hand, along with Jews, Celts, Germans, and Egyptians, were superstitious, irrational, and dangerous to society."

It occurred to me that the first and the twenty-first centuries were not so different. Several of my friends, including Jake, thought unchecked religion led to fanaticism and conflict. It was, they'd say, bad for society. They liked to point to Palestinian suicide bombers and Israeli settlers, to Iraqi Sunni and Shiite militants, to the 9/11 hijackers. And they would point to Christian leaders like the religious broadcaster who publicly recommended the assassination of Venezuela's president. Or the cult leader from Oregon who swore that God told him to kill people. Tacitus and Pliny saw then what many see now: that unrestrained religious zeal gets people to do scary things. And religion's revolutionary potential went well beyond overt rebellion and physical violence. Even the weakest citizen who won't pledge primary allegiance to flag and country can be dangerous. I was about to press the point when Dorothy spoke.

"What did Nero do to the Christians?" she asked.

"It isn't pretty," I said, and resumed reading.

> First, Nero had self-acknowledged Christians arrested. Then, on their information, large numbers of others were condemned—not so much for incendiarism as for their anti-social tendencies. Their deaths were made farcical. Dressed in wild animals' skins, they were torn to pieces by dogs, or crucified, or made into torches to be ignited after dark as substitutes for daylight. Nero provided his Gardens for the spectacle, and exhibited displays in the Circus, at which he mingled with the crowd—or stood in a chariot, dressed as a charioteer. Despite their guilt as Christians, and the ruthless punishment it deserved, the victims were pitied. For it was felt that they were being sacrificed to one man's brutality rather than to the national interest.

(handwritten margin note: Incendiarism: deliberate fire starting)

"Nero made the punishment fit the crime," I said. "He fought fire with fire."

"I was thinking something else," she replied. Apparently she didn't appreciate my sharp wit. "Like master, like disciple."

"What do you mean?" I asked.

"Tacitus said *Christians* got their name from *Christ*. Then he adds that Christ was *executed by Pilate*. So *they* deserved death because *Jesus* did. *They* were crucified under Nero like *Jesus* was crucified under Tiberius. They were enemies of the state like Jesus was an enemy of the state. Jesus said, 'If the world hates you, be aware that it hated me before it hated you. If they persecuted me, they will persecute you'" [John 15:18, 20].

Dorothy continued to impress. My early snobbery was looking more and more, uh, snobbish.

"I've heard that some people today doubt that Jesus ever existed," she continued. "Isn't this proof, from the lips of a pagan, that he did?"

"Well," I replied, "I used to think so. Problem is, we don't know where Tacitus got his information. If this came from official documents, then yes. But what if he learned about Jesus from talking to Christians in Rome or when he was stationed in Turkey?"

"Maybe he read the Gospels."

"Unlikely," I replied. "The parallels aren't close enough. All we can say for sure is that although Tacitus hated Christians, he had no doubt whatsoever about the existence of their leader. Actually, I think the best evidence for the existence of Jesus, outside the New Testament, comes from Josephus."

Extra-Jesus

"Another Roman governor?"

"That's about the only career he didn't try."

Testimonium Flavianum

"About this time there lived Jesus, a wise man, if indeed one ought to call him a man. For he was a teacher of such people as accept the truth gladly. He won over many Jews and many of the Greeks. He was the Messiah. When Pilate, upon hearing him accused by men of the highest standing amongst us, had condemned him to be crucified, those who had in the first place come to love him did not give up their affection for him. On the third day he appeared to them restored to life, for the prophets of God had prophesied these and countless other marvelous things about him. And the tribe of the Christians, so called after him, has still to this day not disappeared."

Josephus,
Jewish Antiquities 18.63

"What do you mean?"

"Josephus went from student to hermit to Pharisee to diplomat to army general to professional scholar."

"Quite a list."

"He was quite a weasel. When he saw that the Romans were going to defeat the rebellion he helped organize, he surrendered. They executed many comrades, but somehow he ended up in Rome with a nice home and sweet job writing history for the emperor."

"What does Josephus say about Jesus?"

"We're not sure."

"I thought you said the best evidence . . ."

"I did. Josephus was born only a few years after Jesus died, and his writings include a clear statement about Jesus. Problem is, it's hard to believe Josephus wrote it. He says Jesus was the Messiah and rose from the dead in fulfillment of prophecy."

"Isn't that what it says in the New Testament?"

"Yes, but Josephus wasn't a Christian. Scholars suspect someone inserted a little pro-Jesus propaganda into their copy of the manuscript."

Blank look.

"Most people who study Josephus think his bit about Jesus is oddly out of place. He is listing crises and tensions, most of them involving Pilate the governor. Halfway through his list is an upbeat, heartwarming account of the Messiah's life, death, and resurrection. It's like slashing your way through the jungle and stumbling onto a café!"

"It won't be long before Brazil has Starbucks."

"They already do. Consider this: no second- or third-century Christian ever quotes this passage to strengthen the case for Christianity. If their copy of Josephus referred to Jesus, why would they ignore it?"

"I thought the best evidence for Jesus outside the New Testament comes from Josephus."

"It does. Even after scholars have separated what Josephus himself wrote from the later Christian bits, Josephus still has a lot to say."

"Like what?"

"Like that Jesus was a wise, popular teacher who performed astonishing deeds; that he was accused by Jewish leaders and crucified by Pilate; and that a band of 'Christians' continued to Josephus's own day."

"And that the band of Christians believed Jesus rose from the dead?"

"Maybe. I don't know. Josephus is solid, first-century Jewish evidence *that* Jesus existed. How much Josephus knew *about* Jesus is hard to say."

I was tired of being the answer guy, so I got her to talk. She said she was joining a group of Christian pilgrims, adding that the one leading the tour had published a book on the End Times.

"The Rapture," she confided quietly, "could happen at any moment."

I glanced sideways, marveling at her confidence. It was as if her little pilgrimage could hasten the end of the age. But although my initial fears about her were confirmed, my feelings of condescension were gone. Perhaps we two weren't so different. Both of us were on Jesus quests, she to confirm her faith and I to test mine. My journey was shaped by my recent encounter with the academy; hers by a long life in the church. We both wanted to know how the future is tied to the past, and we both thought the answer awaited us in the land called Israel.

The only movie I watched on the plane was an old one about the apocalypse. The hero was an unlikely survivor who led a small band—twelve misfits—back from the brink. You could say he founded a little "church" except that he spent most of the movie trying to abandon them and go solo. Another reluctant Messiah.

The man across the aisle—the stout and fearless Pliny—finally awoke as we began our descent into Tel Aviv. Dorothy was in line for the bathroom.

"The younger Ananus, who . . . had been appointed to the high priesthood, was rash in his temper and unusually daring. He followed the school of the Sadducees, who are indeed more heartless than any of the other Jews . . . when they sit in judgement. . . . Ananus thought that he had a favourable opportunity because Festus was dead and Albinus was still on the way. And so he convened the judges of the Sanhedrin and brought before them a man named James, the brother of Jesus who was called the Christ, and certain others. He accused them of having transgressed the law and delivered them up to be stoned. Those of the inhabitants of the city who were considered the most fair-minded and who were strict in observance of the law were offended at this. . . . King Agrippa, because of Ananus' action, deposed him from the high priesthood which he had held for three months."

Josephus,
Jewish Antiquities 20.199–203

"Did you forget aboat James?"

Aboat? Must be from Minnesota. Or Canada.

"Did I forget about James?"

"Josephus says the High Priest tried *the brother of Jesus the so-called Christ, a man named James.*"

"Pliny" turned out to be Professor Carpenter from Montreal, who knew a thing or two *aboat* Josephus. And he knew Professor Guilder. Leaning across the aisle, he explained that Josephus identifies James as Jesus's brother even before providing his name. This, he said, makes sense only if Josephus had already referred to Jesus. So at least a part of the *testimonium* must go back to Josephus. Not bad, detective.

At that point Dorothy returned and retrieved her book, which, in addition to her, um, girth, completely cut me off from the professor. I didn't get to talk to him again until I found him at baggage claim.

"Hey Professor!"

"Welcome to the much-too-promised land."

I asked what he was doing in Israel.

"Giving a lecture in Tel Aviv," he said. "And I'm working on a paper aboat Jewish burial practices. I need to visit some cemeteries and check oat some tombs. Ah, there's my bag. Great to meet you. Keep oat of trouble!"

The professor hoisted a bulging satchel, pivoted, and pressed through the crowd that swarmed the carousel. Perhaps I would do some tomb raiding of my own; you can't come this far just to explore ideas! At that moment, though, the priority was food and sleep. I grabbed my pack off the belt, waved to Dorothy, and headed for passport control. When I passed the interrogation and headed through the door, a wall of heat pushed back. Thankfully the bus was not far away. I climbed aboard and set my face toward Jerusalem.

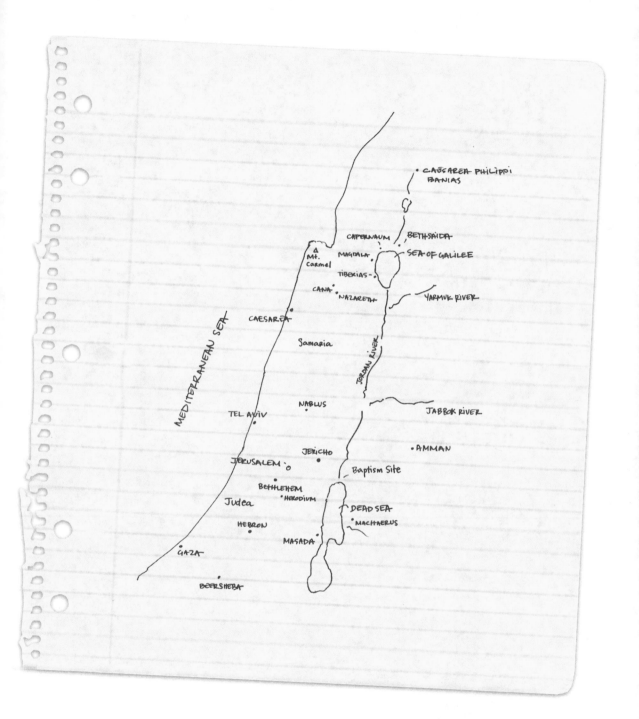

CHAPTER 2

Ghosts at the River

MONTY PYTHON'S LIFE OF BRIAN, SCENE 18

SIMON: I've kept my vow for eighteen years. Not a single, recognizable, articulate sound has passed my lips.

BRIAN: Oh, please. Could you be quiet for another five minutes?

SIMON: Oh, it doesn't matter now. I might as well enjoy myself. The times in the last eighteen years I've wanted to shout and sing and . . .

BRIAN: Shhhh.

SIMON: . . . scream my name out! Oh, I'm alive!

In which Norm has prophet sightings at a riverbank and a fortress, while keeping his distance from two experts on the End Times.

Wonder and Welcome

The shuttle driver between Ben Gurion Airport in Tel Aviv and Jerusalem was possessed. Made me think of Mr. Toad in *The Wind in the Willows*, "before whom all must give way or be smitten."[1] Cigarette in one hand, wheel in the other, he threaded through honking traffic at the speed of radio chatter. When he deposited me north of the Old City, the tip of a lit cigarette pointed the way.

I won't soon forget my first encounter with the Old City. Broad steps descended to the stone bridge that ended at a shadowy opening in the Ottoman Wall. Damascus Gate. My gaze shifted from stones to people and back again, all of it too old and too new to take in. Five armed Israeli soldiers supported a wall near the entrance. Bellowing Arab merchants, old and young, set a cadence for my steps. The human current carried me across the bridge and into the void where the path turned sharply left, then right to emerge into the light of a teeming market.

I must have been weary. The pack must have been heavy. All I remember is childlike wonder. I adjusted my footfalls to the city's rhythm. My journey across the land and into the Gospels was under way. Farther down and farther in. After ten minutes of shuffling I arrived at the hospice.

Professor Guilder had recommended the Austrian Hospice on Via Dolorosa in the heart of the Muslim Quarter. The view from the roof, he said, was epic. Three Palestinian teens slid off the steps to let me ring the buzzer. Inside, up several flights, the vaulted, nineteenth-century lobby was a world away from the street below: a European enclave in an Arab neighborhood in a Jewish state. As I waited for the clerk to finish helping an older couple, I noticed a small shelf wedged with books. Most were in German, but the handful of English titles included a worn *Screwtape Letters* by C. S. Lewis. I snagged it for bedtime reading.

With Germanic efficiency Franz marched me down to the dorms in the basement, listed the house rules, and beat a military retreat. I was more interested in food than conversation, so I let him go, dumped my pack, and headed down El-Wad, the street outside my door. Around a corner at the mouth of an arched tunnel was a falafel stand tended by an eager Arab named Ahmed. Nearby old men shared a water pipe. Women squatted beside mountains of mint and banana leaves. As stomach filled, body remembered that it belonged ten time zones away. I retraced my steps and dropped into bed.

Those first few days in Jerusalem were an intoxicating blend of wonder and welcome. G. K. Chesterton says life is fullest when we experience side by side the strange and the familiar.[2] I was never more alive than during those first few weeks, wandering the streets of the busy Muslim Quarter. Each morning the market magically appeared: spices and fruit, boiled corn, baklava. Young boys trumpeted bargains over the din of Arabic music. At intervals through the day minaret speakers summoned the faithful to pray at the mosques.

One week in, I dreamed I was back in the US, hiking the Sierras. My dog and I rode the shuttle from Mammoth to the valley below and hiked up to Lake Ediza in the shadow of snow-capped Mount Ritter, not far from a jagged range called the Minarets. The dream ended when the sun fell behind the range. I wrote a poem to bring together my two impossibly different worlds.

Minarets

"It means 'trumpets,'"
drawled shuttle driver into rearview mirror.

> "Just after noon we entered these narrow, crooked streets, by the ancient and the famed Damascus Gate, and now for several hours I have been trying to comprehend that I am actually in the illustrious old city where Solomon dwelt, where Abraham held converse with the Deity, and where walls still stand that witnessed the spectacle of the Crucifixion."
>
> Mark Twain,
> *Innocents Abroad*, 415

A razor ridge slices skyward,
heralding something I'm too far below to hear.

It's different with these minarets
here in old Jerusalem, Muslim Quarter.
Every day—five times—trumpets sound sideways:
Allahu Akbar. God is great.

Perhaps city folk wrapped in Hijab or Kefiyeh,
trapped in jostling throng, dodging market cart,
scuffing cobbles on march toward Damascus Gate,
need the reminder.

But there, below towers older than Muhammad,
it is enough
to hear meltwater jostle rock
and watch trees dodge Ediza's gusts.

Enough to follow darkened cloud
scuffing Ritter and Banner
as dusk dons veil and shadows march
as if in step to trumpet's call.

Friday afternoon found me in the Jewish Quarter. I surveyed the sea of men bobbing in prayer at the wall and then explored a maze of tidy stone alleyways where tidy families marched in tidy processions toward the homes where they would share a Shabbat meal. Reminded me of Gimli circling the carpet before her nap. I bought a *Maccabee*—in Israel beer is named after freedom fighters—from a shop owner preparing to close, found a bench, and pulled out *The Screwtape Letters*. One particular letter got my attention. Speaking for the dark side, Lewis writes:

> You will find that a good many Christian-political writers think that Christianity began going wrong, and departing from the doctrine of its Founder, at a very early stage. Now,

Religious Jews Walking

this idea must be used by us to encourage once again the conception of a "historical Jesus" to be found by clearing away later "accretions and perversions" and then to be contrasted with the whole Christian tradition. In the last generation we promoted the construction of such a "historical Jesus" on liberal and humanitarian lines; we are now putting forward a new "historical Jesus" on Marxian, catastrophic, and revolutionary lines.[3]

I knew it would be tempting to fashion Jesus in my image, but I had to know whether historical inquiry could also deepen my faith, whether studying Someone from the past could enrich my worship in the present.

Someone at church once posed an interesting question: *Did I believe in Jesus because of the Gospels, or in the Gospels because of Jesus?* Maybe it was a trick question, a thought experiment, but it helped me clarify where my loyalties lay: with the man whose stories got written up, rather than with the stories themselves.

The idea of a "historical" quest for Jesus made little sense to most of my friends at church. Their four Gospels fit together perfectly. Their Jesus wasn't remotely puzzling. He had fair skin, told stories, smiled at children, and died for our sins. When I spoke of a leathery Jewish prophet who defied authorities and warned of the apocalypse, the response was mostly raised eyebrows and awkward silence. That was when Mom suggested I make a pilgrimage to the Holy Land so I could conduct my quest in Jesus's natural habitat. Maybe our pastor came up with the idea in order to get me out of town. Like the bus driver from Tel Aviv, obsessive types can be dangerous.

Freelance Prophet or Publicity Agent?

I was set to begin my quest when unrest broke out in Bethlehem. In a military operation to arrest "wanted" Palestinians, Israeli forces had killed an eighty-three-year-old woman. Next came street protests, rock throwing, and tear gas, so Bethlehem was placed "under closure," meaning none could enter or leave. I wondered if Herod imposed a curfew on Bethlehem when his troops entered to find the "wanted" newborn who threatened his rule.

"Although the Christian creed contains a number of historical assertions about Jesus, Christian faith as a living religious response is simply not directed at those historical facts about Jesus, or at a historical reconstruction of Jesus. Christian faith is directed to a living person. The 'real Jesus' for Christian faith is the resurrected Jesus, him whom God has made both Lord and Christ.' . . . The real Jesus for Christian faith is not simply a figure of the past but very much and above all a figure of the present, a figure, indeed, who defines believers' present by his presence."

Luke Timothy Johnson, Real Jesus, 141–42

The crisis in Bethlehem forced me to begin my quest where two of the four Gospels began theirs—with John the Baptist. John is everything I'm not. Wild-eyed, unkempt, aggressive. Fearless in corridors of power. Able to survive on honeycomb and bugs. I ate honeycomb as a kid for allergies, but I don't do bugs. In Sunday school we learned that John and Jesus were "cousins" (Luke 1:36) and nearly the same age (Luke 1:26, 44), and that John knew the Coming One had arrived (John 1:29). John told people to repent and blasted Herod Antipas for marrying someone, which got him thrown in prison. Prison provoked a crisis. Why wasn't Jesus more militant? Where was his prophetic indignation (Matt. 3:11–12)? To get some answers John sent messengers to Jesus (Matt. 11:2–6). Next thing you know John is dead.

That was Sunday school. Back then my big question was about the heavenly voice that declared Jesus to be God's Son. Was the voice inside Jesus's head (Mark 1:11 and Luke 3:22) or out where all could hear (Matt. 3:17)? My teacher answered by invoking Winnie-the-Pooh. Remember, she said, the time Pooh clutched a sky-blue balloon and floated up to a bees' nest at the top of a tree? Pooh sang a cloud song so the bees wouldn't suspect he was after their honey. God spoke out of the cloud, she explained, like Pooh. The crowd was like the bees: they knew something dangerous had invaded their world but didn't understand what it was.

Then came freshman New Testament. Pooh was conspicuously absent. Guilder began his lecture by saying Jesus's baptism by John was among the most solid facts we've got—almost as solid as Jesus's crucifixion under Pilate. The reason, he explained over his glasses, was simple: Christians would never invent a story in which Jesus looked inferior to someone else. Not even John.[4] Guilder called this the historian's criterion of "embarrassment" because a story about Jesus undergoing John's baptism—a baptism of repentance—would embarrass Jesus's followers. Ergo, it must have happened.

Guilder next invoked the criterion of "multiple attestation": when stories occur in multiple, independent sources—Mark, Matthew/Luke (when they aren't following Mark), John—the idea must be older than the lot of them and may well be authentic.[5]

Guilder also suggested that Jesus was John's disciple before branching out on his own.[6] Never heard that in Sunday school.

"Think about it," he pressed. "Jesus embraced John's message (cf. Matt. 3:2 with 4:17), submitted to his baptism, and imposed his water ritual on his own followers (John 3:22–24; 4:1–3). Jesus even drew his first recruits from the ranks of John's followers (John 1:35–40)."

A girl in the front row pointed out that most of Guilder's evidence was coming from John, the Gospel Guilder himself considered the least reliable of the

Criteria of Authenticity

Dissimilarity: "Material can be safely attributed to Jesus if it agrees neither with the early church nor with the Judaism contemporary with Jesus" (Sanders and Davies, *Studying the Synoptic Gospels*, 316).

Multiple Attestation: "A passage is more likely to go back to Jesus if it has been preserved in two or more sources which are independent of each other" (ibid., 323).

Coherence: "Material from the earliest strata of the tradition may be accepted as authentic if it can be shown to cohere with material established as authentic by means of the criterion of dissimilarity" (Perrin, *Rediscovering the Teaching of Jesus*, 43).

Embarrassment: "Traditions which would have been an embarrassment to followers of Jesus in the post-Easter period are unlikely to have been invented" (Stanton, *Gospels and Jesus*, 175).

Historical Plausibility: "Jesus can only have said and done what a first-century Jewish charismatic could have said and done" (Theissen and Merz, *Historical Jesus*, 118).

four. Guilder's unibrow arched. Seconds passed. The girl beamed as though she'd scored a point for God.

Guilder rallied.

"We know the Fourth Gospel is reliable here," he said, "precisely because it works so hard elsewhere to depict John as Jesus's subordinate."[7]

The girl stopped taking notes and crossed her arms. I typed faster. That was when Guilder announced that John the Baptist probably didn't point people toward Jesus. The girl slumped. John spoke about sin and imminent judgment, Guilder said, but not about a Messiah.

"Read the Old Testament texts the Gospels use to explain John," he said. "They talk about the coming of God, not the Messiah!"

He made us look them up.

Mark 1:3; Matthew 3:3; Luke 3:4; John 1:23	Isaiah 40:3	"A voice cries out: 'In the wilderness prepare the way of the LORD, make straight in the desert a highway for our God.'"
Mark 1:3 Matthew 11:10 Luke 7:27	Malachi 3:1	"See, I am sending my messenger to prepare the way before me, and the Lord whom you seek will suddenly come to his temple. The messenger of the covenant in whom you delight—indeed, he is coming," says the LORD of hosts.

"We need to imagine," Guilder continued, getting a little preachy, "that John was a prophet of Israel who leveled his critique at Israel (Acts 13:25) and heralded the imminent arrival of Israel's God. Period."[8]

The slumping arm-crosser said something about John being the forerunner, at which point someone else chimed in to ask, if John's only goal was to introduce Jesus, why his movement continued after Jesus appeared on the scene (John 3:22–23; Acts 18:24–25; 19:1–7).

Something didn't seem right. No Jew would describe *God* as "*more powerful than I*" (Matt. 3:11; Luke 3:16). And John would hardly declare himself unworthy to lace *God's* sandals (Mark 1:7). These images worked only to contrast human figures. They made sense only if John expected a prophet or a Messiah or an Elijah—someone strong enough to take the lead in God's next act. As usual, this flash of sheer brilliance didn't strike until after class.[9]

After break, Guilder had us compare John the Baptist as he appears in the Gospels and in Josephus. The overlap is impressive, especially since borrowing in either direction seems unlikely.[10]

	Luke 3 and Matthew 14	Josephus, *Jewish Antiquities* 18.116–119
A man called John the Baptist	**Matthew 14:8** Prompted by her mother, she said, "Give me the head of John the Baptist here on a platter."	*116* But to some . . . the destruction of Herod's army seemed to be divine vengeance . . . for his treatment of John, surnamed the Baptist.
challenged large crowds	**Luke 3:7** John said to the crowds that came out to be baptized by him, "You brood of vipers! Who warned you to flee from the wrath to come?"	*118* When others too joined the crowds about him, because they were aroused to the highest degree by his sermons, . . .
to repent,	**Luke 3:3, 16** He went into all the region around the Jordan, proclaiming a baptism of repentance for the forgiveness of sins.	*117* They must not employ [baptism] to gain pardon for whatever sins they committed,

	Luke 3 and Matthew 14	Josephus, *Jewish Antiquities* 18.116–119
be baptized,	John answered all of them by saying, "I baptize you with water . . ."	*117* he . . . exhorted the Jews . . . to join in baptism. In his view [justice and piety] was a necessary preliminary if baptism was to be acceptable to God.
and perform deeds of righteousness.	**Luke 3:8, 11, 13** "Bear fruits worthy of repentance . . ." "Whoever has two coats must share with anyone who has none; and whoever has food must do likewise." . . . "Collect no more than the amount prescribed for you."	*117* he was a good man and had exhorted the Jews to lead righteous lives, to practice justice towards their fellows and piety towards God. . . . [Baptism was] a consecration of the body implying that the soul was already thoroughly cleansed by right behavior.
This prompted Herod Antipas to fear him,	**Matthew 14:5** Though Herod wanted to put him to death, he feared the crowd, because they regarded him as a prophet.	*118* Herod became alarmed. Eloquence that had so great an effect on mankind might lead to some form of sedition, for it looked as if they would be guided by John in everything that they did.
put him in prison,	**Luke 3:19–20** But Herod the ruler, who had been rebuked by him because of Herodias, his brother's wife, and because of all the evil things that Herod had done, added to them all by shutting up John in prison.	*119* Though John, because of Herod's suspicions, was brought in chains to Machaerus . . .
and, finally, execute him.	**Matthew 14:9–10** The king was grieved, yet out of regard for his oaths and for the guests, he commanded it [John's head] to be given; he sent and had John beheaded in the prison.	*117* For Herod had put him to death, though he was a good man. *119* and there [at Machaerus] put to death.

Given all the agreement, it's no wonder historians are confident that John the Baptist—the "historical" John—was a fiery preacher who stirred up the masses and made authorities nervous. Those same historians, however, point out that the sources diverge sharply at several key points.

	Gospels	Josephus
John's message	Warns of imminent judgment/coming wrath (Matt. 3:7, 10–12; Luke 3:7, 9, 16–17)	No reference to judgment
John's relationship to Jesus	Heralds Christ's arrival as "the one who is more powerful than I" (Mark 1:7; Luke 3:16; cf. John 1:20, 34; 3:30)	No hint of an alliance with Jesus, or that John sent followers to Jesus
Where John was baptizing	In wilderness (Mark 1:4) by Jordan River (Mark 1:5)	No mention of desert or river
Why John was arrested	Antipas is rebuked for his unlawful marriage (Mark 6:18; Luke 3:19)	Antipas feels threatened by John's popularity

The Gospels, Guilder said, have "Christianized" John. They've turned a reformer into a forerunner. A freelance prophet into a publicity agent. Hidden beneath all the Christian overlay, he said, was a zealous Jewish prophet who got in trouble with the authorities.

I told him after class that I wasn't persuaded. It's one thing for the Gospels to exploit John's testimony, I said. Something else for them to kidnap the man and make him read pro-Jesus propaganda into the camera. What did become clear that day was that all four Gospels are heavily invested in John's testimony.[11] Anyone who wants to find Jesus will need to spend time with John. As I planned to do precisely that, I emailed Guilder for advice. His reply was swift, concise, and organized. Typical Guilder.

From: "Randall Guilder" <rguilder@sblusa.com>
Subject: RE: Will the real Baptist please stand?
To: "Norm Adams" <nadams@state.com>

Norman:
On John's relationship to Jesus, I see four options.

1. John was a moral reformer with no urgent, apocalyptic message, very much in line with Josephus's account. Anything beyond that is later Christian fabrication.

2. John spoke only of God's coming judgment but not about any human figure. The early Christians knew Jesus's mission began with his baptism and concluded that John's role was preparatory. John's testimonials and the heavenly voice are narrative inventions designed to make this theological point. The evangelists may have faced competition from the Baptist's followers and thus purposely minimized John's independent significance.

3. John spoke vaguely of a coming one. When John baptized Jesus, he didn't recognize Jesus's significance. If he told people to follow Jesus, it was to expand his base and advance his national campaign. Only Jesus "saw" the Spirit/dove descend and heard the voice (Mark 1:11). John began to see Jesus as a possible messiah only after his arrest (Matt. 11:3).

4. John recognized Jesus at his baptism and publicly declared him to be the coming one (John 1:29–34; Matt. 3:14–17).

I defended number two in class (have you forgotten?), though lately I'm giving number three another look. If you're serious about tracking down *John the Plunger* (Meier's happy phrase), I'm afraid you'll need to trade the comforts of Jerusalem for the heat of the wilderness.

b'shalom
Guilder

Writing on the Wall

The École Biblique et Archéologique Française de Jérusalem is a Dominican school and world-class library five minutes' walk north of the Old City. Guilder's letter of introduction persuaded the librarian, Father Pawel, to give me a tour and assign me a desk. After spending several hours in the books, I had my John quest mapped out.

Kidron Valley Tombs

I bought a five-shekel kebab on the street and headed east along Via Dolorosa for the Kidron Valley. After passing Arab shopkeepers and the soldiers who guard the Western Wall tunnel, I exited the Old City through St. Stephen's Gate and went down into a valley of tombs whose bones patiently await resurrection. At the base of the Mount of Olives three massive tombs are chiseled out of bedrock. On the one known as Absalom's Tomb an anthropologist recently discovered an inscription.

I scrambled up the cliff above the tomb and squinted at a spot just above an opening, where the Greek text had been found. The afternoon shadows finally coaxed the weathered stone into revealing its secret: two faint lines, each about four feet long. According to the report, the inscription reads:

THIS IS THE TOMB OF ZACHARIAH, MARTYR,
VERY PIOUS PRIEST, FATHER OF JOHN[12]

Clambering back down, I found a ledge and dug into my stash of dried fruit and nuts. Not exactly wild honey and locusts, but close. In an article I'd found in the École stacks, Karin Laub explains how a photograph by an art history student brought the letters to light. Émile Puech used paper-mache to create a cast of the inscription. Good thing he'd paid attention in kindergarten.

Although the monument was probably built for the Jerusalem aristocracy, the inscription is too late to be reliable. All we can say for sure is that some fourth-century Byzantine Christian had reason to link this monument to John's father. Perhaps he'd heard the old tale about Herod slaughtering Zechariah in the temple when he wouldn't say where little Johnnie was hiding.[13] I pictured breathless, wide-eyed Byzantine pilgrims standing in my place. Did anyone fact-check the stories they heard from their guides? How much solid history lies embedded in these old legends?

Dusk was settling as I climbed out of the valley. The inscription reminded me that the story of Jesus is a Jewish story—one that includes both prophet and priest. But it also added questions to my growing list. I felt like an old widow going the wrong way in a crowded bazaar. Four ideas took shape, each one moving me further back in time.

1. **The fourth century.** How much myth did Byzantine storytellers weave into their history? For a fourth-century pilgrim, so many holy sites must have made an impression. Things would never be the same back on the farm. If I had to choose between their pious credulity and the suspicions of the modern academy, what would I prefer?

2. **Jesus's early career.** Why did Jesus associate with John? He could have sought the respect of Pharisees, apprenticed with Essenes, or joined a band of rebels. What was it about John's message that earned Jesus's endorsement (Matt. 11:11)?

3. **John's early career.** Why did John forsake his priestly heritage and family to live in the desert and forecast judgment? What caused the break between father and son? Did John's refusal to continue the priestly line provoke outrage? Or did John's father, a poor, rural priest, share John's alienation from the wealthy urban aristocracy?[14]

4. **John's infancy.** Was John the son of a temple priest? Various details (e.g., the division of Abijah in Luke 1:5; the temple ritual in 1:8–10; Zechariah's return home in 1:23) suggest historicity. Other bits may imply poetic license (e.g., the fact that Luke's Gospel *begins* [1:8] and *ends* [24:53] in the temple) or Old Testament inspiration (e.g., John's old, childless parents behave like Abraham and Sarah; John's family mirrors Samuel's). Were the early Christians telling new stories without forgetting the old?[15]

Absalom's Tomb

John the Baptist as a Second Samuel

Luke 1		1 Samuel 1–2	
1:7	a childless couple: Zechariah and Elizabeth	1:2	a childless couple: Elkanah and Hannah
1:9	Zechariah sacrifices in Jerusalem temple.	1:3–4	Elkanah sacrifices in the Shiloh tabernacle.

Luke 1		1 Samuel 1–2	
1:13	God announces, in the temple, that Zechariah's prayer for a son will be answered.	1:17	Eli expresses hope, in the tabernacle, that Hannah's prayer for a son will be answered.
1:57–58	John's birth brings great joy.	1:18; 2:1	Samuel's birth brings great joy.
1:13, 60–63	Choice of name is decided by angel.	1:20	Meaning of name is explained by Hannah.
1:15	not to drink alcohol (a lifelong Nazirite)*	1:11	hair not to be cut (a lifelong Nazirite)*
1:67–79	Zechariah prophesies.	2:1–10	Hannah prays.
3:7–9	John prophesies of coming judgment.	3:11–18	Samuel prophesies of coming judgment.
3:21	John baptizes Jesus.	10:1; 16:13	Samuel anoints Saul and David.

*The **Nazirite vow** described in Numbers 6:1–5 prohibits alcohol, haircuts, and more.

Cresting the knoll on the Via Dolorosa, I spied an oddly dressed pair dragging weathered, overstuffed bags across the cobbles. As I drew closer I heard a British accent.

"Shan't be long now, Sister Sophie."

"So you said five minutes ago," countered a younger, Germanic voice.

"Perhaps the lads at the gate didn't understand."

"Can I help you find something?" I was awash in chivalry.

"Thank . . . you . . . Jesus!" panted the red-faced Sister.

"Ha-llllooo my good man!" The gentleman turned my way. "We're seeking the Austrian Hospice. Don't suppose you've heard of it, then, have you?"

"Heard of it? I'm staying there. Help with the bags?"

More praises shot heavenward as I fell in beside "Prophet Jonathan," who wasted no time announcing their reason for coming to Jerusalem: the "last days" had "drawn nigh," and God had "summoned" them to "forsake" their jobs in London and Amsterdam to "sound a warning" while Messiah Jesus saw fit to "tarry." I'd heard that such types felt drawn to the Holy Land, especially after Y2K and 9/11, but this was my first close encounter.

Warily I guided them around three armed soldiers lounging on the hospice steps, to whom, thankfully, they chose not to divulge their prophetic insights. I steered them to the front desk, picked up a phone message, and turned to leave, when the prophet seized my arm. Pressing a booklet into my hand, he made me promise to join them for dinner. I hesitated, but only for a second. It's not every day you get to dine with a pair of doomsday apocalyptics.

The thesis of their book turned out to be that global chaos and the rise of the antichrist would swiftly follow the formation of an independent Palestinian state. A tangle of **bold fonts**, CAPITAL LETTERS, and exclamation! marks! gave a certain urgency to recent events. Turns out:

- Israel's declaration of independence on May 14, 1948, fulfilled Isaiah 66:7–8.
- The Six Days' War of 1967 and the capture of East Jerusalem (especially the Temple Mount) ended the "times of the Gentiles" (Luke 21:24).
- Saddam Hussein "was" Nebuchadnezzar. Isaiah 13 predicted Iraq's invasion of Kuwait.
- Ezekiel 38 predicted Iran's nuclear program.
- God sent Hurricane Katrina and Ariel Sharon's stroke to condemn Israel for giving up the Gaza.
- God inspired Ehud Olmert to rain judgment on Gaza just as God had David inflict judgment on the Philistines.

On it went. I marveled that these books cleared El Al security. Over dinner I learned that the group my new acquaintances belonged to, Night Watchers, began with a vivid dream that Jesus would return before 2018, seventy years after the birth of Israel in 1948. Meanwhile the world was spiraling toward Armageddon.

I admired their sincerity. And wondered about their sanity. This could be a dangerous place for strange-looking preachers of repentance, judgment, and imminent cataclysm. That's when I was struck by the similarities between these folks and John the Baptist. Was John's message less eccentric than theirs? Were they any less likely to run into trouble with authorities? Would the Baptist have enjoyed any greater credibility among the elites of his day (John 1:19–25)? John was looking less heroic and more, um, bizarre. And his death was making more sense. I was making progress.

Pots and Baths

The phone message was from Jesse, my roommate's uncle and a PhD student at Bar Ilan University. He was borrowing a car and heading down in the morning to the Dead Sea, to the ruins of Qumran. Would I care to ride along?

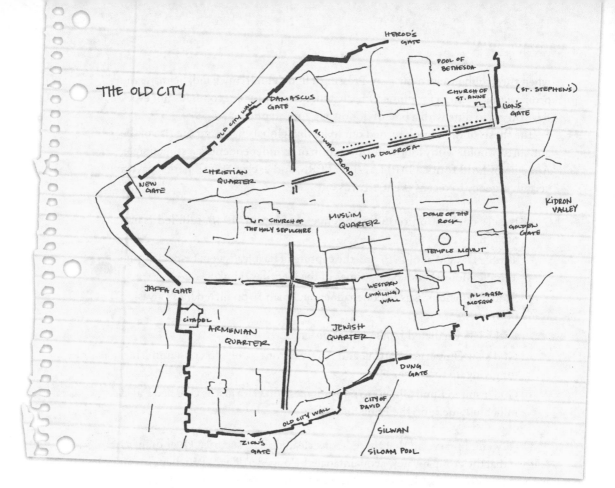

I woke to the *fajr*, the predawn prayer call, and stumbled up the cobbles past sleeping dogs and padlocked shops to Damascus Gate, where Jesse was waiting. He wore a Tilley hat with a chin strap and a vest with about three hundred pockets. Back home this wouldn't work. Out here it was almost cool. As we descended 1,150 meters to the Dead Sea, Jesse pointed first down to rickety, dusty Bedouin camps in the arid ravines and then up to the affluent, sprawling, hydrated Jewish settlement of Ma'ale Adumim on the hills. This land makes you believe impossible things before breakfast.

When we reached the valley floor, we turned south toward the sea just as the sun broke through the haze seeking something to scorch. The ruins, roughly the size of a football field, were hard to miss, perched on a plateau above Wadi Qumran, the deep ravine that funnels seasonal torrents from the heights to their final resting place in the sea. Mental note: return here during a downpour.

When I asked Jesse what brought him again to this desolate spot, he detoured into a lecture on the Dead Sea Scrolls, the ruins, and the community that once occupied them. He was hiding something.

"Eleven caves. Nine complete scrolls. Fragments of hundreds of others," he began. "Greatest archaeological find of the twentieth century. Bedouins found five of the caves; archaeologists the other six. That's eleven caves out of some 270 up there. On the scrolls are books of the Hebrew Bible—especially Psalms, Deuteronomy, and Isaiah—but also prayers and sectarian documents belonging to some kind of apocalyptic, end-times, messianic group. Some say the scrolls have little to do with these ruins, but most say this settlement housed Jewish monks who gathered and copied texts, and stored their scrolls nearby. All that changed when the Romans destroyed the settlement during the Jewish War."

We wandered the settlement, pausing at cisterns, a tower, a pottery workshop, and the room that archaeologist Roland De Vaux dubbed the "scriptorium." From there it wasn't far to the end of the plateau, where we looked across to Cave 4, home for thousands of fragments of hundreds of manuscripts before they were retrieved in 1952.

Between sips of water I asked Jesse whether John the Baptist might have spent time at Qumran. Jesse's Tilley was looking cooler by the minute.

"Well—if John's elderly parents died when he was young (Luke 1:7) and if he spent years in the desert (Luke 1:80), he had to live somewhere."[16]

"But why here?"

"Because we are standing a Frisbee throw from where John baptized. And because the Essenes were known to adopt children and train them in their ways."[17]

"I thought the case would be stronger than that."

Jesse wasn't finished. "If John grew up here it might explain why he remained single and why he baptized. Ever wonder why *water* was so important to John?"

"You read my mind."

"Look over there. And there." Jesse nodded at several plastered cisterns with odd-looking stairways. They could be *mikva'ot*, or purification baths, Jesse explained.[18] "I count ten," he said. "Lots of Jews bathed to remove impurity; these guys devoted a section of their brains to ritualistic lustrations."

"On the west side of the Dead Sea, but out of range of the noxious exhalations of the coast, is the solitary tribe of the Essenes, which is remarkable beyond all the other tribes in the whole world, as it has no women and has renounced all sexual desire, has no money, and has only palm trees for company. Day by day the throng of refugees is recruited to an equal number by numerous successions of personnel tired of life and driven there by ways of fortune to adopt their manners. Thus, through thousands of ages (incredible to relate) a race in which no one is born lives on forever; so prolific for their advantage is other men's weariness of life."

Pliny the Elder,
Natural History 5.17.4

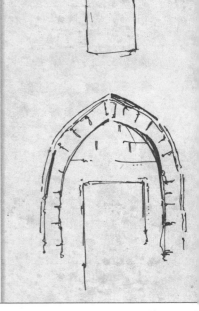

"Let me get this straight: Both John and the folks at Qumran inhabited the *hot* desert and embraced rituals involving *cool* water . . . so they must be related? That's all you got?"

"You're right to be skeptical. The John–Qumran connection is just speculation."

"Why do *you* think these people lived in the desert?" It was Jesse's turn to ask questions.

"Because this is the sort of place Israel's God shows up? Like at the burning bush?"

"The burning bush was in Egypt."

"Yes, but it was in the wilderness, which is my point."

"Mind if I sharpen it?" Jesse asked.

"Please do."

"The Gospels quote Isaiah 40:3 to explain that John is *the voice crying in the wilderness.* A scroll from Cave 1 quotes the very same text to explain what these Qumran folks were doing out here.[19] So both John and Qumran think the last days have begun, and both find the script for their part in Isaiah 40:3."

"Truly you have a dizzying intellect," I said. This guy was not someone to be trifled with.

"Wait till I get going!" he retorted. "Where was I?"

"You were going to tell me why you reject the theory of John's ties to Qumran."

"Right. I don't think it works. For one thing, only in the Fourth Gospel (1:23) do we find the Isaiah quote on the lips of the Baptist. In the Synoptics the author inserts the Isaiah quote. My hunch is that Christians looking back saw that John fit Isaiah's profile and worked the idea back into the story. The Gospels rarely indicate when they've stopped reciting historical events and started explaining what they mean."

Jesse looked east toward a field of oblong rock piles on the edge of the settlement. "Those corpses over there might complain if they heard us comparing John the Baptist to Qumran."

"That's a cemetery?"

"Eleven hundred bodies lined up in tidy rows. Heads all pointing south. *Time* ran an article a few years ago suggesting one of the corpses might belong to John the Baptist!"

"No way."

"Bannus . . . dwelt in the wilderness, wearing only such clothing as trees provided . . . and using frequent ablutions of cold water, by day and night, for purity's sake."

Josephus, *Life* ‖

Scrolls from Qumran

Community Rule (1QS), or *Manual of Discipline*, is sometimes called the "constitution" of the community, since it deals with leaders, new recruits, ceremonies, rules, and penalties.

Thanksgiving Scroll (1QH) or *Hodayot*, contains about twenty-five psalms, written in first person by someone convinced of his lofty mission and of his opponents' wickedness. These may be the actual words of the community's founder, the *Teacher of Righteousness*, whom one scholar has called "the first Messiah."

War Scroll (1QM) describes a final war—forty years long—between the "sons of light" and the "sons of darkness," aided by angels and demons, until God finally weighs in and defeats Satan and his minions.

Copper Scroll (3Q15) names sixty-four locations where buried treasure may be found. Some dismiss the scroll as fanciful; others hope to recover treasures from the temple, buried by priests fleeing the Roman assault of 66–70 CE.

"Way. The skeleton was over at the east end. Very odd—the body was oriented east-west and in some kind of a building. The guy might have been one of the leaders, but the idea that it was John is nonsense. The scholars who led the dig said the idea was someone's publicity stunt."

"So why would these corpses complain?"

"They'd say John's one-and-done baptism wasn't enough. Qumran recruits underwent a watery initiation like John's, but they also dipped themselves *daily* during their two or three years of probation.[20] John wasn't nearly so Type-A. He had followers (John 1:35–44), but he wasn't organizing a commune. He just dunked them and sent them off to be fairer tax collectors and kinder soldiers (Luke 3:12–14). He told people to share extra tunics but never required a common purse."

"Okay," I said. "John was not Qumran's poster boy. But I still see similarities. These folks worshiped and studied . . ."

"And bathed."

"And bathed. But they didn't *sacrifice*."

"Correct. In fact, some scrolls declare the temple hopelessly corrupt. Since Jerusalem didn't follow Qumran's *solar* calendar, the priests were sacrificing on the wrong day!"

"I hate when that happens. My point is that Qumran got along *without sacrifices* . . . and right down the road, nowhere near the temple, the Baptist was declaring forgiveness of sins."

"I see where you're going," said Jesse.

I was on a roll.

"In class we saw that John expected righteous deeds to come *first*, before baptism. On that, the Gospels and Josephus agree. So John's baptism took care of impurities as long as people *first* turned away from sin toward justice. Answer me this: Was John's baptism an end run around temple ritual? Like at Qumran? Was John replacing the temple system with something more, I don't know, spiritual?"

"Some think so.[21] Me? I'm not sure. Maybe John was simply echoing the old idea that righteousness and justice are more important than sacrifice.[22] If John was so antitemple, do you think officials from Jerusalem would line up for baptism?"[23]

Jesse drained his water bottle and continued.

"I'm not sure Qumran was antitemple either. What if they were staying pure out here because God was about to *restore* the temple and invite *them* to run it?"

Jesse rose to his feet and looked around. He had been eyeing a group on the north edge of the site. Their bodyguard's rifle was plainly in view.

Qumran Cave

"Why did we come here today?" I asked suspiciously.

He sat back down. "Recently two archaeologists finished excavating the last and largest cistern," he said. "That one over there. What they found at the bottom was a surprise: three tons of high quality clay. They think this 'proves' the site has no ties to the scrolls. Nor to the Essenes or any other Jewish sect. It was a factory that made pots. And date honey. Period. No spiritual retreat center. No manuscript production. No countertemple rituals. Just pots . . . and honey."

"What about the *scriptorium*?"

"There may not *be* a scriptorium. The only hard evidence is a pair of inkwells and some oil lamps. Whoo-wee. Why no parchment or scribal tools? As for the plastered mud-brick tables and benches, the idea that they were furniture for scribes is just a guess."

With that Jesse became serious. Ducking under a barrier, he lowered himself into the cistern and began scraping hardened clay into his Nalgene.

"Are you allowed to take stuff from an archaeological site?" I hissed.

"No," he said, not looking up.

Jesse said no more until we were back in the car. Since clay has its own properties and mineral composition, he planned to subject part of his sample to "Neutron Activation Analysis" and mix the rest with water so a potter friend could throw him a pot. He planned to compare the results with clay shards from Cave 4 and elsewhere in the region.

"What if this clay doesn't match the scroll jars?" I asked.

"Then the jars probably came from somewhere other than this kiln."

"Like where? Jerusalem?"

"Maybe."

"What would happen if the Essene Hypothesis crumbled? If this place turned out to be a pottery factory?"

"Lots of authors would have to revise their books," Jesse quipped.

"Do you think some scrolls arrived here from other places?"

"Absolutely. These guys probably had a library, but it's unlikely they owned all the scrolls. There are hundreds of scribal hands, with almost no two the same! And the Copper Scroll . . ."

"Copper Scroll?"

"It's a treasure map. If it's not a joke, it describes way too much wealth for this little place."

"So the scrolls are much more than the quirky library of a fringe cult. They testify to the rich diversity of early Judaism."

"And to its apocalyptic worldview."

"Maybe that's why John's fervent message resonated with so many people across society—tax collectors and soldiers, peasants and priests."

"Maybe so."

A Floor and a Roof

It was time to head for the Jordan. Time to ponder John the Baptist's doomsday message and its connection to Jesus. My day at Qumran had convinced me that first-century Judaism was a big umbrella, with lots of room for odd characters and fringe groups. John would have little trouble fitting in. Same goes for Jesus. Makes you wonder why they were executed.

Mark says John did his baptizing in the Jordan not far from Jerusalem (Mark 1:5). John's Gospel consistently puts the Baptist's activities *east* of the Jordan, in Perea (John 1:28; 3:26; 10:40).[24] This fits nicely with Josephus's claim that when John was arrested he was taken bound to nearby Machaerus (*Jewish Antiquities* 18.119). And it suited me very well because the traditional baptism site on the Israeli side, the Monastery of St. John, is in a military zone and is accessible only on Orthodox feast days.[25]

When forty-six years of belligerency ended with the Jordan–Israel peace treaty of 1994, archaeologists were eager to track down "Bethany beyond the Jordan" (John 1:28). Sure enough, on the Jordan's east bank, along the Wadi Kharrar, they uncovered extensive Byzantine ruins exactly where the ancient sources said they should be. Hermit caves, baptismal pools, churches—amazing what you find when you clear away a few land mines.[26] So the combined witness of the New Testament, later traditions, topography, and now archaeology makes a persuasive case that John performed more than a few baptisms in the vicinity.

Locating a site is one thing. Getting there is another. I took a bus to the Allenby Bridge, a curiously unofficial crossing between the West Bank and Jordan. Air-conditioning on Palestinian busses is called window shades. To leave Israel you pay a hefty exit tax, answer lots of questions, and then wait for a shuttle across no-man's-land, the wilderness that John once called home. John survived months, years, out there. I *might* last a day.

Beneath the bridge the Jordan was muddy, narrow, and slow. Growing villages and agriculture now siphon most of the water before it reaches the Dead Sea, except in winter, when for a few weeks the Jordan reclaims its mythical stature as a river. More security screening and passport inspection on the other side. Beyond a swarm of taxi drivers, I found an old bus willing to make the grinding, sweaty ascent to Jordan's hilly capital. The total distance from Jerusalem to Amman is about forty miles. It took me four hours.

In Jesus's day, Amman was called Philadelphia and belonged to the Decapolis, the league of city-states that buffered the Roman Empire against enemies to the east. Although Jesus traversed this region (Mark 5:1–2; 7:31), I'd bet that a Galilean rabbi and his "unschooled ruffians" avoided the major pagan centers.

I didn't. I headed downtown to see the Roman theater, and then across the street to a narrow, twisting staircase that ascends to the ruin-strewn acropolis. A small museum up there is home to the Copper Scroll, the Dead Sea treasure map Jesse told me about. I arrived at the door without a ticket. The guard shrugged and let me pass.

To unroll the scroll they had to cut the corroded metal lengthwise into segments. I spotted them immediately: several dozen curved green strips. It is easy enough to translate, I'm told, but nearly impossible to follow its cryptic directions. Were second temple riches still out there? Does this scroll point us to the temple treasury? The ark of the covenant? Would treasures from the second temple settle any disputes, or would they simply incite militants to blow up the Dome of the Rock?

From the hilltop a road snaked down to the city center, where I boarded a bus bound for Madaba, home of St. George's Church and its astonishing mosaic map of the Holy Land. Though I wrongly assumed the driver would know where to let me off, I eventually found the church, where, protected only by rope and a sign, a colorful sea of ancient ceramic shows dozens of towns and holy sites from Lebanon to Egypt. Here was Jerusalem with its streets, gates, and houses. There was the Jordan River with fish swimming *upstream* to avoid a salty death in the Dead Sea. Each tiny tile offers a glimpse of the way things were, and of what Christians believed, in the sixth century.

I was struck by the prominence the map gave to John the Baptist. Just west of the Jordan, not far from Jericho, the map reads:

BEΘABAPA
TOTOYAΓIOY IWANNOY
TOY BAΠTICMA
TOC

My guide book said *Bethabara*[27] meant "place of crossing over." The map marked a ford in the river. The significance of the place was explained with red letters: "the [place] of the baptism of Saint John." Apparently pilgrims wanted to know where Jesus was baptized so they could follow his example.

I spent the night in Madaba on the roof of a low-end hotel near St. George's. My roof-mate was Bernie, a British university student on a two-month trek. I first met him in the tiny "lobby," where he was arguing for a discount. It was a game— British wit against Arab determination. Like the day Britain relinquished its Mandate over Jordan, the Arab won.

Raised Catholic, Bernie felt grateful for his childhood encounter with religion, since it meant he was now an *informed* atheist and not an unreflective one like his friends. On the roof Bernie wanted to know why I believed in God. "Good" and "bad" were social constructs, he said. Nothing more. A neuroscience major, he thought emotions were the result of stimulation in some corner of the brain. Someday, he suggested, they'll locate the god-sensing zone and be able to create "authentic" encounters with the deity by firing lasers into our skulls.

Madaba Map of Jordan River

A bare mattress and a grubby blanket did little to shield me from the cool night. Dogs and roosters conspired. My mind churned.

Was I foolish to think that coming here would bring me closer to Jesus? Could mosaics and theaters do for me what textbooks could not? Was I foolishly looking for the Grail—for evidence to persuade the Bernies of the world, and myself, that we Christians got it right?

Then I saw her. No, not Bathsheba on a roof nearby. Low in the sky, fiery orange and almost full, the moon was caught in a tangled web of antennas, water towers, and protruding rebar. Suddenly my rooftop was sacred, my soul pierced. If Bernie's brain was acting up, he didn't let on.

Down to the River

Standing on the bank of the Jordan, I pictured John shaking a fist at the crowds. If the summaries in Matthew and Luke do him justice, John was feisty and fearless. And he could smell pretexts for injustice a Roman mile away.

Luke 3:7–9, 16–17 (RSV; cf. Matt. 3:7–12)	Old Testament Echoes?
He said therefore to the multitudes that came out to be baptized by him, "You brood of vipers! Who warned you to flee from the wrath to come? Bear fruits that befit repentance, and do not begin to say to yourselves, 'We have Abraham as our father'; for I tell you, God is able from these stones to raise up children to Abraham. Even now the axe is laid to the root of the trees; every tree therefore that does not bear good fruit is cut down and thrown into the fire." . . .	"I have winnowed them with a winnowing fork in the gates of the land; I have bereaved them, I have destroyed my people; they did not turn from their ways." (Jer. 15:7 RSV) "See, the day is coming, burning like an oven, when all the arrogant and all evildoers will be stubble; the day that comes shall burn them up," says the Lord of hosts. . . . (Mal. 4:1)
John answered them all, "I baptize you with water; but he who is mightier than I is coming, the thong of whose sandals I am not worthy to untie; he will baptize you with the Holy Spirit and with fire. His winnowing fork is in his hand, to clear his threshing floor, and to gather the wheat into his granary, but the chaff he will burn with unquenchable fire."	

When I showed Bernie Luke's accounts of John's preaching, he wasn't impressed. All that brimstone sounded to him like the violent God of the Old Testament. Bernie had decided to join me for the day to see Bethany, where John baptized, and Machaerus, where he lost his head. We agreed to share the cost of a taxi. He didn't even haggle over the price. Now, standing on an unremarkable patch of dirt on the bank of an unimpressive stream, Bernie looked trapped. For him I represented the religious dark ages, when medieval gods consigned the unbaptized to the inferno.

"You'd like the way Josephus tells the story," I suggested. "Not a trace of fanaticism. No flames, not even a pitchfork." According to Josephus, John simply told folks to honor God and be nice.

"Problem was," I continued, "it's hard to imagine city folk hiking all the way out here in the heat just to hear John tell them to play nicely. And harder to imagine *that* kind of John incurring anyone's wrath. John must have been edgier, more dangerous, than Josephus lets on."

I spoke as if the idea had just dawned on me. Actually I stole it from John Meier, a New Testament professor at Notre Dame who has authored several massive volumes on Jesus. His work makes my expedition look like an Easter egg hunt. As it happened, Professor Meier was staying at the École when I arrived. I was hoping to find him in the bowels of the library, surrounded by weathered tomes or pouring over parchments with a magnifying glass. Instead I spotted him shuffling across the courtyard, late for a meeting. When I asked him *which* John seemed more credible—the apocalyptic John in the Gospels or the moralistic John of Josephus—he looked at his watch and suggested I look at volume two of his opus, *A Marginal Jew*. I told him volume two wasn't on the shelf. I didn't tell him that it was sitting mostly unread in my cubicle.

It worked. Meier set down his bag and put his fingertips together, like Mr. Burns in *The Simpsons*. "Josephus," he began, "had no use for a fiery day of judgment, especially one that would make ethnic ties irrelevant. No use for a judgment meted out by a mysterious figure, nor for one

"For Herod had put [John] to death, though he was a good man and had exhorted the Jews to lead righteous lives, to practice justice towards their fellows and piety towards God, and so doing to join in baptism. In his view this was a necessary preliminary if baptism was to be acceptable to God. They must not employ it to gain pardon for whatever sins they committed, but as a consecration of the body implying that the soul was already thoroughly cleansed by right behavior."

Josephus, *Jewish Antiquities* 18.117

"Josephus .... presented a distinctly non-apocalyptic portrait of Judean culture. ... The recently failed revolt in Judea, which had brought the Jews such bad press, had been partly fueled by apocalyptic hopes—the anticipation that God would choose that moment to intervene in world affairs and restore Israel's glory. ... Josephus wants no part of this 'deliverance' mentality."

Steve Mason, *Josephus and the New Testament*, 223–24

that could be avoided by submitting to a baptism of repentance. Josephus had little use for such disturbing ideas. In fact, if the Synoptic portrait of the Baptist did not exist, we'd have to invent it to supply what Josephus must have suppressed or simply didn't know."[28]

"So if Josephus knew that John thought the end was near, he would have kept that to himself?" I asked.[29]

"I would if I were being paid *by* Romans to write *in* Rome *for* Romans," Meier quipped, adjusting large square glasses that liked to slide down his nose. "Not only was Josephus basking in imperial support, but he'd also landed Roman citizenship. Provocative rhetoric about an angry god raining down judgment could jeopardize everything."[30]

Back on the riverbank, Bernie acknowledged that Josephus had reason to soft-pedal John's message. Maybe the Gospels' depiction of an angry prophet condemning injustice and heralding a new age wasn't so bad after all. Echoes of Bob Dylan, Bernie said.

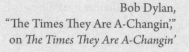

Gather 'round people wherever you roam
. . . admit that the waters around you have grown
. . . accept . . . that soon you'll be drenched to the bone.
. . . the times they are a-changin'.

Bob Dylan,
"The Times They Are A-Changin',"
on *The Times They Are A-Changin'*

"If John believed the times were a-changin'," he started, "why not head for the city? Why stand at a desert crossroads when you can set up your soapbox in the marketplace? Every zealot knows you gotta take your message to the people."

Bernie knew whereof he spoke; two of his friends died when a suicide bomber took his apocalyptic message to the London Underground. And Bernie was right about the desert. From the parking lot we had ridden

Jordan River South

the shuttle bus across a moonscape and then hiked through a thicket to the river. Nothing we had seen made this spot an obvious choice. Even in John's day there were no settlements in the area, only roads. Most of his preaching would have fallen on the thorny ground of distracted merchants or the rocky soil of weary travelers (Mark 1:5; Matt. 3:5). It made no sense.

Near us at the river were two armed, chain-smoking Jordanian soldiers (there, evidently, to shoot us before we waded across to the West Bank), an Italian couple who might have been on their honeymoon, and our official guide, Mahmoud.

"You not know why thees place important?" Mahmoud had been listening.

"Not really."

"Thees where the Jewish cross into Palestine."

He wasn't talking about 1948. The map in my Bible showed we were very near the Israelites' camp on the plains of Moab (Num. 33:48–50) and the spot Joshua chose to lead Israel across the Jordan into the land (Josh. 3–4). Indeed, we were almost in the shadow of Mount Nebo, Moses's last known whereabouts, from which he looked across to Canaan and promptly died (Deut. 32:48–52; 34:1–6).

In Guilder's class we read about "Theudas," another freelance "prophet" who emerged a decade or so after John. People flocked to the river to see him reenact Joshua's miracle crossing of the Jordan. Fadus, the Roman procurator, saw Theudas's riverbank theater as politically subversive: if the masses thought too much about the golden days of Joshua's conquest, anti-Roman violence was sure to break out. A Jewish intifada.

Was John's message similarly subversive? Was he reenacting the Jordan episode that began Israel's conquest?[31] Was he showing those with eyes to see that God's people—the righteous among them at least—were on the march?

I glanced at our guide, a Jordanian Palestinian, wondering what he thought about ancient Israel's occupation of the land. Mahmoud was pointing at the river.

Theudas

"When Fadus was procurator of Judaea, a certain imposter named Theudas persuaded the majority of the masses to take up their possessions and to _follow him to the Jordan River. He stated that he was a prophet and that at his command the river would be parted and would provide them an easy passage._ With this talk he deceived many. Fadus, however, . . . sent against them a squadron of cavalry. These fell upon them unexpectedly, slew many of them and took many prisoners. Theudas himself was captured, whereupon they _cut off his head_ and brought it to Jerusalem."

Josephus,
Jewish Antiquities 20.97–99

"But a Pharisee in the council named Gamaliel, a teacher of the law, held in honor by all the people, stood up and . . . said to them, ' Men of Israel, take care what you do with these men. For before these days Theudas arose, giving himself out to be somebody, and a number of men, about four hundred, joined him; but he was slain and all who followed him were dispersed and came to nothing.'"

Acts 5:34–36

"Thees where e-LEE-yah dee-VIDE dee waters."

I looked again at the map in my Bible. Sure enough, from Jericho Elijah and Elisha traveled east (2 Kings 2:4–5) to the Jordan (2:6–7) and across, miraculously, to the east bank (2:8–9). The most direct route would land them pretty much ... exactly ... *here*. Which meant *here* was where the chariot of fire appeared and the whirlwind carried Elijah away, leaving Elisha to fend for himself (2:11–12).

I was on to something. Wouldn't the crowds of John's day, if they knew their Elijah traditions, experience collective déjà vu (John 1:21, 25)? Before them stood someone who demanded unswerving loyalty to Yahweh, who promised divine fire, and who challenged the ruling elites. Even Jesus saw John as an Elijah figure (Matt. 11:14; 17:12–13; cf. Mark 9:13).[32]

John, however, begged to differ (John 1:21). He couldn't see himself in the prophetic big leagues. Just call me a *voice*, he said (John 1:23). I am *not worthy* (Mark 1:7). Think of when Wayne and Garth in *Wayne's World* met Steven Tyler and Joe Perry from Aerosmith.

Does John's *location* tell us something about his *expectation*? Did he come here because he expected Elijah to return (Mal. 4:5) to the spot of his departure (2 Kings 2:11)? Was John like Elisha, waiting for his mentor? Waiting for the one who would summon God's fire against the unrighteous of his day, as Elijah did against the prophets of Baal (1 Kings 18:37–38)? Waiting for the one who would bring reconciliation between fathers and children (Mal. 4:6)? Did John come to the Jordan not because he thought he *was* Elijah but because he knew he *wasn't*?

"If John came here to witness Elijah's second coming," Bernie said, "he must have been disappointed."

"That's the sixty-four-thousand-dinar question," I said. "*Was* he disappointed?" As Jesus's reputation spread, people had plenty of reason to call him a prophet, even an Elijah (Mark 8:28), what with his band of disciples, his northern origins, and rumors about feeding the hungry and raising the dead. What if John was among those who saw in Jesus signs of Elijah's return?

Brain activity slowed as we began the sweaty hike back to the visitors' center, where thirsty tourists must run the gauntlet of shops that sell vials of Jordan water and sand art from Petra. We roused our taxi driver, who drove us in silence for Mukawir.

I would return to the Elijah question back at the École, where it became clear to me that the Gospels cast *both* John *and* Jesus as Elijah figures. Contrary to my expectations, the tighter Elijah parallels were with Jesus. Jesus, however, seems to have had mixed feelings about the connection, and he happily let John have it.[33]

Parallel	Elijah		John as Elijah	
Location of ministry	lived in the wilderness and along the Jordan River	1 Kings 17:3–6; 19:3–4, 15; 2 Kings 2:6–7, 13–15	appears in the wilderness and baptizes in the Jordan	Mark 1:3–5, 9; Luke 3:2–4
Clothing	identified by apparently odd attire: hairy garment and leather belt	2 Kings 1:8	described by apparently odd, nomadic attire: camel's hair and leather belt	Mark 1:6; Matthew 11:8
Judgment to come	warned of coming judgment	1 Kings 17:1; 2 Kings 1:10–12, 16	warns of one to come who will burn the chaff	Matthew 3:12
Fire from heaven	spoke of fire from heaven	1 Kings 18:23–25, 38; 2 Kings 1:10–14; 2:11	warns of one who will baptize with the Holy Spirit and fire	Matthew 3:11; Luke 3:16–17
Call to repent	turned people back to God; his return would reconcile parents and children	1 Kings 17:24; 18:20–40; 21:28–29; Malachi 4:5–6	turns people back to God	Luke 1:16–17; 3:10–14
Confronts rulers	confronted kings and leaders about sin	1 Kings 17:1; 18:15–19; 21:17–27; 2 Kings 1:3–4, 16	confronts Herod Antipas, Pharisees, and Sadducees about sin	Matthew 3:7–10; Luke 3:19–20
Opposed by rulers	Ahab tried to kill Elijah; wife Jezebel threatened to kill him but was thwarted	1 Kings 18:9–14; 19:2, 10, 14	imprisoned by Herod Antipas; wife Herodias conspires to have John executed; thwarted, then successful	Luke 3:20; Mark 6:16–29; Matthew 14:1–12

Parallel	Elijah (or Elisha)		Jesus as Elijah	
Forty days in the wilderness	traveled forty days and nights without food, from near Beersheba to Horeb (Sinai)	1 Kings 19:8	spends forty days and nights in the wilderness without food	Mark 1:12–13 (Matt. 4:2; Luke 4:1–2)
Calls disciples	while traveling, found farmer Elisha plowing; put his mantle on him; Elisha followed	1 Kings 19:19–21	while traveling, summons fishers Simon and Andrew, James and John; they follow	Mark 1:16–20 (Matt. 4:18–22)
Disciples leave family	let Elisha kiss his parents before leaving home	1 Kings 19:20	won't let one would-be disciple bury his father and another bid farewell to those at home	Matthew 8:21–22; Luke 9:59–62
Miracle: widow's son raised	in an upper room in Zarephath, raised a woman's dead son by lying on him and praying	1 Kings 17:17–24	in funeral procession at gate of Nain (2 miles from Shunem), raises widow's son by speaking	Luke 7:11–17
Miracle: child raised	behind closed doors in Shunem, raised to life a woman's son by lying on him and praying	2 Kings 4:32–37	in home of Jairus, raises daughter to life by speaking; commands parents to tell no one	Mark 5:35–43 (Matt. 9:23–26; Luke 8:49–56)

Parallel	Elijah (or Elisha)		Jesus as Elijah	
Miracle: the hungry are fed	asked widow for bread, but she had only a little flour; flour/oil lasted until the rains; Elisha had loaves and grain given to the people, though his attendant thought it wasn't enough; there were leftovers	1 Kings 17:8–16 (cf. 2 Kings 4:1–7); 2 Kings 4:42–44	twice asks disciples to feed the crowds; they have only a few loaves and fish; crowd eats, has leftovers; John 6:14: people think Jesus is "the prophet who is to come into the world"	Mark 6:32–44 (Matt. 14:13–21; Luke 9:10–17; John 6:1–15) Mark 8:1–10 (Matt. 15:32–39)
Promise of return	God promised to send Elijah again before the Day of the Lord	Malachi 4:5	various ones think Jesus is John the Baptist, Elijah, Jeremiah, or a prophet, but he is the Christ	Matthew 16:14 (Mark 8:28; Luke 9:19); Mark 6:15 (Luke 9:8)
Fire from heaven	twice called fire down on the men of Ahaziah, king of Samaria	2 Kings 1:9–16	rebukes disciples for wanting to call down fire on inhospitable Samaritans	Luke 9:51–55 (12:49–53)
Departure and ascension	Elisha watched Elijah ascend into heaven on a whirlwind	2 Kings 2:10–11	discusses his "exodus" with Moses and Elijah; time for his being "taken up"; disciples watch him ascend on cloud	Luke 9:30–31; Luke 9:51; Acts 1:9–11

Peering through Haze

Apart from a flat tire, our trip to Mukawir went smoothly. To get to the isolated fortress of Machaerus you hike down to a saddle, cross an aqueduct, and ascend a steep path to the plateau. It was easy to see why Herod the Great built a palace here; the height would intimidate assailants, and the location was perfect for defending against nearby Arab tribes. And it was easy to see why Lucilius Bassus, the Roman legate, seized it from rebels to destroy it.[34]

As we climbed across the meager ruins on the summit, I struggled to re-create the resplendent palace described by Josephus: Somewhere here John lost his head. It couldn't have been there in the bathhouse, or there in the private quarters. I paused on the pavement in the courtyard, picturing holy John, in chains, entertaining degenerate Antipas (Mark 6:20). From the courtyard, I moved south across the remains of what my book called a *triclinium*, a U-shaped dining room. The triclinium was divided into two parts, one smaller than the other. It took a moment for this to sink in. Mark says Salome *entered* the men's area to dance, *left* to consult with her mother, and *returned* to request John's head. The men must have dined in the larger room while Herodias dined with the women in the smaller one next door. If so, I was standing in the very room where John's dripping head first went on display.

At the west end of the plateau, I looked out over what Josephus calls "ravines of a depth baffling to the eye"—steep and desolate wadis, terraced by wind and weather. The thick haze shrouding the far shore of the Dead Sea made me think of John squinting into the future, hoping to discern the shape of things to come. So much about prophecy I didn't understand. Did Jewish seers see with crystal clarity?[35] Were they the ancient counterparts to Prophet Jonathan and Sister Sophie, privy not only to God's view of current affairs but also to transcripts and high definition images of the future?

"[Herod] enclosed an extensive area with ramparts and towers and founded a city there, from which an ascent led up to the ridge itself. Furthermore, on the top, surrounding the actual crest, he built a wall, erecting towers at the corners, each sixty cubits high. In the center of the enclosure he built a palace with magnificently spacious and beautiful apartments; he further provided numerous cisterns at the most convenient spots to receive the rain-water and furnish an abundant supply. . . . He stocked it with abundance of weapons and engines, and studied to make every preparation to enable its inmates to defy the longest siege."

Josephus, *Jewish War* 7.164

"Herod . . . gave a banquet for his courtiers and officers and the leading men of Galilee. For when Herodias' daughter came in and danced, she pleased Herod and his guests; . . . And she went out, and said to her mother,' What shall I ask?' And she said, 'The head of John the baptizer.' And she came in immediately with haste to the king."

Mark 6:21-25 RSV

From the haze of his cell, John sent to ask Jesus if he was the One to Come (Matt. 11:3). Preachers like to describe John's predicament here as his dark night of the soul. We should never doubt in the dark (of a rat-infested prison) what God tells us in the light, they say. Fair enough, but if Israel's prophets saw through a glass darkly[36] and could describe only what they saw, then John's question to Jesus may have been a sign of emerging faith, not a confession of doubt. John expected someone tougher, more fiery, less forgiving, and Jesus wasn't fitting the profile. With Jesus's reputation for miracles and preaching, John was beginning to wonder whether Jesus might be the Elijah-figure of his dreams,[37] and whether God's arrival would be marked more by deliverance than by condemnation. Maybe John's question was a plea for help. Weren't Messiah-types supposed to *free* prisoners (Isa. 61:1)?

However clear his vision and firm his convictions, John's preaching career was cut short. Literally. Antipas thought John's popularity could spark an uprising, Josephus says. If John's followers were expecting imminent judgment and divine rescue, and if tax collectors (Luke 3:12–13) and soldiers (Luke 3:14) were rethinking their loyalties, how long would it be before someone tried to move history along by staging a coup? Like most Roman autocrats, Antipas was big on preemptive strikes.[38]

The basic facts of John's death are clear, but sorting out the details is tricky, since the testimonies of our key witnesses—Josephus (*Jewish Antiquities* 18.109–119) and Mark 6:17–29[39]—diverge at key points. Much of the divergence may be editorial spin. For Josephus, John's death is a back story, included only to explain why God let Herod suffer at the hands of the Nabateans.[40] In the Gospels, John's death is a major event, not only because it removes Jesus's competition (John 3:30) but also because it vividly demonstrates to Jesus the perils along his own path (Matt. 4:12; 13:57; 14:13; Mark 6:30–31). Four differences stood out to me.

"When others too joined the crowds about him, because they were aroused to the highest degree by his sermons, Herod became alarmed. Eloquence that had so great an effect on mankind might lead to some form of sedition, for it looked as if they would be guided by John in everything that they did. Herod decided therefore that it would be much better to strike first and be rid of him before his work led to an uprising, than to wait for an upheaval, get involved in a difficult situation and see his mistake."

Josephus, *Jewish Antiquities* 18.118

"By illustrating the fate of a true prophet (martyrdom), John's sad end foretells what is in store for Jesus. . . . The fate of the forerunner is that of the coming one."

W. D. Davies and D. C. Allison, *Matthew*, 2:476

1. Where did John's death occur?

Mark's readers might assume the dastardly deed was done at Antipas's estate in Tiberias, since his guest list included "the leaders of Galilee" (Mark 6:21).	Josephus locates John's imprisonment at the Machaerus fortress in Perea (*Jewish Antiquities* 18.119).

2. Who was Herodias's first husband?

Mark and Matthew say he was Antipas's half-brother Philip (Mark 6:17; Matt. 14:3).	Josephus says he was Antipas's half-brother Herod, son of Mariamme (*Jewish Antiquities* 18.136), and further that Philip was the uncle, and then husband, of Salome, Herodias's daughter (*Jewish Antiquities* 18.137).

3. What part did Herodias play?

Mark and, less so, Matthew blame Herodias for the execution (Mark 6:24–26; Matt. 14:8–9).	Josephus places all blame on Antipas, saying nothing about a party where Herodias demanded John's head (*Jewish Antiquities* 18.116, 118).

4. What motivated Antipas to have John killed?

Mark says Antipas feared John, heard him gladly, and protected him (initially) from Herodias (Mark 6:20). Matthew says Herod personally wanted to execute John but feared the people, who regarded John as a prophet (Matt. 14:5).	Josephus says John's popularity motivated Antipas to have John executed (*Jewish Antiquities* 18.118).

Several harmonizations are possible. Perhaps Antipas, for his birthday, hosted a *Galilean* delegation in *Perea*. Or Mark kept silent about the location to make John look more like Jesus. Or maybe Josephus had no record of the party, or he ignored it because it would complicate his tidy account of why God caused Antipas's military defeat. As for Herodias's first husband, Josephus clearly calls him Herod, not Philip (*Jewish Antiquities* 18.130–42), prompting some conservative scholars to speak of "Herod Philip," even though no ancient source equates the two. "Salvation by conflation," complains John Meier.[41]

Minor glitches aside, however, I found it surprisingly easy to stitch the Gospels and Josephus together into a single, coherent story.

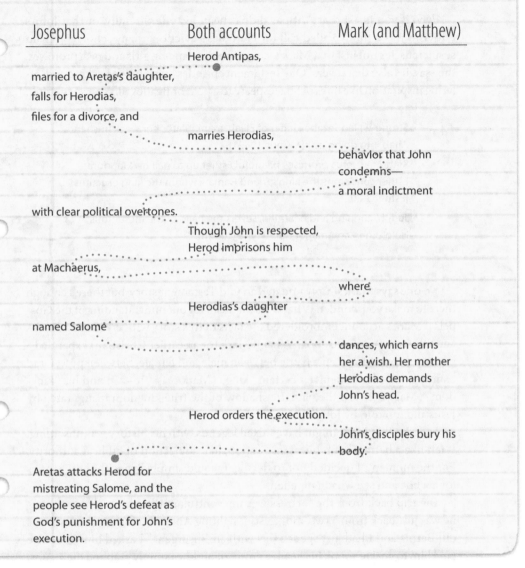

Josephus	Both accounts	Mark (and Matthew)
	Herod Antipas,	
married to Aretas's daughter,		
falls for Herodias,		
files for a divorce, and		
	marries Herodias,	
		behavior that John condemns—
		a moral indictment
with clear political overtones.		
	Though John is respected, Herod imprisons him	
at Machaerus,		
		where
	Herodias's daughter	
named Salome		
		dances, which earns her a wish. Her mother Herodias demands John's head.
	Herod orders the execution.	
		John's disciples bury his body.
Aretas attacks Herod for mistreating Salome, and the people see Herod's defeat as God's punishment for John's execution.		

It's a great story, full of love, unfaithfulness, betrayal, escape, revenge, murder, and retribution—routine stuff for the inbred and decadent Herodian family. Not surprisingly, many scholars find the birthday-dance/head-on-platter scene to be historically unlikely. Bultmann called it a legend.[42] Others chalk it up to courtroom gossip or marketplace buzz.[43] After all, what ruler would give away *half* his wealth? And what woman would forgo untold riches just to settle a score?

Even if you insist that Antipas didn't mean his offer literally, or that John's criticism was a thinly veiled call for Herodias's eviction, many scholars remain suspicious. It's not just that Mark's story includes dancing girls and rash promises, they say. It's also that several Old Testament episodes linger in the background, offering inspiration like lines of Shakespeare to a poet or Beatles riffs to a songwriter.

- Strong-willed Jezebel, hater of Elijah, manipulates her weak husband Ahab into doing evil (1 Kings 18–21).
- King Ahasuerus promises beautiful Esther up to half his kingdom. Esther condemns the king's friend Haman, whom the king executes (Esther 5–7).
- Judith, cunning and beautiful, severs the head of the murderous Holofernes, commander of Assyria (Judith).[44]

No one says Mark simply updated an Old Testament story, but there's enough there to make you wonder. What would it mean for our understanding of the Gospels if Mark's account embroidered the facts of this story with creative additions and Old Testament allusions? What if Mark (or an earlier Christian) expanded a historical core into an epic battle between male and female, between power and cunning, in order to depict a certain "king" (Mark 6:14, 26–27) and his "kingdom" (Mark 6:23) as the pathetic shadow of the true kingdom inaugurated by Jesus and foretold by John?

The idea that Mark might have mixed legends with his history was unsettling. It felt like a betrayal of biblical inspiration, like a rejection of biblical authority. For the moment, I decided not to decide. I would simply live with these stories for a while and see what happened.

The trip back from the fortress was uneventful, until our taxi driver told us he was just back from a two-month stint fighting American forces in Iraq. Turns out Bernie and I had just spent a day with an "insurgent." I asked him if anyone paid him to go. He shook his head; a group of buddies simply grabbed their guns, piled into a car, and went.

"Who cared for your family while you were gone?" I asked.

"My father."

"Did your wife want you to go?"

His reply was confusing, but apparently her wishes were not relevant. This was a man's world. War was a guy thing.

"Will you go again?"

"Maybe yes. Maybe not."

Israeli immigration at the crossing was a sea of Palestinians—men in long lines, women tending children on the floor nearby. Someone pointed out the queue for foreigners, and I was through in minutes. Wide is the chasm between safe and suspect, between powerful and powerless. As the service taxi pulled into East Jerusalem, I decided I wasn't ready to edit Salome's dance from the screenplay of history. Perhaps I worried that Jesus's dance upon the waves of Galilee might be next. Or perhaps I was simply becoming less troubled by historical loose ends. Either way, I knew that the journey ahead would return often to the bustling crossroads where history meets story.

Machaerus

CHAPTER 3

Room at the Inn

In which Norm skirts a checkpoint, smokes with wise men, and takes reading lessons from a filmmaker.

MONTY PYTHON'S LIFE OF BRIAN, SCENE 1

WISE MAN 2:	We must see him. We have brought presents.
MANDY:	Out!
WISE MAN 1:	Gold, frankincense, myrrh.
MANDY:	Well, why didn't you say so? He's over here.
	. . . Sorry this place is a bit of a mess.

Ibn Allah

At the center of the Christmas story is the scandalous claim that Jesus was born of a virgin. I once thought Christians were the only ones to believe such a thing. That was before my field trip to the embattled West Bank city of Hebron, where I hoped to see some of Herod the Great's best-preserved leftovers.

Moments after the service taxi deposited me downtown a stranger offered to help. Through bustling market, past loaded donkeys, spice shops, and falafel stands, he led me to a military checkpoint beyond which Palestinians like him could not go. An Israeli soldier, peering through a peephole, directed me down the (evacuated, "sterilized") streets of the Old City, which I followed until the ancient walls of Herod's compound rose up before me. Within them were the tombs of Abraham, Sarah, and family. I was standing on holy ground. And I was being followed.

It was a kid. I said, "Hi." The kid decided to appoint himself as my guide. He, Safwat, led me through a maze of alleys back to the market, where I met his friends, and from there to his home, where his parents invited me to stay for the night. On their roof they pointed out the onion domes of the Russian church guarding the "oaks of Mamre," where Ibrahim welcomed and fed three strangers—strangers who, over a meal, promised Sarah she would soon have a son (Gen. 18:1–15). There was I, also a foreigner, also embraced, protected, and fed—not with curds and homegrown calf, but with rice and homegrown grapes. Like their patriarch, they honored the stranger among them. If only I could promise, like the three strangers, that within the year their deepest yearning would be fulfilled.

At dusk a water pipe appeared, along with three generations of Muslims who asked, between puffs, about my family and about what Christians believed. "Muhammad is our prophet," they explained in jagged English. Christians believe that `Isa (Jesus) was a prophet, I responded, but also God's son. "Ibn Allah." The response was immediate. Wagging fingers and shaking heads informed me, as one lost and needing directions, that `Isa was the son of Mary. Period. No father. Not Joseph. Not God. They knew nothing of the raging academic debates, nor of the real reason I was there. They were simply a gracious Muslim clan enjoying the rare chance to talk with, and straighten out, a Christian. For them, the virgin birth was not a problem. Just as long as I didn't try to make Jesus a god. There is no God but Allah.

That night on the roof, serenaded by roosters, I felt the strangeness of Christian belief descend on me with new weight. For the first time I sensed the true scandal of the Trinity. In what sense was Jesus the *Son* of God? Why are devout Muslims, and Jews too, so troubled by Christian theology?

One Story yet Two

Before venturing to Bethlehem I needed to review the story. I knew Matthew had the bit about the wise men following the star and Luke had shepherds watching flocks by night. After that things got fuzzy, the cure for which was the École. After a few hours with a synopsis, I had organized the stories into a table.[1]

Details shared by Matthew and Luke	Matthew	Luke
Joseph is a descendant of King David.	1:16, 20	1:27, 32; 2:4
Mary and Joseph are betrothed to each other but don't yet live together and haven't had sex.	1:18	1:27, 34
Mary is a virgin who conceives through the Holy Spirit, not through Joseph.	1:18, 20, 23, 25	1:27, 34–35, 37
An angel announces to Joseph (Matthew) or Mary (Luke) the forthcoming childbirth.	1:20–23	1:30–35

Details shared by Matthew and Luke	Matthew	Luke
The angel directs that the child is to be named Jesus.	1:21	1:31
The angel predicts that Jesus will be a savior.	1:21	2:11
Jesus is born after Mary and Joseph have begun to live together.	1:24–25	2:5–6
Jesus is born in Bethlehem.	2:1, 5, 8, 16	2:4–6, 11, 15
Jesus is born during the reign of Herod the Great.	2:1	1:5
Jesus grows up in Nazareth in Galilee.	2:23	2:39
John the Baptist is Jesus's forerunner.	3:11	1:76; 3:16

The parallels did not add up to obvious borrowing in either direction, which probably meant that any ideas they share must be older than either one. Maybe a lot older. Some similarities were more striking than others. Unsurprising was the common reference to Nazareth as Jesus's hometown, since this detail appears elsewhere in the Gospels.[2] Jesus's ties to Galilee were widely known (John 7:41, 52). Also predictable were the references to Herod the Great, whose feats of engineering still littered the land; whose body, according to Josephus, was buried just five miles from Bethlehem; and whose tomb was discovered only a few years ago. Two parallels stood out: the miracle of Mary's virginity and the location, Bethlehem.

I built another table for bits found only in one Gospel or the other.

Matthew only

1:18–19	Joseph's desire to divorce Mary
1:20–25	An angel's annunciation to Joseph in a dream
2:1–12	A star appears to the wise men, who travel to Jerusalem, meet Herod, and worship Jesus in the "house" in Bethlehem.
2:13–15	Jesus's family flees from Bethlehem to Egypt.
2:16–18	Herod's slaughter of Bethlehem's boys two years old and younger
2:19a	Herod the Great's death
2:19b–21	An angel instructs Joseph in a dream to return to Israel.
2:22–23	Joseph fears Archelaus, so the family moves north to Nazareth.

Luke only

1:5–25	Elizabeth, Zechariah, and the angel's annunciation of John's birth during reign of Herod
1:26–56	Gabriel's annunciation to Mary; Mary's three-month visit to Elizabeth
1:57–80	The birth and naming of John; Zechariah's prophecy
2:1–5	The census requiring Joseph to travel from Nazareth to Bethlehem
2:6–7	No room in the inn, so Jesus is laid in a manger.
2:8–20	Angels appear to the shepherds, who find Jesus in the Bethlehem manger.
2:21–38	Eight-day-old Jesus is presented in the temple; Simeon and Anna recognize God at work.
2:39	Jesus's family returns home to Nazareth.
2:41–51	Jesus in the temple at age twelve

A pair of differences stood out. One concerned the itinerary of the holy family. According to Luke, Joseph and Mary began in Nazareth, traveled to Bethlehem because of the census, then returned without incident to Nazareth (2:39), perhaps after a month or so when mother and child were ready to travel. Matthew, however, says nothing about a census and seems to imply that the family began in Bethlehem (2:1), shifted to Egypt (2:14), then settled in Nazareth because it wasn't safe to return to Bethlehem (2:22–23).

A second difference had to do with the central character. Matthew consistently focuses on Joseph, with no hint that Mary has a clue about Jesus's origins, his destiny, or the risks they will face along the way (1:19–25; 2:13–14, 19–22). Luke shines the spotlight on Mary (1:26–56; 2:7, 19, 34–35, 48–49, 51), hiring Joseph almost as a stage prop, a token father figure who can help establish Jesus's Davidic lineage (1:27; 2:4–5, 16, 33).

I was curious to know what Guilder would say about Mary's virginity, so I fired off an email. His reply, across ten time zones, was surprisingly detailed. And he signed off using his *first* name. It was like an invitation to join his inner circle. Should I accept? Did I want to find a home in the academy? Could scholarship be a way to live out my faith, or would I waste my time in endless deconstruction and demystification? The prospect of getting paid to pursue interesting and (one hopes) important questions had a certain appeal. But would I, like many in the "guild," find more delight in disabusing the church of false notions than in nourishing it with true ones?

Misconception

Guilder's thumbs down on the virgin birth came as no surprise; he sided with the majority of his peers. I was eager to get to Bethlehem, but I wanted to give his comments the time they deserved. Here's the exchange—my original post, Guilder's reply, and my follow-up.

From: "Norm Adams" <nadams@state.com>
Subject: Did a virgin give birth?
To: "Randall Guilder" <rguilder@sblusa.com>

Greetings to you again, sir, from the bowels of the École Biblique. I hope your students are making life interesting. I'm wondering if you might weigh in on the little matter of the virgin birth. Your comments in class were evasive as I recall. Perhaps you didn't want to step on toes. Do you reject the V.B. because these sorts of things don't happen?

Norm

From: "Randall Guilder" <rguilder@sblusa.com>
Subject: RE: Did a virgin give birth?
To: "Norm Adams" <nadams@state.com>
Attachments: GuilderStevens.jpg

Norman—good to hear you still walk the earth. Yesterday during Personnel Committee I was desperately wanting to join you.

The infancy narratives present some of the heftiest challenges to interpreters, not least of which, of course, is the claim that Jesus's mother was a virgin! You're too young to remember when the infamous Jesus Seminar finally tackled the Gospel infancy narratives. These guys managed to agree on only two points: Jesus was Jewish and his mother's name was Mary! They voted against conception without intercourse—Joseph was their prime suspect—but they wouldn't take a stand on whether the Holy Spirit played a role in Mary's impregnation, since, they said, such claims are theological, not historical. I avoid the topic in class, but since you asked, several thoughts.

1. Silence

Our earliest sources (Paul & Mark) seem to know nothing about Jesus's birth, virgin or otherwise. Indeed, according to Mark 3:20–21 it looks like Jesus's family was unprepared for his early popularity. Only in the birth narratives of Matthew and Luke do we learn that Jesus was conceived by the Spirit (Matt. 1:18–25; Luke 1:35).

2. Different paths

Both Matthew and Luke affirm the virginal conception, but they follow different paths to get there. In Matthew (1:23), the virgin birth fulfills a prophecy (Isa. 7:14). In Luke, the fact that Jesus's father was divine (1:32, 35) explains why Jesus is to be called *Son of God*. Matthew's Jesus fulfills the Jewish Scriptures; Luke's appeals to gentiles raised on Greco-Roman myth. These are not contradictory, but they are different. How did this come about?[3]

3. Greek parallels

The notion of a virgin birth was unknown in 1st c. Judaism, but was well established in the Hellenistic world, about which Bultmann says: "The idea of the generation of a king or hero from a virgin by the godhead was widespread" (*History of the Synoptic Tradition*, 292). Here's Justin Martyr, a 2nd-century Christian, summarizing the complaint of his non-Christian Jewish opponent Trypho:

> Moreover, in the fables of those who are called Greeks, it is written that Perseus was begotten of Danae, who was a virgin; he who was called among them Zeus having descended on her in the form of a golden shower. And you ought to feel ashamed when you make assertions similar to theirs, and rather [should] say that this Jesus was born man of men. And if you prove from the Scriptures that He is the Christ, and that on account of having led a life conformed to the

law, and perfect, He deserved the honour of being elected to be Christ, [it is well]; but do not venture to tell monstrous phenomena, lest you be convicted of talking foolishly like the Greeks. (*Dialogue with Trypho*, 67)

I'm attaching a handout that contains the text of several pagan birth legends. Wouldn't someone who was raised on these stories be tempted to compose a comparable narrative for Jesus? Wouldn't they want Jesus to out-Alexander Alexander and out-Caesar Caesar?

4. Jesus's legitimacy

Lately it has been sexy (sorry) to suggest that Jesus's birth was illegitimate—that Mary was seduced or raped. It is clear that rumors of illegitimacy were in the air (Matt. 1:19–20; Mark 6:3), though I think Joseph was the father, as the two genealogies imply (except for two words in Luke 3:23 [*hōs enomizeto*; "as was thought"]). Explicit allegations that Jesus was illegitimate do not emerge until the 2nd & 3rd centuries. In the 2nd-c. *Acts of Pilate* 2:3, we read:

> The elders of the Jews answered and said to Jesus, "What should we see? First, that you were born of fornication; second, that your birth meant the death of the children in Bethlehem; third, that your father Joseph and your mother Mary fled into Egypt because they counted for nothing among the people."

Likewise Celsus (c. 177–180), the anti-Christian whose works are preserved in quotations by Origen (c. 248):

> [Celsus] accuses [Jesus] of having "invented his birth from a virgin," and upbraids Him with being "born in a certain Jewish village, of a poor woman of the country, who . . . was turned out of doors by her husband . . . because she was convicted of adultery; that . . . she disgracefully gave birth to Jesus, an illegitimate child." (*Against Celsus* 1.28)

> [Celsus says] that when she was pregnant she was turned out of doors by the carpenter to whom she had been betrothed, as having been guilty of adultery, and that she bore a child to a certain soldier named Panthera. (1.32; see also 1.69)

Rabbinic literature attributes to 2nd c. rabbis the ascription *Jesus, son of Pantera*. Later traditions identified *Ben Pantera* with *Ben Stada*, someone who knew black magic and was crucified on Passover (R. Brown, *Birth*, 536). Did such polemic circulate in the first century? Might NT accounts of Jesus's birth be meant to refute rumors of illegitimacy?

I'll soon be sending you a chapter of my book. Don't hold back; I can be dull. Mark it up and send it back—department pays postage. Oh, I'm scanning a photo of an old friend. Mitchell Stevens taught early Judaism for years at a few east coast schools but abruptly quit 4 years ago to move to Jerusalem. I heard he was guiding, but that can't be why he left a tenured post. I'll wager he's up to something. If you spot him let me know.

Shalom and salaam.
Randall

From: "Norm Adams" <nadams@state.com>
Subject: **RE: Did a virgin give birth?**
To: "Randall Guilder" <rguilder@sblusa.com>

Dear Dr. Guilder:
Thanks for your email! My $0.02.

I recall you saying in class that no Jewish interpretation of Isaiah 7:14 before Christianity envisioned a virginal conception. If so, would not Matthew need to be convinced of the virgin birth before turning to Isaiah 7:14? (R. Brown, *Birth*, 149–53, is helpful here.) Likewise, if Luke doesn't allude to Isaiah 7:14, might not this suggest that Isaiah was not the starting point for Christian ideas about Jesus's birth?

I studied the Greek parallels and now have more questions than ever!

1. Would the earliest Christians have known these pagan nativity myths? And, if they did, would they find anything about them attractive? (Don't these stories usually entail sex with the gods?)
2. The lapse between the alleged miracle birth and the narrative about it is consistently longer than the 70 or so years between Jesus's birth and the Gospel records. Would not a shorter gap between the event and the write-up leave less time for myths to arise?
3. Compared to Suetonius on Octavius and Plutarch on Alexander, Matthew and Luke seem far less legendary. Do you agree?
4. Why didn't you consider the Hebrew tradition of miracle birth? All the matriarchs of Israel—Sarah, Rebekah, and Rachel—had problems bearing children. Same with Hannah, mother of Samuel, and Elizabeth, mother of John the Baptist. Doesn't Mary's pregnancy echo a very *Jewish* theme?
5. You suggest that Matthew and Luke might have been tempted to craft their birth narratives in response to pagan competition. Couldn't it work the other way around? Might not some pagan accounts be composed in response to the rise of Christianity?
6. If Luke embellished the speeches of Mary (1:46–55), Zechariah (1:68–79), and Simeon (2:29–32), he could certainly adopt a similar approach to his narrative. But can we not allow for a blend of history and legend? Must we choose pure fact or pure fiction?
7. If Matthew and Luke were principally concerned to protect Jesus's (and Mary's) honor, wouldn't they be more likely to affirm, rather than deny, Joseph's paternity? Charges of illegitimacy may have influenced Matthew and Luke, but if the argument rests on alleged innuendoes like John 8:41 and Mark 6:3, I'm not persuaded.

Off to Bethlehem tomorrow. Finally.
Norm

The picture showed Guilder somewhere in the Middle East. Beside him was a tall man under an Indiana Jones hat who was holding a ratty map and frowning impatiently. I printed out the picture and stuffed it in my pack, where it became another layer on a rising tel. Perhaps there were layers to the virgin birth as well: historical, literary, traditional, theological. Could I follow a Jesus whose conception was completely normal? How would a "normal" conception alter my perceptions of Jesus? Of the Gospels? Could Joseph's son also be the Son of God? The Sin Bearer? Would an "illegitimate" Jesus be a better advocate for the poor and marginal? I packed up my questions and prepared to depart for Bethlehem.

Three Pagan Birth Narratives

(from Cartlidge and Dungan, *Documents for the Study of the Gospels*, 131–33, 211. Text from Loeb Classical Library or Penguin Classics.)

1. The birth legend of **Alexander the Great**, born in 356 BCE, preserved by Plutarch (*Alexander* 2.1–3.2) in 75 CE:

Alexander was a descendant of Herakles, on his father's side, through Karanos; on his mother's side he was descended from Aidos through Neoptolemos; this is universally believed. It is said that Philip [Alexander's father] was initiated into the mysteries at Samothrace with Olympias [Alexander's mother]. . . .

The bride, before the night in which they were to join in the bride chamber, had a vision. There was a peal of thunder, and a lightning bolt fell upon her womb. A great fire was kindled from the strike, then it broke into flames which flashed everywhere, then they extinguished. At a later time, after the marriage, Philip saw a vision: he was placing a seal on his wife's womb; the engraving on the seal was, as he thought, in the image of a lion. The men charged with interpreting oracles were made suspicious by this vision and told Philip to keep a closer watch on his marital affairs. But Aristander of Telmessus said [the vision meant that] her husband had impregnated her, for nothing is sealed if it is empty, and that she was pregnant with a child whose nature would be courageous and lion-like.

On another occasion, a great snake appeared, while Olympias was asleep, and wound itself around her body. This especially, they say, weakened Philip's desire and tenderness toward her, so that he did not come often to sleep with her, either because he was afraid she would cast spells and enchantments upon him, or because he considered himself discharged from the obligation of intercourse with her because she had become the partner of a higher being.

. . . After the vision [concerning the snake], Philip sent Chairon of Megalopolis to Delphi [to learn its meaning]. He brought an oracle to Philip from Apollo: Philip was henceforth to sacrifice to Zeus-Ammon and worship that God especially. Furthermore, he was to put out the eye which spied on the God through the crack in the door, the God who, in the form of a serpent, had lain with his wife. And Olympias, as Erastosthenes says, when she sent Alexander on the campaign [against the Persians], told him alone the forbidden secret of his conception, ordering him to act worthy of his birth.

2. The birth legend of **Octavius** (Caesar Augustus), born in 27 BCE. The historian Suetonius (*The Deified Caesar* 94.4), writing in 120 CE, claims to have read this story "in the books of Asclepias of Mendes":

When Atia had come in the middle of the night to the solemn service of Apollo, she had her litter set down in the temple and fell asleep, while the rest of the matrons also slept. On a sudden a serpent glided up to her and shortly went away. When she awoke, she purified herself, as if after the embraces of her husband, and at once there appeared on her body a mark in colors like a serpent, and she could never get rid of it; so that presently she ceased ever to go to the public baths. In the tenth month after that Augustus was born and was therefore regarded as the son of Apollo. Atia too, before she gave him birth, dreamed that her vitals were borne up to the stars and spread over the whole extent of land and sea, while Octavius dreamed that the sun rose from Atia's womb.

3. The birth legend of **Apollonios of Tyana** (first century CE), preserved by Philostratus (*Apollonios of Tyana* 1.4–5) in 218 CE.

While his mother was pregnant with him the shadowy figure of an Egyptian God appeared to her, namely Proteus, who can change his form at will according to Homer. She, not frightened at all, asked him to whom she would give birth. "Me," he said. "But who are you?" she asked. "Proteus," he replied, "the Egyptian God." . . .

It is said that Apollonios was born in a meadow near the temple which was recently dedicated to him there. And the manner in which he was born should not be left unknown for when the hour of birth had drawn nigh to his mother, a vision came telling her to go to this meadow and pick some flowers. Well, she had no sooner arrived when she fell asleep lying in the grass, while her maidservants wandered over the meadow picking flowers. Then some swans which dwelt in the meadow came and formed a ring around her while she slept and as is their custom suddenly flapped their wings and honked all at once, for there was a light breeze blowing across the meadow. She jumped up because of the sound and gave birth, for any sudden panic will cause birth to take place even before its time. The inhabitants of that area say that at the same time she was giving birth a bolt of lightning seemed to strike the earth and then bounce back upward into the air where it vanished. By this sign the Gods, I believe, revealed and foretold that Apollonios would become superior to all things earthly, even drawing near to the Gods and soon.

O Little Town

Since Bethlehem is only five miles south of Jerusalem, I thought my pilgrimage would be more authentic if I walked. That was before the weather turned hot. Conceding defeat, I boarded a service taxi loaded with Palestinians. To my surprise, just before the main Bethlehem checkpoint the driver abruptly turned west. When he stopped, we piled out onto a nondescript mound of dirt and broken concrete. This was Beit Jala, someone said, the back door into Bethlehem. Just over the mound taxis were waiting. If Joseph, Mary, and Jesus could sneak out of town, I supposed I could sneak in.

I must have been hoping for a Hallmark Bethlehem of docile animals and bath-robed shepherds. Maybe a little snow. What I found was a crowded city whose twenty-eight thousand residents clogged narrow streets and busy markets. From the taxi window I saw buildings scarred with bullet holes, announcing like acne on teenagers the awkward fragility of the times. I expected hordes of tourists (over a million a year, I'd heard), but there were more UN vans than tour busses. I found myself one of a handful of foreigners in a Palestinian sea. Bethlehem's economy depends on showing hospitality to Christian pilgrims. That, and selling carved olive wood camels. All of which makes an intifada—like the one that began in September of 2000—particularly troublesome. The uprising had emptied hotels, closed shops, and pushed thousands of Palestinians to the brink.

Professor Guilder warned me about all this, and he told me about the Franciscan monastery in Manger Square next to the Church of the Nativity. These were the monks, he said, who were trapped in the church compound—"voluntary hostages," they called it—with about two hundred Palestinian militants for some forty days back in April of 2002. Rather gutsy, those Franciscans. Nonviolent. Nonpartisan.

Church of the Nativity Entrance

Ready to die to protect a holy site. They went without food, water, medicine, and electricity, hoping to prevent what some might call another "slaughter of the innocents." It worked.

This was not the first threat to the Church of the Nativity's survival. It withstood Persian and Muslim attacks. Earthquakes and fire failed to bring it down. As I approached across the open square, I was amazed to see so tiny a doorway, half hidden behind a massive buttress. What had been in the sixth century a grand entrance had been reduced by Crusaders and again by Muslims in order to control traffic and keep out the carts. It occurred to me that this moment, this threshold, was a milestone for me. A metaphor. I had traveled far, bearing weighty questions and more than a little intellectual pride. Now, as I arrived, I had no choice but to stoop.

Perhaps because so much of the ancient church was hidden by later structures, the inside seemed surprisingly big. In *The Last Battle*, C. S. Lewis describes the response of Tirian, Narnia's last king, when he charged through the door of what he thought was a small, thatched stable in the woods.

> "It seems, then," said Tirian, smiling himself, "that the Stable seen from within and the Stable seen from without are two different places."
>
> "Yes," said the Lord Digory. "Its inside is bigger than its outside."
>
> "Yes," said Queen Lucy. "In our world too, a Stable once had something inside it that was bigger than our whole world."[4]

I crossed the threshold ahead of Walid, a gentle man who had approached me in the plaza to offer his guiding services. He scurried to uncover fourth-century mosaic fragments hidden beneath the sixth-century floor of Justinian, and he pointed out darkened twelfth-century Crusader art painted on the red limestone pillars of the original Constantinian church. Then, finally, he pointed me toward the birth cave, into which we descended through a narrow, steep staircase not far from the high altar. The Armenian fathers, having just finished their Mass, were retreating to their monastery. Incense hung thick in the air. The rough, blackened cave walls were mostly veiled in heavy fabric. Birthplace and manger both were overlaid with marble and silver. For better or worse, generations of Christians had transformed a rustic cave into a dazzling, flickering shrine whose shape and appearance bore scant resemblance to the original.

What would Mary and Joseph think, I wondered, of all this display of devotion? All the finely tuned ritual, the territorial protection of holy space, the tour guides, the controlled access? Could Mary have imagined centuries of public worship on the spot where she, very privately, crouched to push her child into the world? Part of me wanted to complain with Jerome, who, Walid told me, preferred the old rough-hewn manger to the silver one that replaced it. A larger part of me wanted to wrap myself in so many years of liturgy and tradition, and to sit at the feet of ancient saints, whose faith, I imagined, would wash away my doubt. My double-minded musings ended abruptly when a flock of Italian pilgrims descended, with candles and cameras, into the cave.

The Refugee Camp Talks

From Manger Square I rode a taxi to Deheisheh refugee camp on the edge of town. A journalist I'd met in Jerusalem had told me it had a guesthouse. Every move of the holy family, I thought as we rode, seemed etched in stone. Walid had shown me not only the birth cave and the manger but also the cave where Bethlehem's mothers hid from Herod and, down the road, the spot where Mary nursed her infant! To much of this I attached no historical significance, yet I marveled at the importance time could attach to place. How much about Jesus's beginnings could we know for sure? Which spots were simply identified to round out a pilgrim's itinerary? How much was fact and how much fiction?

The name of the guesthouse, *Ibdaa*, means "creation," explained Ziad, the director. In the midst of conflict and destruction, they dared to create something—peace, dignity, hope—out of nothing. Ziad drained his coffee cup and sent me on a tour of the refugee camp with a volunteer named Jihad who translated his name "Holy Fight." As we walked, Jihad recounted the camp's troubled history

since displaced Palestinians first arrived in 1948. The camp is now home to eleven thousand, of whom six thousand are kids. Nearby a loudspeaker blared. It was the closing ceremony of a youth camp, Jihad explained, run by Hamas, the Islamist organization well known for its charity networks. And suicide bombers. And Qassam rockets. I thought back to summer camp in the States and wondered what the speaker was saying. Hamas had no use for Ibdaa, Jihad said. We're not Islamic enough.

As it turned out, two professors and two students from an American seminary were staying at Ibdaa. One of the students, gray ponytail, black beard, wanted to talk.

"Ever smoked Nargile, Norm?" asked Wayne.

"Nar-GEE-lay?"

"Hookah. Shisha. Hubbly-Bubbly. Think: caterpillar in *Alice in Wonderland*."

"Oh, right. A water pipe. Sure."

"We're gathering at sunset up on the fifth floor to smoke and talk. Y'interested?"

Sunset over Bethlehem, hubble-bubble, and theological banter: life is good.

The smell of cappuccino greeted me on arrival. Wayne's efforts soon yielded gray plumes of sweet-smelling haze. We puffed quietly for several minutes, gazing over a tangle of unfinished buildings and telephone cable. Tans faded to browns. Gray shadows faded to deep purple. For the moment all was well in the West Bank.

"What's on your mind, Norm?" It was Professor Conrad—tall and wiry, completely bald, but scarcely forty. Taking the pipe, he puffed several times and glanced my way through the mist.

"The Nativity Church," I began. "Do you guys think it marks the spot?"

"Helena sure did."

"Helena?"

"The mother of Constantine." The professor liked to move sideways through conversations. "When Constantine ended persecution in the early fourth century and decided to erect churches in the Holy Land, he appointed Helena as lead archaeologist."

Bethlehem Traditions

Justin Martyr (100-165), <u>Dialogue with Trypho</u> 78.5: "Since Joseph had nowhere to lodge in that village, he lodged in a certain cave near that village; and while they were there, Mary brought forth the Messiah and laid him in a manger."

Protoevangelium of James (c. 150) 17-18: "And he took her down there [from a donkey] and said to her: 'Where shall I take you and hide your shame? For the place is a desert.' And he found a cave there and brought her into it, and left her in the care of his sons and went out to seek for a Hebrew midwife in the region of Bethlehem."

"She was very eager to sweep away centuries of pagan debris," Conrad continued, rubbing his head. "Locals helped her choose the site for the new church."

"What are the chances that her sources were reliable?"

"Pretty good, I'd say. Christians had maintained a continuous presence.[5] Justin Martyr, a second-century local, refers to 'a certain cave' in the area. Origen says the cave was attracting pilgrims in the third century. Saint Jerome complains that pagans have been violating the site for almost two hundred years."

"But three centuries is a long time."

"Norm, you're thinking like a good American." Hani, the other student, was talking. He was younger than Wayne, with Arab features and an British accent. "Americans think in decades. Europeans think in centuries. Here in the Middle East, we think in millennia."

Conrad took several long draws on the pipe and continued. "The Bethlehem cave tradition is simply too strong, too early, and too diverse not to be taken very seriously."

The other professor was Dr. Modred—short, stocky, fifty-something—a biblical scholar who thought sleeveless vests were cool. He added a fresh coal to the pipe and handed me the hose.

"Norm," he said, "is that why you're here? Are you studying archaeology?"

"No," I replied. "I'm studying Jesus. Actually, I'm *following* Jesus. I didn't bring a shovel. Just questions."

"Like what?"

"Like why Matthew and Luke don't agree on the Christmas story."

I pulled out my notes on the Gospels, rehearsed some of the basic differences, and inhaled my share of smoke. For a brief moment I was boy Jesus among the rabbis. Embarrassing now, thinking back.

Into the room at that point came "Max," visiting from New York, there to produce a documentary about the camp. Apparently Max was her real name. She'd heard about our soirée and

Bethlehem Traditions

Origen (185–254), <u>Against Celsus</u> 1.51: "In conformity with the narrative in the Gospel regarding His birth, there is shown at Bethlehem the cave where He was born, and the manger in the cave where He was wrapped in swaddling-clothes. And this sight is greatly talked of in surrounding places, even among the enemies of the faith, it being said that in this cave was born that Jesus who is worshipped and reverenced by the Christians."

Jerome (342–420), <u>Epistle 58 to Paulinus</u> 3.5: "Even my own Bethlehem, as it now is, that most venerable spot in the whole world . . . was overshadowed by a grove of Tammuz, that is of Adonis; and in the very cave where the infant Christ had uttered His earliest cry lamentation was made for the paramour of Venus."

asked to film it. When she later mailed me a DVD of the evening, I was able to create this transcript.

Conrad: I think you overstate the tensions between Matthew and Luke. I can imagine a single story that harmonizes both accounts.

Me: Harmonization is what we do every Christmas at church. Wise men and shepherds have to jostle for room around the manger.

Conrad: Aren't some harmonizations more plausible than others?

Max: If it takes harmonization to get tourists to buy from the local olive wood carvers, I'm all for it!

Conrad: So let's see: Mary and Joseph come from Nazareth because of the census, as Luke suggests. They find temporary accommodations, deliver the holy child, and encounter the shepherds. For some unexplained reason they remain in Bethlehem.

Hani: Any Palestinian could explain why. The economic benefits of living on the edge of Jerusalem are many.

Conrad: Right, so they move into a house for about two years, at which point the wise men arrive and the family escapes Herod's clutches by fleeing to Egypt, as we read in Matthew. En route back from Egypt they decide to return to Nazareth, where they settle down permanently.

Modred: Bravo, Conrad! A nicely woven cord! How far will it stretch? If we are going to twist two strands together, mustn't we also explain how they first got separated? How could Matthew ignore the annunciation to Mary and the census? And why would Luke ignore the star, the magi, the slaughter, and the narrow escape?

Conrad: You tell me. You're the New Testament scholar on this trip. I do church history.

Me: Some would say Matthew gives us Joseph's angle, and Luke, Mary's side of things.

Modred: Surely young Mary would have been awed by a caravan of exotic magi. And be forever marked by her baby's brush with death. I think we're better off saying that Jesus's birth didn't unfold exactly as written in either Gospel. Matthew and Luke grounded their stories in historical reality but felt a certain artistic freedom in the telling. That's how all stories were told back then.

Me: *How much* artistic freedom? Where does history stop and poetry kick in? How do we know we're not reading fiction?

Max: Or . . . watching *docudrama?*

Me: Huh?

Modred: Say more, Max.

Max: Docudrama. It's a genre of film. Actually, it combines two genres: documentary and drama. When it's done well, it offers a powerful, artistic interpretation of real events. Of course, the camera has to take a certain angle so it's always somebody's interpretation and never the full story. But it doesn't pretend to be.

Me: So it's not the same as "Reality TV."

Max: Not even close. So-called Reality TV uses "real" people to run a game show. Docudrama uses "fake" actors to reenact real history. Think of *Malcolm X* or *Schindler's List* or *JFK* or *Apollo XIII*. Each one tells a "true" story, but it's not necessarily "factual" at every turn. Screenwriters simplify, embellish, rearrange, and interpret to draw in the audience and clarify the moral of the story as they see it.

Me: Is that what Matthew and Luke are doing?

Max: Don't look at me. I make films.

Modred: Max is right: Matthew and Luke hold their "cameras" at different angles. Matthew's opening scene, his genealogy, ties Jesus firmly to Father Abraham and to King David. He never misses a chance to show how Jesus fulfills Scripture,[6] and how Jesus is the royal one who triumphs over danger. Luke's Jesus, like the reigning emperor, appears on the scene as a peaceful Savior. His birth foreshadows his vocation: to challenge the supremacy of a pagan empire and bring salvation to the world.

COMMENT: Modred rambled for a while about how Matthew's roots were sunk deep in the Old Testament. I watched Wayne and Hani, evidently used to his monologues, maneuver into more comfortable positions. Max kept the camera rolling but went for a Pepsi. Rather than bore you with the details, I've created a(nother) chart.

Old Testament Parallels to Matthew's Infancy Narrative

Joseph, son of Jacob

Genesis 37:5, 9, 19	God speaks to Joseph in dreams.	Matthew 1:20–21; 2:13; 2:19–20	In a dream an angel tells Joseph • not to divorce Mary • to flee to Egypt • to return to Israel.
Genesis 37:27–28	Joseph is sold and taken to Egypt, where he eventually protects Jacob's clan from starvation.	Matthew 2:14	Joseph descends to Egypt to protect his family.

Joseph, father of Jesus

Moses

Exodus 1:22	Pharaoh ordered all male Hebrew babies thrown in the Nile.	Matthew 2:16	Herod had soldiers massacre all boys in Bethlehem under two years old.
Exodus 2:15	Pharaoh tried to kill Moses, so Moses fled.	Matthew 2:13–14	Herod tried to kill Jesus, so Joseph took him and Mary away to Egypt.
Exodus 2:23	Pharaoh died.	Matthew 2:19	Herod the Great died.
Exodus 4:19–20	"The LORD said to Moses	Matthew 2:19–20	"When Herod died, an angel of the Lord suddenly appeared in a dream to Joseph
	in Midian:		in Egypt and said,
	'Go back to Egypt;		'Get up, take the child and his mother, and go to the land of Israel,
	for all those who were seeking your life		for those who were seeking the child's life
	are dead.'		have died.'
	So Moses took his wife and his sons, put them on a donkey, and		Then Joseph got up, took the child and his mother, and
	went back to the land of Egypt."		went to the land of Israel."

Jesus

It looks like Matthew—whatever else he is doing—portrays Jesus as another Moses.[7] Messiah mirrors Lawgiver. Hero of first exodus foreshadows hero of second. When I pointed out that some of the parallels weren't very close, Modred said this was evidence that Matthew was weaving the Old Testament together with real history and not just making stuff up. When I asked him about Herod's slaughter of the male children, things got interesting.

Me: Do you think Herod sent death squads to kill all male children under two?

Wayne: Bruce Cockburn. Nice.

Modred: I think Matthew constructed the slaughter of the innocents from Pharaoh's massacre of the Hebrew boys in Exodus 1–2. It's part of his Jesus–Moses typology.

Me: So it didn't happen?

Conrad: I'm not ready to say that. This episode fits perfectly the character of Herod; he would slaughter his own mother if that would help him stay in power!

> The child is born in the fullness of time. Three wise astrologers take note of the signs . . .
> . . . Herod, a paranoid man . . . ,
> when he hears there's a baby born King of the Jews, sends death squads to kill all male children under two.
>
> Bruce Cockburn,
> "Cry of a Tiny Babe,"
> on *Nothing but a Burning Light*

A nearby minaret sounded the evening call to prayer as the sun slipped from view. We paused to listen.

Conrad: Besides the actual story in Exodus, plenty of legends about Moses were floating around out there. Moses had been destined from birth to be Israel's savior.

> "His Jesus was not the unbegotten phantom of docetism but the upshot of a history, Israel's *telos*. Thus the newness we do encounter in Matthew is that of completion . . . : there is repetition and the past lives on. Indeed, the old vindicates the new, through the resemblance of the two. In Judaism the present was regularly legitimated by the past: memories were the measure of all things. . . . So too, with qualification, was it for Matthew. For him discontinuity would have been falsehood, for truth required continuity. Jesus and the new creation wrought by him therefore had their significance confirmed by resonant links with the past, that is, with Israel's history. . . . Jesus brought to fulfillment the history of Israel; and it was axiomatic, given the past's paradigmatic character, rooted in the consistency of God, that the end be like the beginning of that history."
>
> Dale C. Allison Jr.,
> *New Moses*, 273–74

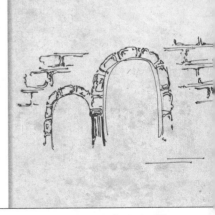

Pharaoh ordered the Hebrew boys drowned because he heard that Israel's liberator had been born. And so on.

Modred: Another legend says that God reassured Moses's father in a dream.

Me: Could Matthew have known those traditions when he sat down to write about Jesus and Herod?[8]

Conrad: I think so, though he might not have known where the history ended and where the legends began.

Max: That's my biggest challenge in making this documentary: sorting out the difference between history and myth, between memory and imagination.

Modred: You're not alone. Did any of you see that painting of Joseph and Mary in the church?

Me: I did. Joseph has a towel on his head and carries a staff. Mary is riding a very tired donkey.

Max: *What rough beast slouches towards Bethlehem to be born?*

Me: Huh?

Wayne: Yeats. Nice.

Modred: So Joseph has a staff and Mary rides a "rough beast." Where's this from?

Hani: No idea. Around here women walk and men ride the donkeys.

Modred: Norm, you have a Bible. Read Exodus 4:20.

Me: Let's see . . . "So Moses took his wife and his sons and mounted them on a donkey, and returned to the land of Egypt. Moses also took the staff of God in his hand." [NASB]

Modred: Wife, donkey, staff, Egypt—it's all there. When Christian artists tell the story of Jesus, they instinctively look to Moses.

Max: Maybe Matthew and Luke were the first Christian artists.

Modred: Not bad. For the early Christians Jesus was the new lawgiver, the prophet whom they dare not ignore.[9]

Me: Where I come from, appeals to the past are passé. Even pathetic. Anyone who lives in the past is like Uncle Rico in *Napoleon Dynamite*.

Hani: It's not like that here. Here if you ignore the past you betray everything. The present is just the latest chapter of an ancient story.

Modred: That sounds like the Gospels: Jesus is the latest chapter of the story of Israel. You could even say Jesus *was* the story of Israel.

Me: Jesus *was* Israel?

COMMENT: Modred launched into a monologue about how Matthew's Jesus relived Israel's troubled story but got it right. Where the nation stumbled Jesus stood firm and all that. Hani and I took notes. Wayne's head bobbed. I've inserted Modred's main points into another table.

Like Israel, Jesus . . .	Israel's story	Jesus in Matthew
Went down to Egypt	Genesis 46:3–4	2:13–14
Was protected by Joseph	Genesis 45–48	2:14
Saw a new king emerge	Exodus 1:8	2:15a
Was called out of Egypt	Exodus 6	2:15b, 19–20
Was "baptized" in the Sea/Jordan	Exodus 14–15	3:13–15
Was called "God's Son"	Exodus 4:22–23; Hosea 11:1	3:17; 17:5
Was led into the wilderness	Deuteronomy 8:2a	4:1
Endured forty years/days of testing and fasting	Deuteronomy 8:2b–3	4:2
"Conquered" the land	Joshua	4:23–25
Had twelve sons/tribes/disciples	Genesis 46	10:2–4
Met God on a mountain	Exodus 19	17:1–3

Me: I'm still not clear on what happened here, in Bethlehem. Do parallels like these mean the Gospels care more about allusions than reality?

Conrad: *I've been to the mountaintop.*

Me: Huh?

Wayne: Martin Luther King Jr. Nice.

Hani: Stop showing off.

Wayne: I'm not the one quoting poets and preachers.

Conrad: King loved to describe the struggle for justice using the language of Exodus. *I've been to the mountaintop. I've looked over and I've seen the Promised Land. I may not get there with you but we, as a people, will get to the Promised Land.*[10]

And so we still have a long, long way to go before we reach the promised land of freedom. Yes, we have left the dusty soils of Egypt, and we have crossed a Red Sea

> that had for years been hardened by a long and piercing winter of massive resistance, but before we reach the majestic shores of the promised land, there will still be gigantic mountains of opposition ahead and prodigious hilltops of injustice.[11]

        Me: Where are you going with this?

  Conrad: Was King distorting the truth? Was he showing disregard for the historical reality of his day?

        Me: Clearly not.

    Hani: So when Matthew and Luke depict the present using stories from the past, they aren't necessarily guilty of distortion. They aren't automatically antihistory.

Modred: Good, and there's more. When we borrow from the past, we attach significance to the present. King's quest for racial justice was not a random power struggle; he believed the God of the exodus was going to liberate his people once more.

        Me: So borrowing from the past adds weight to the present.

Modred: You're getting it.

        Me: Okay, but . . .

  Conrad: But what?

        Me: Well, we can fact-check Martin Luther King Jr. We can't fact-check the Gospels. Maybe Matthew used scriptural language to describe what really happened. Maybe he used it to write fiction. How do we know whether the Gospels used Scripture to interpret or to create history?

    Hani: You're asking whether they *scripturized* history or *historicized* prophecy.[12]

        Me: Huh?

    Hani: Sorry. That's the way John Crossan would ask the question.

        Me: I need to do graduate school.

  Wayne: Does any of this help us with the star? Was it a supernova? A comet? A conjunction?[13]

  Conrad: Whatever the star was, Babylonian astrologers decided its position signified the birth of a Judean king. Do you recall what the magi asked when they got to Jerusalem?

        Me: *Where is the one born King of the Jews?*

  Conrad: That doesn't sound like a request for directions. They wanted a tour of the royal nursery and a glimpse of the king's successor.

Modred: Maybe so, but I think the answer is textual, not celestial. In Numbers 24 Balaam sees a *star* rising up from Jacob. In other words, he sees a Jewish king rising to defeat Israel's enemies. Matthew turns Balaam's metaphorical star into a real one.

Me: So a star didn't hover over the manger?

Modred: Stars can't hover over a single house!

Conrad: If the magi headed for Bethlehem, it was not because the star turned ninety degrees but because somebody told them about Micah 5:2. Once they reached the village, it wouldn't have been hard to find the newborn.

Modred: Whether or not the star is a metaphor, Matthew uses the wise men as a preview of coming theological attractions.

Max: That's film-speak. I like it.

Modred: Matthew's Gospel ends with Jesus's Great Commission, right? *Make disciples of all nations.* The wise men are the teaser; their worship at the beginning of the story foreshadows the nations' faith at the end.

Me: Reminds me of "Journey of the Magi." The magi are haunted by the past but compelled by it to look ahead.

Wayne: T. S. Eliot. Nice.

Hani: Shut up, Wayne.

> We returned to our places, these Kingdoms,
> But no longer at ease here, in the old dispensation,
> With an alien people clutching their gods.
> I should be glad of another death.
>
> T. S. Eliot, "Journey of the Magi"

At that moment we heard loud voices outside (in the dark) and glass breaking. The professors disappeared down the stairs, followed closely by Max and her camera. From the window the rest of us could see two teens facing off. The smaller one held a broken bottle like a sword. Suddenly Conrad came into view. He approached the pair slowly, hands out. The shouting ceased. The bottle clinked to the ground. As suddenly as they appeared, the two boys were gone.

That night in bed my head buzzed with pipe smoke. I dreamed I was an angry kid on the streets of Bethlehem. One minute I was menacing innocent bystanders with a broken bottle, the next I was asking for help to find my way. My dreams are never very subtle. Could I handle the jagged edges? The loose ends? The shadows? It helps when you encounter wise men along the way, but still.

I returned to Jerusalem in the morning, this time through the checkpoint. As I waited in line, four Palestinians up ahead were commanded, at gunpoint, to drop their pants. No suicide belts. Just underwear, shame, and resentment. Suddenly my personal woes seemed trite. Back in Jerusalem I went straight to the Ali Baba Internet Café and fired off another email to Guilder, this time about the census in Luke 2.

From: "Randall Guilder" <rguilder@sblusa.com>

Subject: **RE: Con-census**

To: "Norm Adams" <nadams@state.com>

Norman—I read of your smoke-filled evening with interest; a delightful diversion during yesterday's faculty meeting. (Enrollment report, housing policy, senate elections—every bit intolerable.)

Now concerning the matters about which you wrote: Luke's census (2:1–5). For me it is a delightful example of Lukan *creativity*. He has to get the family from Nazareth (where everyone knows they're from) to Bethlehem (where Messiahs are supposed to be born) so he invents an imperial edict to bring it to pass! To treat Luke's census as historical is to face several problems.[14]

- **Timing.** Luke 2:2 says a tax census in the days of Quirinius brought Joseph, Mary, and Jesus to Bethlehem. Luke mentions this census (and accompanying tax revolt) again in Acts 5:37. Josephus says Quirinius was the Syrian legate who took charge of Judea, Samaria, and Idumea in 6 CE when Caesar banished Herod's son Archelaus (*Jewish Antiquities* 17.355; 18.1–2; 20.102; *Jewish War* 2.117–118; 7.253). So Luke thinks Herod the Great was still alive at the time of the census (1:5; cf. Matt. 2:1) even though he died in 4 BCE, ten years earlier.
- **Travel.** It isn't clear that Rome would have required its subjects to travel. Would all Jews throughout the empire have to return home to Judea? Some scholars have suggested that the journey of the holy family reflected regional, Jewish concerns about ancestral land rather than Roman policy. Or that Joseph owned taxable property

in Bethlehem. But Luke 2:4 says Joseph had to travel because of ancestry, not real estate. And verse 7 implies that Joseph had no home of his own in Bethlehem.

- **Ancestry.** Why would Joseph have to return to the town of an ancestor who lived some 40 generations earlier? If every grandson could trace his lineage that far back, there'd be thousands, millions, of taxpayers descending on tiny Bethlehem! (Solomon had 1,000 wives.) Some suggest that only those with clear royal ties would have to travel, but this makes no political sense, as E. P. Sanders (*Historical Figure of Jesus*, 86) points out:

> Augustus supported Herod. He would not have asked members of a royal family that had been out of power for over 500 years, and that had been superseded by two successive dynasties (the Hasmonean and the Herodian), to register in some special way. He would not have wanted the social tension that reviving hopes of a Davidic kingdom would have created.

- **"First."** Some scholars have rendered Luke 2:2 "this census happened *before* Quirinius . . ." but I don't think this works. And Rome wouldn't undertake a census in Herod's realm; Herod could handle that for himself. Only when Judea came out from under Herodian rule (in 6 CE) did Rome, through Quirinius, conduct its own registration.

I conclude that Luke, writing eighty years after the fact, has conflated two tumultuous episodes, the death of Herod the Great and the transition from Archelaus to Quirinius. I don't blame him. Both episodes saw public riots involving Galilean rebels named Judas (*Jewish War* 2.56, 118)!

Shalom/salaam
Randall

I wanted to give Luke the benefit of the doubt, but I had to admit that Luke's census was historically problematic. Do we know enough about Quirinius's career to dismiss Luke's version of events out of hand? Enough about Rome's tax policies in its territories? Should Josephus's names and dates be used to correct Luke's, when Josephus himself was known for twisting the facts?

When all else fails, there's Google. My search for *Quirinius* produced an impressive ninety-four thousand hits. Several posts by Stephen Carlson caught my eye.[15] Carlson has proposed a different translation of Luke 2:2: "This *became a very important* registration when Quirinius was governing Syria." According to Carlson, verse 2 is a parenthetical digression to the effect that, though Joseph's travel to Bethlehem was occasioned by Augustus's decree (i.e., the registration of 8 BCE), the most important registration from Augustus's policies was the one that took place when Quirinius was governor (and that led to the revolts in Galilee). Thus Luke is distinguishing the registration that Joseph obeyed from that most prominent one in 6 CE, not confusing it. Carlson's proposal, that Luke has linked together more than one Roman census, was promising. Time would tell, I thought, how well it would fare among the critics.

There was a time when I imagined that all my questions would divide into neat piles—clear and unclear, open and shut, critical and trivial. Historical issues were distinct from scientific questions. Literary issues were not theological. I pictured myself taking inventory, working systematically through the piles, and finishing off with a little Christian garage sale. That was then. Now, as I wandered the backstreets of the Christian Quarter, passing sober Copts and scurrying Franciscans, I saw that many of my questions intersected. My historical quest for Jesus could not avoid a literary quest for the Gospels, those strange books—part biography, part novel, part sermon—that told a scandalous tale about the son of Mary who was also the Son of God. How do the Gospels work? What sort of books are they? With what might they be compared?

CHAPTER 4

Mist and Mystery

In which Norm rides a pickup, learns from a siren, dances at a wedding, and finds true love.

MONTY PYTHON'S LIFE OF BRIAN, SCENE 5

BRIAN: Who cured you?

EX-LEPER: Jesus did, sir. I was hopping along, minding my own business. All of a sudden, up he comes. Cures me. One minute I'm a leper with a trade, next minute my livelihood's gone. Not so much as a by-your-leave.

World without Transcendence

I needed a night at the movies. I missed the sloping seats, the sticky floors, the dimming lights that announced my departure for another world. It didn't have to be Middle Earth or Hyperspace; Wallace and Gromit's garden would do. Just let me suspend my disbelief for ninety minutes or so.

Keith Hopkins says believing in miracles is like going to the movies. When we tell miracle stories we escape into fantasy. We flee life's gray predictability to enter the luminescent Gospel World where anything can happen. According to Hopkins, "religious discourse itself is bracketed off from the mundane world."[1]

The idea that miracles inhabit the realm of sacred imagination has obvious appeal. It would explain, for example, why I've never seen one. I've heard the stories, some from credible sources, but I've never actually been on hand when the lame walk or the blind see. (Televangelist sleight-of-hand doesn't count.) For me, miracles mostly belong to *back then* or *over there*.

But Hopkins's tidy proposal also has its downside. It means we have to inhabit a world without transcendence—a *Truman Show* world, where any hint of another reality is hastily dismissed. In such a world God, like Christof, conspires to hide all signs of his existence. It's a dominion haunted by the ghost of Rudolph Bultmann, where New Testament miracle stories, including the one about Jesus rising from the grave, are either declared preposterous or deftly demythologized.[2] This move seemed hasty to me. It is one thing to say that nature-reversing, doctor-defying miracles are rare.[3] Quite another to rule them out.

In the film *Stigmata*, God delivers an urgent message through Frankie Paige, a nonbelieving hairstylist from Pittsburgh. To determine whether Frankie's "stigmata"—physical marks of crucifixion—are genuine, the Vatican dispatches priest-sleuth Father Andrew Kiernan, who discovers more than his superiors intended. The film's stinging indictment of institutional Christianity almost overwhelms another theme: the modern tension between science and religion, between skepticism and faith. Cardinal Houseman spells out the stark alternatives: Andrew, he says, "can't decide whether he's a scientist or a priest." Andrew's own assessment of his plight, offered in confession to Brother Delmonico, is parallel: "I travel around the world investigating miracles, and then I disprove them. The real miracle is that anyone believes anything. I don't know what I'm doing, to tell you the truth."

As the story unfolds, Frankie transmits a message from Jesus reportedly so radical that it threatens to topple St. Peter's itself, and Father Andrew learns that the church will do anything to keep that message from getting out. Along the way Frankie's faith is born and the priest's is reborn, though not before they bear witness to raw, otherworldly power. Miracles, it turns out, change everything.

Miracles in the Gospels

 7 exorcisms (none in John)

14 healings

 3 raisings of the dead

 9 nature miracles (stilling storm, walking on water, feeding two crowds, cursing fig tree, coin in fish's mouth, two catches of fish, water into wine)

Mine was not a quest for raw, unearthly power. Bleeding statues and scratching demoniacs weren't for me. Hopkins says miracles belong in some other world; I wanted to locate Jesus's miracles in this one. I wanted to see if Jesus's miracles had more credibility, if they made more sense, as part of a life lived out in the mundane, profane world of first-century Palestinian Judaism.

Several questions asserted themselves: Can we evaluate Jesus's "miracles" using historical criteria? Are some miracle stories more believable than others? Did the early Christians invent miracles to boost Jesus's stature? Can we make historical sense of Jesus only if we grant the possibility of "transcendence"?

There were certainly plenty to choose from. Mark is littered with wonders—half the space he devotes to Jesus's life (not counting the last week) is allotted to miracles. Granted, historical inquiry can never prove the miraculous. Historians trade in probabilities, not certainties. But perhaps a little digging could tilt the balance of probability, or test the plausibility, of a story or two.

According to Guilder, modern scholars agree that Jesus was known in his day as a doer of extraordinary deeds. Ancient folk didn't doubt the supernatural, he said. They hadn't heard that nature's "laws" were immutable, so their question was not whether miracles happened but where, and by whom they were done. Even Jesus's opponents didn't deny that Jesus had special powers; they just debated their source (Mark 3:22).

I'm not sure how long I slept, face in a book, in the basement of the École, but the puddle of drool on the page wasn't pretty. The library's bookshelves leaned in as I regained consciousness. Forget the illiterate, drooling masses, they whispered. How about the empire's educated, urban elites? How would they react to rumors of the miraculous? Cicero, statesman from the time of Julius Caesar, came to mind. For Cicero, "The impossible never has happened and . . . the possible need not excite any wonder" (*On Divination* 2.49). "That which could not have happened never did happen; and that which could have happened is no portent; therefore, in any view, there is no such thing as a portent" (2.61). "What would be the sense in the sick seeking relief from an interpreter of dreams rather than from a physician?" (2.123). Cicero would surely have applied the same logic to Jesus's miracles: they had natural explanations or they didn't happen.

This approach to Jesus remains popular. According to the late Morton Smith, "Rationalists long assumed that miracles do not occur and that the gospel stories of Jesus' miracles were legendary. . . . Then came the discovery that blindness, deafness, loss of speech, paralysis, and the like might occur as hysterical symptoms and be 'cured' instantaneously if the hysteria suddenly ceased."[4] For Smith, Jesus "cured" people by his uncanny ability to heal psychological disorders and calm troubled minds. In Jesus's day, of course, enlightened folks like Cicero and Smith held little sway over the weary ones who lived day to day with sick and insane relatives. For folks like these, the arrival of Jesus would have been cause for hope and celebration.

An Angel and a Spa

The cats were at war. Gray tumbled with black on the stone ledge of the library window, in the tight space between the glass and the bars. One moment they were deadly serious, the next, mischievous and playful. I'd come to Israel on a sober quest for Jesus, but sometimes I just needed to play. Mom always said we do our best thinking as whole bodies, not detached heads. (John the Baptist would agree.) So with stray cats and Mom's voice as inspiration, I abandoned my Dominican oasis and ventured onto the cobbles of East Jerusalem.

At opposite ends of the Old City are two ancient pools—Bethesda and Siloam—twin anchors for twin healing stories in the Gospel of John. I headed south toward Bethesda, staying in the cool of the afternoon shadows. Then down the broad steps and through Damascus Gate, along El Wad, and east onto the quieter Via Dolorosa. Just inside St. Stephen's Gate I reached St. Anne's. Monastery, gardens, Crusader church, home of Jesus's grandparents, ancient pool—this place had it all.

According to John 5:1–17 it was during a pilgrimage to Jerusalem that Jesus, on a Saturday, visited a pool near the "Sheep Gate" (through which animals passed bound for the temple). I doubt Jesus came for a swim; to reach the pool he'd have to traverse a sea of invalids (John 5:3, 13), an oozing rash of untouchables, including at least one who'd been sick for thirty-eight years.

Scholars say the original Gospel of John didn't include verses 3 and 4—the part about angels infusing the water with energy

"Few serious historians now deny that Jesus . . . performed cures and did other startling things for which there was no obvious natural explanation."

N. T. Wright, *Jesus and the Victory of God*, 188

"Jesus was one of these 'men of deeds.' Indeed to his contemporaries it was the most remarkable thing about him. During his lifetime he was known primarily as a healer and exorcist."

Marcus Borg, *Jesus: A New Vision*, 60

"The question that Jesus' contemporaries asked about his actions was whether or not it was God who acted through him. Jesus' enemies did not suspect him of fraud, but of healing by calling on a demonic power."

E. P. Sanders, *Historical Figure of Jesus*, 160

enough to heal the first one to jump in. The logic seems solid: it doesn't sound like John's diction, and the best manuscripts omit these verses entirely.[5] That said, verse 7 makes it clear that many in Jesus's day—the rabble if not the elites—thought of God's power as magical, detached, and floating, perhaps out there on the surface of the water.[6]

As I circled the cluster of ancient pools, peering down on worn steps and recesses, I imagined hordes of magic-tinged invalids inching across the pavement on a slow-motion scramble for wholeness. They were waiting, with odds equal to a widow's at a lottery booth—waiting for a miracle.

> Nothing left to do when you're begging for a crumb
> Nothing left to do when you've got to go on waiting
> Waiting for the miracle to come.
>
> Leonard Cohen,
> "Waiting for the Miracle," on *The Future*
>
> So how come history takes such a long, long time when you're waiting for a miracle?
>
> Bruce Cockburn, "Waiting for a Miracle," on *Waiting for a Miracle*

Against this backdrop of Jewish folklore and superstition, Jesus makes quite an impression. As John tells it, Jesus said nothing about the pool's magical properties; he simply responded to human need: "Do you want to be made well?" Then: "Stand up, take your mat and walk" (vv. 6, 8). Jesus doesn't wait for the random act of a cosmic Life Guard. Nor does he acknowledge the pool's mystique. Rather, he behaves as though he can summon God's power to heal whenever he chooses.

It seems unlikely Jesus's followers would make all this up. For one thing, John's knowledge of these pools at a place called Bethesda has been confirmed by archaeology.[7] For another, the invalid's behavior defies stereotypes. He doesn't seem overly enthused about being cured (like the "ex-leper" in *Life of Brian*). And he offers no thanks when healed. Instead he tattles to the authorities and gets Jesus in trouble. This isn't *proof* that a certifiably lame man began to walk without surgery or therapy, but it did rein in my skepticism.

I lingered over the tangle of basins, baths, steps, and walls, trying to pinpoint the five pools of John 5:2, when my solitude was interrupted by several dozen Asian pilgrims sporting matching visors and name tags. Their local guide, umbrella in hand, spoke English while someone translated. I was a Western buoy bobbing on an Oriental sea. I lingered to listen.

Not long after Jesus's death, the guide explained, Jerusalem suffered a pair of horrific defeats at the hands of the Romans, so that by 135 CE they angrily converted

Jerusalem into a thoroughly pagan city, calling it *Aelia Capitolina* and dedicating it to Zeus. Excavations show, she announced, that during this pagan period the Bethesda pool continued to function as a cultic healing center. People still thought the place had curative powers, except that now the credit went to Asclepius, the god of medicine. By the fifth century, pagan worship gave way to the first of several Christian churches, the last of which was the stunning twelfth-century Romanesque Church of St. Anne, which stood nearby.

It took a moment for all this to sink in. This place had memory. For Jews, then Romans, then Christians, these pools localized the power to heal. This space had for centuries been liminal, a threshold to another world. It was The-Wood-between-the-Worlds.[8]

It was as if Jesus came here because it was the sort of place healings *ought* to occur. Did he mean to repudiate the magic water of folk Judaism? Subvert the cultic rituals of Greco-Roman religion? Whatever the reason, Jesus seemed to behave as if his mere presence was sufficient to guarantee that healing powers would flow. Jesus simply didn't fit our mundane world with its diseases and deformities, rituals and superstitions. I split the crowd, crossed the courtyard, and exited to the street. If Jesus escaped throngs of invalids (John 5:3, 13), I could squeeze past a few tourists. Pagan spas reminded me of Jake, my self-identified "pagan" roommate back home and a university spa regular. He was pre-med, so I emailed him for information about Asclepius.

Light at Tunnel's End

The next day, after a late breakfast and several hours of journaling, I set out for the pool of Siloam. In Jesus's day the pool lay within city boundaries; today it lies well beyond the Ottoman walls. The route I chose to get there was underground.

A 538-meter tunnel, chiseled in bedrock back in the days of Hezekiah, still directs spring water from the Gihon spring downhill to Siloam.[9] It was completely dark and barely wide enough for one, the ceiling varying from five to maybe fifteen feet. The water flowed crisp and fresh, rarely rising above my knees. Ahead of me a young family

> "To see the numbers of maimed, malformed and diseased humanity that throng the holy places and obstruct the gates, one might suppose that the ancient days had come again, and that the angel of the Lord was expected to descend at any moment to stir the waters of Bethesda. Jerusalem is mournful, and dreary, and lifeless. I would not desire to live here."
>
> Mark Twain, *Innocents Abroad*, 399

> "It is easy for modern people to see in folk religion only a naïve preoccupation with the marvelous, but at the very least folk religion made life bearable and hopeful for people who experienced the regularities of the world as oppressive, confining and inhuman."
>
> Richard Bauckham, "Coin in the Fish's Mouth," 244

Roman Pool of Siloam

waded, their patriarch bravely singing Hebrew folk songs to comfort his children. I turned off my light to amplify the echoes and inched forward, one hand probing for the ceiling and the other tracing the wall. So *this* was blindness.

The darkness made me metaphorical. The tunnel was my Jesus quest. If water is flowing, there can be no dead end. The channel was narrow with abrupt jogs and misleading spurs, but if I felt my way I could trace the path of countless others and arrive eventually at my goal. It didn't matter that I couldn't see; what mattered was what I would find at the end.

If this were in the States, some genius would have chiseled it wider to create a tube run or installed hand rails. At the bottom would be a gift shop with Hezekiah T-shirts and bobbleheads. Things are different here. When I emerged from the darkness, I found myself alone in a rectangular pit, open to the sky but walled high on all sides. So this was the famous pool where the blind man found his sight. I found a ledge along the wall, dug out my Bible and began to read from John's Gospel, chapter 9.

The story begins with a poke at Jesus's disciples, who assume that blindness is sin's punishment. Like the folk magic up at Bethesda, the disciples' theology here is mechanical and formulaic: present illness must mean past wickedness. So to be blind from birth means to suffer punishment by God for the sin of one's parents (Deut. 5:9).

Precisely this sort of karma is what Jesus rejects. Not radical enough. The man was born blind, Jesus says, so God's power could show itself. Years of cruel darkness led to a singular moment of joyous enlightenment, to a dazzling encounter with the Light of the world. Initially Jesus's explanation seemed no more palatable than the disciples'. Does God afflict innocent people in order to demonstrate, years later, healing power? This kind of God would surely not be safe. But was he good?

As my eyes adjusted to midday, I remembered a blind old Arab I'd seen just inside Damascus Gate, shuffling along the cobbles on the arm of his dutiful grandson. In my mind *he* was the one Jesus instructed to find his way here, and it was his young helper who washed off the indignity—the muddy spit Jesus smeared on his eyes. As I conjured the scene, the first thing the old man saw was his grandson's face.

The miracle story in John is surprisingly brief—briefer than many synoptic episodes. To some this suggests that John's account is "primitive" and maybe au-

thentic.[10] As for the long, heated aftermath (John 9:8–41),
many chalk that up to freehand composition—John refers obliquely to life in the late first century, when Jewish Christians have been tossed out of the synagogue
for loyalty to Jesus (v. 22) and when the chasm between
Christians and "Jews" (9:18, 22) is growing.[11]

This could explain why John calls Jesus's opponents
"Pharisees" one minute (9:13, 15, 16, 40) and "Jews" the next
(9:18, 22). It might also explain the Pharisees' hostility toward a
poor beggar whose crime was washing his face and deciding his healer was a prophet. Like the Jewish Christians of
John's day, the beggar could *see* what the synagogue elite
could not (9:39–41): that Jesus was Israel's Messiah (9:22),
the Son of Man (9:35), and coming Judge (9:39). Whatever
we make of the miracle itself, John seems eager to get on to
the debate about Jesus's identity: was he a Sabbath-breaking
sinner or the Light of the world (9:5, 16, 24–25, 29–33)?

As I rose to depart, a solitary religious Jew descended from
the street and strode past me toward the tunnel. Without
looking around, he stripped off his blacks and whites, hopped
buck naked into the pool, and plunged beneath the surface. My
gentile eyes grew wide. I had stepped back in time. Here was
a ritual bath at Qumran. Here, a baptism at the Jordan. Smiling
to myself, I left him dripping and climbed the steps to the street.

Suddenly, a loud voice. "My friend! My friend! You have come!"

It was Ismail, a man I'd met in the Kidron Valley who had urged
me to visit the excavations by the pool. Ismail was a (Palestinian)
worker, not the (Israeli) archaeologist overseeing the dig, but he
was eager to tell me what he knew. Turns out that what I *thought*
was the Roman Pool of Siloam wasn't. The collection pool at the
end of the tunnel was built in the fourth century to commemorate
the Gospel miracle. But the *Roman* pool was several yards farther
south and unknown until 2004, when city workers had to repair
a sewer pipe. Ismail showed me the exposed stone steps—fifteen
of them—running for several hundred feet along the east edge of
the pool. Coins found beneath the steps, he said, confirmed that
the pool was in use in Jesus's day.

Even partially excavated, the bone-dry pool was grand—large
enough to supply water to locals and pilgrims and, because it was
spring fed, able to serve as a Jewish ritual bath. Why would Jesus

"It is this episode, more
than any other in the Fourth
Gospel, which portrays the
parting of the ways between
Judaism and early Christianity."

John McHugh,
"In Him Was Life," 150

"About one thing we can be
sure: the Johannine community
parted ways with the synagogue
and established an independent
community congruent with
increasingly independent strains
of thought and a sectarian
mentality."

Steven Wilson,
Related Stangers, 72–73

compel the blind man to visit such a public venue? To guarantee that the miracle would be noticed? To provoke an encounter between ritually clean Jews and an unclean beggar (John 9:8)? Did water symbolize Jesus's power to cleanse and heal? To quench spiritual thirst?

A gruff voice summoned Ismail back to work. He swung onto a ladder and disappeared down a hole, leaving me alone beside the *real* Siloam pool.

Was this the site of a bona fide miracle? Three Gospel details made me think that the story went back a ways, perhaps right back to Jesus.[12] First, John mentions Siloam in passing as if everyone knew it, even though at the time of writing (after Jerusalem's destruction in 70 CE), the pool was almost certainly buried under rubble. Here's Josephus on the mayhem of the war: "On the following day the Romans, having routed the brigands from the lower town, set the whole on fire as far as Siloam; the consuming of the town rejoiced their hearts, but they were disappointed of plunder, the rebels having cleared out everything before they retired to the upper city" (*Jewish War* 6.363). John's story takes us back to a time when the pool was well known.

Second, John says Jesus was in town for the Feast of Booths, a national campout commemorating Israel's exodus from Egypt (John 7:2, 8, 10–11, 14, 37).[13] According to traditions recorded in the Mishnah, this was when the priests processed down to the Siloam pool to retrieve water for use in the temple. Maybe Jesus was creating an alternative procession, offering himself as the true water that brings light (8:12; 9:5) and life (7:38).

Third, Jesus's behavior here is earthy. Magical, but in a mundane sort of way. No disciple would make this up.[14] Nor is this the only saliva story in the Gospels. Mark describes Jesus up in Galilee putting fingers in a deaf man's ears and saliva on his tongue (Mark 7:33–37). A chapter later Mark has Jesus in Bethsaida (not Bethesda) spitting on a blind man's eyes (Mark 8:22–26). Neither Matthew nor Luke repeats Mark's saliva stories, perhaps due to the *ick* factor. The similarities between Mark's story and the one in John 9 have encouraged some to think that we have got "independent versions of the same source."[15]

Mark 8:22–26	John 9:1–7
They came to Bethsaida. Some people brought a blind man to him and begged him to touch him. He took the blind man by the hand and led him out of the village; and when he had put saliva on his eyes and laid his hands on him, he asked him, "Can you see anything?" And the man looked up and said, "I can see people, but they look like trees, walking." Then Jesus laid his hands on his eyes again; and he looked intently and his sight was restored, and he saw everything clearly. Then he sent him away to his home, saying, "Do not even go into the village."	As he walked along, he saw a man blind from birth. His disciples asked him, "Rabbi, who sinned, this man or his parents, that he was born blind?" Jesus answered, "Neither this man nor his parents sinned; he was born blind so that God's works might be revealed in him. We must work the works of him who sent me while it is day; night is coming when no one can work. As long as I am in the world, I am the light of the world." When he had said this, he spat on the ground and made mud with the saliva and spread the mud on the man's eyes, saying to him, "Go, wash in the pool of Siloam" (which means Sent). Then he went and washed and came back able to see.

I'm not convinced. Saliva plays such different roles in the two stories. John's spit-mud represents the disease; Mark's spit is the cure. Mark's Jesus seems to tinker until he gets it right (Mark 8:23, 25); in John, Jesus isn't even around at the moment of the miracle, nor does he inquire later how things turned out (John 9:35). Rather than assume that John and Mark preserve two accounts of the same event, why not conclude that Jesus used spit more than once?[16] If John 9 doesn't recall a genuine episode from Jesus's life, it was certainly the sort of thing Jesus was known to do.

> Lord, spit on our eyes so we can see
> How to wake up from this tragedy
>
> Bruce Cockburn,
> "Broken Wheel," on *Inner City Front*

Holy Woman, Holy Man

The sun was setting as I entered the Old City, this time through Zion Gate into the Armenian Quarter, the most secretive corner of the city. As I passed the entrance to the little Syrian Orthodox Church of St. Mark, a woman clad in black from shoes to scarf warmly beckoned. Inside the church Yustina pulled back a heavy curtain to reveal the gilded altar. Then she showed me a faded icon of Mary and Jesus that was painted, she assured me wide-eyed, by Doctor Luke himself. Perhaps it was the way she combined intensity with innocence. Perhaps it was her adorable accent and broken English. Whatever it was, I wanted to believe her that this little church rested on the original house of Mary, mother of John Mark (Acts 12:12). Could this be the site of the Last Supper (Luke 22) and the Spirit's descent (Acts 2)? Was this where Peter fled after his escape from prison (Acts 12)? All this happened, she explained, "in dee-howse-down." Yustina led me down to a simple room unfurnished except for an altar, at which point she asked to sing the Lord's Prayer in Aramaic, "dee ling-wudge of Jesus!" Eyes closed, her face radiated tranquility. Her beautifully haunting voice was at home in the ancient tongue. No performance this. I almost converted to Orthodoxy on the spot.

Yustina told me that since her arrival from Nineveh five visitors to St. Mark's had experienced miracles. On one occasion she applied oil to a Bulgarian woman dying of cancer. When she returned home her tumor was gone. I learned also of a Korean Buddhist, sick with TB, whose faltering prayers to the Jesus he didn't know led to healing and to devoting his life to care for the poor. "Vee haff a g'date Gad," Yustina would slowly repeat, eyes closed and hands on breast. We have a great God.

I left St. Mark's a tangle of doubt and delight. My guide book confirmed that a church did indeed occupy the spot at least as far back as the fourth century. Before that, who knew? Although there was more work for archaeologists down there, the chance of anyone getting permission to excavate was remote.

Questions about the site gave way to ones about the saint. Had the simple prayer of a righteous Syrian dissolved a tumor? Or had Yustina's stories improved in the telling? Either way, I had just encountered a living, Aramaic-speaking, storytelling, Lord's Prayer–praying follower of Jesus. Part of me wanted to file Yustina's oral traditions under *pious fiction*. Another part told me where to come if ever I needed a miracle.

Dark was falling when I reached the Muslim Quarter. The warm glow of the Ali Baba Internet Café on Via Dolorosa drew me in. Filling every seat were young boys playing Counter-Strike, stemming the tide of terrorism one click at a time. The shop owner shooed the youngest one away to make room. Jake's reply to my query about Asclepius was in my inbox.

From: "Jake Atkins" <jatkins@state.com>
Subject: **Know anything about Asclepius?**
To: "Norm Adams" <nadams@state.com>

Yo Norm.

School is humming along. Yesterday Nelson began his lecture on chronic diseases with a parody of the Beatles' song "Yesterday." I think someone's posting it on Youtube.

> Leprosy, bits and pieces falling off of me,
> I'm not half the man I used to be,
> Oh I contracted leprosy.

Don't be planning a quest for the "historical" Asclepius. Not enough to go on. According to my History of Medicine notes he's first mentioned in Homer when his sons, a pair of "good healers," join the attack on Troy. By the time of Pindar in the 5th c. BCE, Asclepius has become larger than life:

> *All those who now came with a tumor on the body that grew*
> *by itself,*
> *or with limbs damaged by grey iron or by a stone flung from*
> *a distance,*
> *or with bodies scorched by the burning heat of summer or*
> *by winter,*
> *he set free from whatever torments each individual suffered,*
> *treating some with mild magical spell,*
> *giving others a healing drink or binding dressings with*
> *ointment about their limbs.*
> *He restored others to health through amputation.*[17]

Sunburn, blindness, infertility, amputation—whatever your ailment, Doctor Asclepius is in. He even gets in trouble—struck by lightning—for trying to bring someone back from the dead! Those midlevel gods should know their limits.

Eventually Asclepius becomes the divine son of Apollo, born in Epidaurus, Greece. Shrines and temples spring up, not just in his home town but also in Cos, Athens, Corinth, Rome, and Pergamum, home of my man Galen (130–201 CE), a giant of ancient medicine. But these temples aren't just temples. *Au contraire*. By 2nd century, they are full-service, five-star health spas with dining rooms, libraries, theaters, dorms, baths, stadiums, and gymnasiums!

The best part is how Asclepius heals. At sundown a priest ushers sicko into the inner sanctum and tucks him in. During the night Asclepius appears, if not in person then in a dream or as a sacred dog or snake. If you're not healed on the spot, he tells you what to do in the morning. Sometimes there's a fee, and don't forget to offer something on the altar. One guy who neglected the thank-offering became blind all over again.

Found this story about a guy whose faith needed a boost.

> Cleimenes from Argus, lame in his body. He entered the healing room and slept, and saw a vision: he dreamt that the god wound a red woolen bandage round his body and led him a little way outside the sanctuary to bathe in a pool. The water of this pool was exceptionally cold. When he hung back in cowardice, Asclepius said that he would not heal people who were too cowardly for this, but only those who came into his sanctuary to him with the good hope that he would not do anything evil to them, but would send them away healthy. When he woke up, he bathed and emerged without any physical defect.[18]

That's all I got. Do you see parallels with Jesus? Was he just one more Greco-Roman holy man?

Gotta go. Med school applications. It will be a miracle if I get my first choice.
Jake

What struck me was the time span between the "historical" Asclepius and the divine wonder worker of the same name; Asclepius took centuries to transition from doctor to hero to god. That got me wondering about other ancient holy men. It took me a day at the École to track down some of the more familiar wonder workers.

Wonder worker	Date	Oldest source attributing wonders	Date	Gap
Asclepius	pre-Homer	Pindar	fifth century BCE	???
Pythagoras	560–490 BCE	Iamblichos	245–325 CE	800 years
		Porphyry	222–305 CE	
Empedocles	484–424 BCE	Diogenes Laertius	250 CE	700 years
King Pyrrhus	319–272 BCE	Plutarch	46–120 CE	400 years
Honi/Onias	d. 65 BCE	Josephus	mid-90s CE	158 years
Hanina ben Dosa	mid-first century CE	Mishnah	200 CE	150 years
		both Talmuds	400–550 CE	350+ years
Apollonius of Tyana	late first century CE	Philostratus	218 CE	130 years
Asclepiades	124–40 BCE	Pliny the Elder	23–79 CE	115 years
Jesus	**c. 30 CE**	**Mark**	**c. 70 CE**	**40 years**
Vespasian	9–79 CE	Tacitus	56–115 CE	30 years
		Suetonius	69–122 CE	40 years
Eleazar	mid-first century CE	Josephus	mid-90s CE	0 years

The time lapse between historical figure and surviving miracle story is more than a century in all but three cases from the first century.[19] Vespasian is said to have hesitantly restored a man's sight (using spittle, by the way) and another man's limb. As for Eleazar, Josephus (*Jewish Antiquities* 8.46–49) says he saw him extract a demon by holding a root to a man's nose. (I'd rather watch Bear Grylls eat maggots.) By contrast, the glut of surviving miracle stories about Jesus is embarrassing. Several ideas took shape in the fog:

1. The ancient world knew many magicians and diviners.
2. Some heroes were less miracle *worker* and more miracle *predictor*.

3. Very few *eyewitness* accounts of miracles in the ancient world survive.
4. Surviving sources provide surprisingly few *names* of individual wonder workers. We know of relatively few who had clear reputations for miracles in their day.

No wonder Jesus drew a crowd.

A Free Lunch

The sun rose warm over my shoulder as I peered south across the mist that shrouded the Sea of Galilee. A staircase of bleached buildings ascended from the far shore. Modern Tiberias. The ancient city was founded in 19 CE, a few years after Tiberius became emperor and a decade before Jesus began drawing crowds and preaching about how cities on hills can't be hidden (Matt. 5:14). Built to replace Sepphoris, Tiberias was the glitzy new capital of Antipas's territories and was supposed to convince Rome that little Antipas was just as loyal as his dad.

Birds chirped and swooped across the glassy surface—flaming yellow, incandescent black, turquoise with wings dipped in white. Fish jumped nervously beneath circling gulls. Half-submerged reeds along the shoreline testified to drier times. Beside me a rough-hewn cross cast a long shadow on the water. Listing badly, it seemed more concerned to claim territory than to preach the gospel.

I had taken the bus to Tiberias the night before, then hitchhiked here to Tabgha, a monastery that marks the site where Jesus multiplied loaves and fish (Mark 6:32–44; 8:1–10). Nearby the Church of the Primacy of St. Peter localizes the final chapter of John's Gospel, where Jesus builds a fire and serves breakfast. Uphill to the north a church commemorates the Sermon on the Mount (Matt. 5–7); along the shore to the east is Capernaum, Jesus's home base (Matt. 4:13; 9:1; Mark 2:1). I had arrived, in other words, at Historical Jesus Ground Zero. Jesus knew this shore, these hills, very well.

Brother Samuel, a thirty-something Benedictine in board shorts and sandals, had shown me to my cot in a large army tent, hidden from the busloads who file into the Multiplication Church to see its lively fifth-century mosaics. Next to the tent the brothers had dammed a natural spring to create a narrow pool. The place was perfect; if Jesus didn't feed crowds here, he should have.

I was hungry but had packed little food. The monks' pantry was closed until evening, and the nearest restaurants were miles away in Tiberias. The fact that I was not the first one to seek after Jesus on an empty stomach offered little consolation.

The feeding of the multitude is the only miracle story found in all four Gospels. Since John's version doesn't seem indebted to the other three, the odds are good that *something* historical happened—some "especially memorable communal meal of bread and fish."[20] Or were there two meals? According to Matthew and Mark, a feeding miracle happened twice. I sprawled out on my cot with Bible and synopsis to sort out all this food.[21]

Synoptic meal one (Mark 6:32–44; Matt. 14:13–21; Luke 9:10–17)	Synoptic meal two (Mark 8:1–10; Matt. 15:32–39)	John's version (John 6:1–15)
Common to All		
• Somewhere in Galilee, Jesus worries about thousands of hungry followers.		
• The disciples indicate they haven't enough food for the crowds, producing only a few loaves and fish.		
• Jesus has the people sit down, takes the food, gives thanks, and has the disciples pass it out.		
• Everyone has plenty; leftovers are gathered up in containers.		
Similarities and Differences		
five thousand men	four thousand men	five thousand men
Seated on grass (Mark: green grass), thus springtime		Seated on much grass, around Passover, thus springtime
A deserted place (Luke: Bethsaida)	A deserted place	
Near the Sea of Galilee	Near the Sea of Galilee	Near the Sea of Galilee
Jesus climbs a mountain afterward.	Matthew: it happens on a mountain.	It happens on a mountain.
Crowd arrives and is fed on same day.	Crowd is there three days before feeding.	Crowd arrives and is fed on same day.
Mark: Two hundred denarii might feed them.		Two hundred denarii wouldn't be enough.
Five loaves and two fish	Seven loaves and a few fish	Five loaves and two fish of young boy
Jesus blesses the food.	Jesus gives thanks for the food.	Jesus gives thanks for the food.
Twelve baskets of leftovers	Seven hampers of leftovers	Twelve baskets of leftovers
Next: night walk on water	Next: the dangers of the Pharisees	Next: night walk on water

Sea of Galilee

There are strong similarities between the six accounts. On the one hand, John's version has more in common with Mark 6 (and pars.) than Mark 8 (and par.), but the large number of overall parallels might suggest that a single event lies behind all six. With eyes closed and stomach empty, I pictured the earliest teachers and troubadours telling their favorite Jesus stories over a good meal. I imagined them swapping episodes and collecting memory fragments like leftover bits of bread, and then carefully arranging their pieces into a continuous, compelling narrative. It would be easy, I thought, for different versions of the same episode to emerge and circulate independently. This would explain why Luke and John speak only of a single meal.

On the other hand, Mark (followed by Matthew) describes two meals and portrays the disciples as no wiser on the second occasion (Mark 8:4) than on the first (Mark 6:35–37).[22]

> "Do you have eyes, and fail to see? Do you have ears, and fail to hear? And do you not remember? When *I broke the five loaves for the five thousand*, how many baskets full of broken pieces did you collect?" They said to him, "Twelve." "And *the seven for the four thousand*, how many baskets full of broken pieces did you collect?" And they said to him, "Seven." Then he said to them, "Do you not yet understand?"
>
> Mark 8:18–21

Did Mark double up his meal story for dramatic reasons? Mark likes to emphasize the spiritual dullness of Jesus's disciples.[23] What better way than to include back-to-back, identical feeding stories that leave on them almost no positive impression? And wouldn't this set the stage brilliantly for Peter's dramatic insight, eight verses later, that Jesus is the Christ (Mark 8:29)?

Maybe it was my stomach talking, but it seemed less important to decide on the number of meals than to sort out what happened. Did Jesus feed a crowd with someone's sack lunch? Cicero's ghost whispered a logical alternative: each person got the tiniest piece but appreciated the gesture. Or maybe a child's generosity (John 6:9) triggered a wave of sharing. Or the disciples had a stash in a nearby cave. With due respect to Cicero and his modern counterparts, however, these sorts of explanations struck me as ingenious but implausible.

A squeal and a splash interrupted my musings. The spring-fed pool was off-limits to tourists, so the noise was puzzling. Nothing could have prepared me for what I saw when I poked my head outside the tent. Five or six severely handicapped children lined the walkway on the pool's far edge, some on mats and others in wheelchairs. Only one could hold up her head without assistance. It was a modern Bethesda, except we were in Galilee and they weren't waiting for the waters to stir. Beside each child was an attentive caregiver. The only child in the pool floated safe in the arms of his caregiver. His facial contortions could only mean delight.

As a solitary outsider witnessing this moment of grace, these secret acts of holy compassion, I felt my eyes themselves become pools. Here before me were the "little ones" whose angels behold the face of God (Matt. 18:10), the children to whom belongs the kingdom (Matt. 19:14). These were the "least" among us, to whom we may offer food, drink, and clothing on behalf of the King (Matt. 10:42; 25:40). The harshness of their plight washed over me. Ages ago Galilee's shores welcomed a miracle man. Would they not welcome one again? Or was I already witnessing a miracle in the unreported, unheralded tenderness of six saints who offered these children as much joy as their little bodies could endure?

The synoptic feeding stories are similarly understated and noncommercial. Jesus feels pity for the crowds (Mark 6:34; 8:2–3) but appears almost reluctant to feed them (Mark 6:35–38; 8:3–6). The grand moment of miraculous "multiplication" goes entirely unreported (Mark 6:41–42; 8:6–7). Only in John's version do the crowds seem impressed (6:14–15). The recorded surplus of leftovers is all that confirms that a miracle has occurred (Mark 6:43; 8:8). And no sooner is everyone fed than Jesus slips away (Mark 6:45; 8:10). If this was a pious legend invented to advertise Jesus's ability to meet our needs, the story's creator gets full points for subtlety.

Food for Thought

The water in the pool was surprisingly cold. This confirmed all my stereotypes about monks and self-mortification. I was climbing out when one of the angelic caregivers announced she was heading into Tiberias. I asked to tag along. This was my chance to check email and buy food. It was also my chance to speak to a member of the opposite sex.

"Did you hear the news?" Anna asked, as we pulled out of the parking lot. She looked to be in her mid-twenties, strong, with a ruddy complexion and intense eyes.

"The news?"

"Eighteen-year-old Palestinian blew himself up this morning in Netanya. Four people dead. Two girls, two women. Dozens wounded. First suicide bombing in months."

"Maybe that's why we heard sirens this morning."

"Israeli troops have reoccupied Tulkarim. A Palestinian policeman is dead, and five Islamic Jihadists are in custody. This place is crazy." Anna pounded the steering wheel of the old monastery pickup. "Can you imagine parents letting their child kill himself to kill other children?"

"Why do you come here, Anna?"

"For the children. This is my third time."

Anna first came on a pilgrimage from Holland. She stayed on to help a German nonprofit that worked with the handicapped and has returned each year since. In silence we followed Route 90 west and then south along the shore.

She pointed out Magdala, home to Mary Magdalene. "Do you think Jesus was married to Mary Magdalene?" she asked.

"Sounds like you've read *The Da Vinci Code*."

"Just seen the movie."

"No, I don't think Jesus was married. It's true that most good Jewish boys got married, but not all of them. Prophets like Jeremiah were called to forgo marriage during times of crisis. There was a celibate community down by the Dead Sea. Saint Paul commended celibacy. Maybe he got the idea from Jesus."[24]

"But Dan Brown quotes a secret gospel that describes Jesus's marriage to Mary."

"None of the gnostic Gospels say Jesus was married. My professor did a whole lecture on this when the movie came out. In the gnostic Gospels Mary Magdalene gets close to Jesus, not so she can sleep with him but to learn his secrets. Turns out his secrets sound suspiciously like the beliefs of second-century gnostics."

I followed Anna into a grocery store, where I stocked up on pita, hummus, apricots, and walnuts. After we loaded her supplies into the truck, I found an Internet café and shot a quick email to Guilder. I wanted his take on the "nature miracles," for which the multiplication of the loaves and fish was a nice test case. I was back in Jerusalem before he replied, but I'm inserting it here.

From: "Randall Guilder" <rguilder@sblusa.com>
Subject: **Food for thought**
To: "Norm Adams" <nadams@state.com>

Hello Norman:

Blame my slow reply on grading. That and the fact that my favorite TA has graduated. Good to hear you've made it up to the Galilee. Yes, the so-called nature miracles are suspect across the academy.

Most of us doubt Jesus controlled the weather. As for Jesus feeding the multitudes, I see at least three other stories lurking behind the Gospels' accounts.

1. Old Testament stories of miraculous provision.
1.1. Moses's manna
Every Jew knew that Israel survived on manna during her forty years in the wilderness (Exod. 16; Josh. 5:12). John 6 (vv. 31–32, 49, 58) shows Jesus out-Moses-ing Moses. If Jesus was a prophet like, or greater than, Moses, his followers would have expected proof. Moses fed a nation with heavenly food, but they died. So Jesus, who descended like manna, must feed the world, and those who eat must never die. The Israelites weren't supposed to collect the surplus manna; Jesus has his followers collect the leftovers. Etc.

1.2. Elisha's loaves
First century Jews would know of Elisha instructing his servant to give twenty loaves of bread and some grain to one hundred people, and pledging there would be more than enough to eat (2 Kings 4:42–44). In the Gospels Jesus is greater than Elisha (cf. Matt. 12:6, 41–42).

I would guess these two stories influenced the telling, and the hearing, of the Gospel loaves and fishes story. As for whether they can explain the origin of the Gospel feeding episodes, I am doubtful. The OT stories don't provide enough detail, and the parallels aren't close enough. I think Moses and Elisha inspired the early Christian storytellers to remember a large-scale communal meal with Jesus as a miracle of feeding.

2. Eucharist traditions.
The Last Supper was a meal of bread and *wine*, not *fish*. Nevertheless, the influence of Eucharist traditions on our story was almost inevitable. Have you seen the loaves and fish mosaic under the altar in the *Multiplication* church at Tabgha? The mosaic has only four loaves. Why aren't there five? Because the fifth loaf is the Communion bread on the altar.

Mark's 2nd feeding miracle includes two stages, each with its own prayer. This parallels Mark's two-stage account of the Last Supper.

Mark 8:6–7	Mark 14:22–23
Then . . . he took the seven loaves,	While they were eating, he took a loaf of bread,
and after giving thanks he broke them	and after blessing it he broke it,
and gave them to his disciples to distribute;	gave it to them,
and they distributed them to the crowd.	and said, "Take; this is my body."
They had also a few small fish;	Then he took a cup,
and after blessing them,	and after giving thanks
he ordered that these too should be distributed.	he gave it to them, and all of them drank from it.

I say we've caught Mark in the act of shaping one story to evoke another. A memorable meal in the wilderness foreshadows the Last Supper, which in turn foreshadows a death in Jerusalem and a messianic banquet still to come.

As for the Fourth Gospel, how can **John** devote five chapters to Jesus's final meal with his disciples (13–17) without mentioning the Eucharist? Answer: because John 6 already smuggled it in, in the meal of loaves and fishes and the *bread of life* discourse that follows. John's earliest readers could not read John 6:11, 23, and 51–58 without thinking of Christian communion.

Was the Last Supper the *source* for a loaves-and-fishes legend? I don't think so. The Eucharist tradition explains why the loaves get more attention than the fish, but it can't explain why the fish are there at all, or why the meal includes nothing to drink. Again, I'd bet that there was a memorable meal in the Galilean countryside not far from the sea.

3. Jesus's Practice of Shared Meals

Jesus was widely known for his radical ideas about food. He liked to tell stories about food, he taught his disciples to pray for their daily bread (Luke 11:3), and he imagined the coming kingdom as a banquet (Luke 13:29). More than a few observers contrast Jesus's love for food and drink with John the Baptist's self-denial (Matt. 11:18–19; Luke 5:33; 7:33–34). Even the risen Jesus shared meals of bread and fish with his disciples (Luke 24; John 21). He challenged his followers not to use mealtimes to enforce social status (Luke 14:8–24), and he himself often chose the "wrong" eating companions (Mark 2:15–17; Matt. 9:10–11; Luke 5:29–30; 7:39; 15:1–2). This "open commensality," as Crossan calls it, is so consistent that we would be surprised if several meals didn't stand out in the memory of his followers.

Shalom/salaam

Randall

Water-Walking

On the drive back from Tiberias, Anna offered to stop at a kibbutz to show me a first-century fishing boat. She was in no hurry to return to Tabgha and maybe a little too eager to spend time with me. Just off the main road, the guard at the gate to Kibbutz Ginnosar directed us to the Yigal Allon Museum, a new building designed to handle hordes of tourists. The air-conditioning alone was worth the price of admission. Anna steered me past the gift shop and toward the glass doors that led to the display room.

The boat on display had a story to tell. Back in the eighties an extended drought caused the water level of the Sea of Galilee to drop sharply, exposing wide muddy flats where, in 1986, two local fishermen stumbled onto the outline of a buried ancient boat. The excavation took weeks and the preservation ten years, but today the boat sits proudly on display—a blue-collar fishing vessel from the first century. Built to be rowed or sailed, it was, they say, large enough to seat at least thirteen.

On a wall nearby a display tells the story of a tragic naval episode during the Jewish struggle for independence from Rome. By 67 CE the local rebellion was heating up. After Tiberias surrendered, the Romans moved north and camped just the other side of Migdal, a mile or two from where the boat was found. Rebels and legionnaires clashed on land and water. Imagine peasants waging war against the tenth legion in fishing boats and homemade rafts! When it was over, seven thousand Jews were dead. They called it the naval Masada.

While I was reading the story on the wall, Anna was deciding that this was *the* boat that Jesus's disciples used for one of their getaways.

"Size, age, type, location—it all fits. This is the Jesus boat!" she said.

I couldn't tell if she was serious. We bought drinks at the snack shop and got to talking about Jesus's adventures on or near the sea. Here's a list of water episodes in Mark's Gospel.

1:16–20	Walking along the shore, Jesus recruits four fishermen, Simon and Andrew, James and John.
2:13	Jesus teaches along the shore.
3:7–12	Crowds find Jesus along the shore. He heals and casts out demons, with a boat standing ready.
4:1–2	Jesus teaches another large crowd by the sea, seated in a boat.
4:35–41	That evening, Jesus sets sail with his disciples and has to calm a life-threatening storm.
5:1–2	Jesus arrives by boat at the country of the Gerasenes, where he meets a demoniac.
5:13	When Jesus casts demons out of the man, they cause pigs to stampede and drown in the sea.
5:21	Jesus returns by boat to the other side.
6:32	Jesus and his disciples try to escape the crowds by boat.
6:34	Going ashore, Jesus encounters a multitude.
6:45	After feeding the multitude, Jesus sends his disciples away by boat.
6:47–53	Jesus walks on the sea to meet his disciples, calm the storm, and travel with them to Gennesaret.
8:10	After feeding the second multitude, Jesus and his disciples depart to Dalmanutha.
8:13–14	Jesus leaves the Pharisees with his disciples, who forget to bring bread.

Three out of four Gospels tell the story of Jesus walking on water. The similarities and variations among them are worth a careful look.

Matthew 14:22–33	Mark 6:45–52	John 6:15–21
Immediately he made the disciples get into the boat and go on ahead to the other side, while he dismissed the crowds.	Immediately he made his disciples get into the boat and go on ahead to the other side, to Bethsaida, while he dismissed the crowd.	When Jesus realized that they were about to come and take him by force to make him king,
And after he had dismissed the crowds,	After saying farewell to them,	
he went up the mountain by himself to pray.	he went up on the mountain to pray.	he withdrew again to the mountain by himself.
When evening came, he was there alone,	When evening came, the boat was out on the sea, and he was alone on the land.	When evening came, his disciples went down to the sea, got into a boat, and started across the sea to Capernaum. It was now dark, and Jesus had not yet come to them.
but by this time the boat, battered by the waves, was far from the land, for the wind was against them.	When he saw that they were straining at the oars against an adverse wind,	The sea became rough because a strong wind was blowing.
		When they had rowed about three or four miles,
And early in the morning he came walking toward them on the sea.	he came toward them early in the morning, walking on the sea. He intended to pass them by.	
But when the disciples saw him walking on the sea, they were terrified, saying, "It is a ghost!" And they cried out in fear.	But when they saw him walking on the sea, they thought it was a ghost and cried out; for they all saw him and were terrified.	they saw Jesus walking on the sea and coming near the boat, and they were terrified.

Matthew 14:22–33	Mark 6:45–52	John 6:15–21
But immediately Jesus spoke to them and said,	But immediately he spoke to them and said,	But he said to them,
"Take heart, it is I; do not be afraid."	"Take heart, it is I; do not be afraid."	"It is I; do not be afraid."
Peter answered him, "Lord, if it is you, command me to come to you on the water." He said, "Come." So Peter got out of the boat, started walking on the water, and came toward Jesus. But when he noticed the strong wind, he became frightened, and beginning to sink, he cried out, "Lord, save me!" Jesus immediately reached out his hand and caught him, saying to him, "You of little faith, why did you doubt?"		
When they got into the boat, the wind ceased. And those in the boat worshiped him, saying, "Truly you are the Son of God."	Then he got into the boat with them and the wind ceased. And they were utterly astounded, for they did not understand about the loaves, but their hearts were hardened.	Then they wanted to take him into the boat, and immediately the boat reached the land toward which they were going.

Of the three versions, John's account seems the least miraculous yet the most mysterious. Jesus's disciples row several miles, but we don't know how far they are from shore when they see Jesus "walking on the sea and coming near." The disciples "wanted to take him into the boat," but "immediately the boat reached the land." It's like John himself can't quite sort out what happened.[25]

In Mark's account Jesus, from the shore and in the dark, saw them caught in the storm but inexplicably "intended to pass them by." When he got into the boat, the winds ceased, leaving the disciples "utterly astounded" because "their hearts were hardened."

Matthew closely parallels Mark, except for a twist at the end. Peter asks to join Jesus, manages a few steps, and begins to sink. Jesus chides him as "one of little faith." When Jesus climbs aboard, the winds cease, as in Mark. But unlike Mark's hard-hearted crew, Matthew's sailors are moved to worship.

Anna became visibly distressed.

"Which is it?" she asked, grabbing my sleeve. "Were the disciples hard-hearted or eager to worship? You can't have opposite endings to the same story."

"I know what you mean," I said. "Mark's solitary Jesus stills storms but leaves his disciples adrift in spiritual turmoil. Matthew's Jesus, the faithful companion, bolsters Peter's faith and catches him when he falls."

"Someone is making stuff up."

A siren sounded. The pitch rose as it drew near, the Doppler effect urging each wave of sound to arrive earlier than the last. I imagined the boat pressing across the lake, piling up ripples at its bow. Then I had an idea.

"The museum wants Christians like us to picture Jesus in the boat, right? But they also want Jews to imagine the boat carrying freedom fighters during the Jewish War."

"More tourists that way."

"Right. So the same boat connects some people with the founder of Christianity and others with the Jews' struggle for survival. A single boat tells two stories! Do you see?"

Anna looked at her watch and jumped. Her child care shift started an hour ago.

"Bet you can't guess the name of the Jewish rebel leader," I said on our way back to the truck.

"I give up."

"Jesus ben Shafat, or something."

"So either way it's the *Jesus* boat."

On the drive back to Tabgha Anna pointed out that an ancient *boat* was not the same as an ancient *event*.

"It's an analogy," I said. "Christians and Jews use the same facts to tell very different stories. Rabbi Jesus sets sail to escape the crowds and return to preach another day; rebel Jesus pushes out to sea to escape the Roman sword and return another day to fight."

"Putting out into the lake just far enough to leave the Romans within bowshot, they then cast anchor and, closing up their vessels one against another like an army in line of battle, they kept up as it were a sea-fight with their enemy on shore.
. . . They hovered round the [Roman] rafts, occasionally even approaching them, now flinging stones from a distance at the Romans, now scraping alongside and attacking them at close range. . . . Their stones produced nothing but a continuous rattle in striking men well protected by armour, while they were themselves exposed to the arrows of the Romans. . . . One could see the whole lake red with blood and covered with corpses."

Josephus,
Jewish War 3.469, 524-25, 530

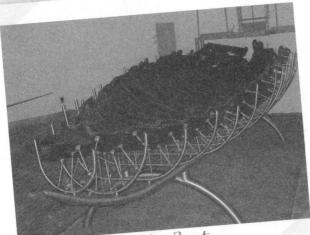

Galilee Boat

Anna was evidently not impressed by my little thought experiment and kept eyeing her watch.

"Your point is . . . ?"

"That maybe Matthew and Mark approached the tradition in the same way. What if each of them saw Jesus's sea voyage as a 'fact' but used it tell a different story? Both stories announce the arrival of God's rule in Jesus.[26] Both depict the sea as a hostile force that can be subdued only by God's authority. But one of them, Mark, wants his readers to remember the disciples' blindness, while the other, Matthew, wants to depict the disciples as models of, well, discipleship. Which is why he includes, maybe even creates, a story about Peter following Jesus on the water."[27]

"Are you saying the Gospels are unreliable?"

"Only if reliability means lockstep conformity to modern ideas about how history should be written. What if an ancient author thought the best way to remain faithful to his story was to blend historical facts with embellishment? What if this was the best way to convey what he cherished most about his hero? My prof used to say there's nothing like an old photograph to distort reality. I think he's right. Sometimes we're better off ignoring the photo and studying the portrait."

"Or the Gospel?"

"Or the Gospel."

Dialogue with the Devil

We knew something was wrong as soon as we pulled into Tabgha. The gate barring tourists from wandering the monastery gardens was flung wide. Behind the trees an emergency vehicle flashed its lights. Anna knew immediately what was wrong.

"One of the children's had a seizure," she called over her shoulder as she sprinted off.

Rather than swell the crowd of spectators, I unloaded groceries. I didn't hear until later that little Shmuel went into a convulsion, struck his head on a railing, and stopped breathing. Paramedics were able to stabilize him but couldn't tell if there'd been brain damage. He was now in Tiberias for observation and tests.

Nightfall brought quiet but little comfort. The world's brokenness weighed heavy. First a desperate teenager detonates himself on a busy crosswalk, and then a severely handicapped child suffers a grand mal seizure. Violence and evil, like the shadows beyond my tent, take many forms. It was almost 3:00 a.m. when I gave up on sleep, clicked on my Maglite, and flipped to the story in Mark 9:17–27 of Jesus healing a child afflicted by seizures.

In our day, recurring seizures signal epilepsy, and multiple voices indicate a split personality. In Jesus's day, such symptoms pointed toward a spiritual presence, a demon whose oppressive grip required extra strength to break. According to Mark, Jesus saw his campaign as a direct challenge to the devil's dominion.[28] When Jesus cast out demons, it not only showed kindness and restored health but also reclaimed for God territory previously held by Satan. Only when Satan is bound can the liberating, reconciling rule of God advance. Only when winter's icy grip is broken can springtime dawn.

> But no one can enter a strong man's house and plunder his property without first tying up the strong man; then indeed the house can be plundered.
>
> Mark 3:27

I'd seen enough icy hostility, hatred, and despair at a single West Bank checkpoint to convince me that the world was desperate and broken. I didn't doubt that evil was real. But was evil personal? Could one have a dialogue with a devil? Banish a demon? Guilder didn't believe in evil spirits. Yesterday's demons are today's psychological disorders, he would say in class. I would point to texts like Mark 1:32, 34; 3:10–11; and 6:13, where Mark shows he can distinguish between sickness and demon possession.[29] Guilder showed us Acts 10:38, where Luke says Jesus went about "*healing* all who were oppressed by the devil."

> The whole world's broke and it ain't worth fixing.
>
> Tracy Chapman,
> "New Beginning," on *New Beginning*

"And don't forget Luke 4:39, where Jesus *rebukes* a fever," he added. "Doesn't that confuse spiritual and medical categories?"

"Touché," I said. But then, succumbing to a precocious impulse, I told him his modern, Western, medical account was one more "totalizing metanarrative."

"Touché," he said back, and laughed. "But pots like you shouldn't call kettles black." He thought my allegiance to historic Christianity was just as "totalizing" as his to modernity. Maybe so, but I didn't see a way to dispense with Satan and still make historical sense of Jesus. A week later, after too much time in the library, I sent him a pompous email about how the popular "tendency to psychologize, rationalize, and pathologize" demonic possession reflected "the reductionisms of Western ego-, logo-, and ethnocentrism."

"What have you been reading?" he shot back, and demanded a photocopy in his box by the end of the day.[30] Such was the life of a lowly TA.

The following weekend Guilder invited some of his students over to watch *The Exorcism of Emily Rose*. Interesting movie. It's the trial of a priest who gets convicted of negligent homicide for deciding his parishioner needed exorcism instead of medical help. In her closing statement, the priest's lawyer, herself an agnostic, challenges the jury to recognize the limits of our knowledge.

> Angels and demons. God and the devil. These things either exist, or they do not exist. . . . Do I really believe that this tragedy is the work of the devil? To be honest, I don't know. But I cannot deny that it's possible. The prosecution wants you to believe that Emily's psychotic epileptic disorder was a fact because facts leave no room for reasonable doubt. But this trial isn't about facts. This trial is about possibilities.[31]

Back in Mark 9, what troubled me most was Jesus's stark outburst in verse 19: "You faithless generation, *how much longer* must I be among you? How much longer must I put up with you?" Not the sort of remark disciples were likely to invent or repeat; it was *their* unbelief and *their* inability to cast out demons (in spite of empowerment; 6:7, 13) that evoked Jesus's stinging indictment. What did Jesus mean by "how much longer"? Jesus must have thought the tide was about to turn.

But which way? Did Jesus expect God's people would soon rise to embrace the kingdom in its fullness (cf. 9:1)? Or did his disciples' spiritual impotence foreshadow his own approaching rejection and death (cf. 8:31; 9:9, 31)? The tone of this verse reminded me of Jesus's much harsher rebukes delivered against three towns nearby (Matt. 11:20–24; cf. Luke 10:13–15). Evidently Jesus thought his deeds were more than sufficient to demonstrate that God was at work, that the kingdom was at hand.

My favorite line in the story has always been the father's plaintive cry: "I believe; help my unbelief!" (Mark 9:24). I've echoed this plea in more than a few prayers. Even before freshman year, doubt had become my companion. Only recently, I realized as I finally drifted off to sleep, had doubt become a *welcome* companion,

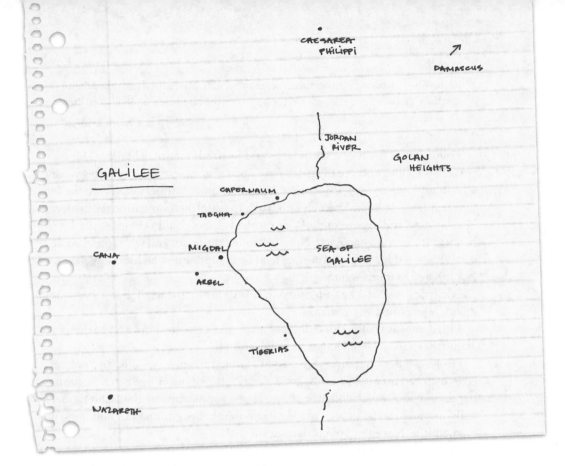

one that stirred me and exposed my limitations, one that brought the world into sharper relief, like the adrenaline-induced clarity I enjoy when venturing on my own into strange lands.

Geography of the Kingdom

I woke early and decided it was Capernaum day. Capernaum is the setting for several miracle episodes and, as it turns out, the target of one of Jesus's harsh rebukes. I wanted to know more about Jesus's comings and goings and more about his close encounters with demons. It was an easy three-mile walk along Galilee's rustic north shore, the same stretch of pebbles and reeds Jesus traversed to encounter Simon and Andrew and then, soon after, James and John.

> As Jesus passed along the Sea of Galilee, he saw Simon and his brother Andrew casting a net into the sea—for they were fishermen. And Jesus said to them, "Follow me and I will make you fish for people." And immediately they left their nets and followed him. As he went a little farther, he saw James son of Zebedee and his

brother John, who were in their boat mending the nets. Immediately he called them; and they left their father Zebedee in the boat with the hired men, and followed him.

Mark 1:16–20

Following in the footsteps of Jesus and his fresh recruits (Mark 1:21), I arrived at the village before the gates were open. The placard was unambiguously Christian: *Capharnaum The Town of Jesus*. One other visitor waited with me for the attendant. He looked vaguely familiar: a youthful forty-something with blond hair, a goatee, and a warm smile. Wire-rimmed glasses couldn't hide the sparkle in his eyes. It was Jonathan Reed, New Testament professor and veteran archaeologist. I had used his book *Excavating Jesus* for a sophomore archaeology paper, a fact I shared to impress him.[32]

"Call me Jonathan," he said. "But don't blame me for the whole book. I cowrote it with John Dominic Crossan."

Jonathan was waiting for a documentary film crew to show up, so when the attendant let us in he offered to show me around.

"In Jesus's day," he said as we passed chiseled fragments, mills, and presses, "the town had no gates or walls. Just a sleepy little fishing village extending three hundred meters or so along the shore. Home for maybe one thousand farmers and fishermen. So far no sign of a theater, public baths, commercial buildings, or marketplace. Not even a public latrine."

"Where's Main Street?"

"There wasn't one. Just narrow alleys. Houses were made of unhewn fieldstones, mud, wooden beams, and thatched roofs. Typical rustic Galilean hamlet, sustained by a nearby trade route and excellent fishing."

"Amazing that Jesus spent so much time here."

"Location. Location. Location."

"Excuse me?"

"Capernaum was Peter's hometown. The first healing story in Mark's Gospel happens here when Jesus heals Peter's mother-in-law. Jesus probably got the spare room and plenty of home cooking."

"Is that it?" I asked. "Free room and board?"

"There were political reasons as well," Jonathan continued. "After John the Baptist was beheaded for denouncing Herod Antipas, Jesus had good reason to move to the edge of Herod's territory. If things heated up, he could slip across into Philip's domain."[33]

I looked over the tangle of ruins, none of it monumental or impressive by Roman standards.

"If Jesus had an adopted 'hometown,'[34] why did he tell people he was homeless?"

"Right. 'The Son of Man has nowhere to lay his head.'" Jonathan paused. "Have you noticed *where* Jesus is when he utters those words?

"Umm."

"Matthew 8:20 says Jesus made that pronouncement here in Capernaum. In Luke 9:58, Jesus speaks those words on the road as he heads south through Samaria. I don't think Jesus felt at home here or anywhere. Settling down didn't fit with his geography of the kingdom of God."

"Geography of the kingdom?"

Whatever the phrase conveyed about Jesus's mission, it described nicely my attempt to meet the prophet in his world rather than transport him into mine. A spiritual quest in a physical place. Kingdom geography.

"Sure!" Jonathan seemed eager to explain. "After Jesus healed Peter's mother-in-law, Mark says he healed many others (1:32–34) and then snuck out of town for morning prayers (1:35). When his disciples tracked him down, it was to hear him announce he was taking his kingdom message on the road (1:36–38)."

"Jesus's radical message wasn't the sort of thing you dispatch from the head office."

"Nope. It's hard to grasp how countercultural Jesus's vision was unless you walk the Galilean countryside from one of these villages to the next. Try it some time. The empire had its throne in Rome. Pilate had his seaside palace in Caesarea. Antipas had his sparkling capital over there in Tiberias. The kingdom Jesus proclaimed had nothing. When Jesus abandoned home and possessions, it was to demonstrate with his life what he said with his lips: that where God rules, wealth is not a measure of status or success. God's people don't cling to things tightly; they don't amass wealth at another's expense. They share freely and refuse to participate in injustice and oppression."[35]

"What's that?" I asked, abruptly. We were approaching the remains of a large building on the north side of the site. Partial walls enclosed several Corinthian columns and the remains of a lintel.

"He left Nazareth and made his home in Capernaum by the sea, in the territory of Zebulun and Naphtali, so that what had been spoken through the prophet Isaiah might be fulfilled: 'Land of Zebulun, land of Naphtali, on the road by the sea, across the Jordan, Galilee of the Gentiles—the people who sat in darkness have seen a great light, and for those who sat in the region and shadow of death light has dawned.'"

Matt. 4:13-16

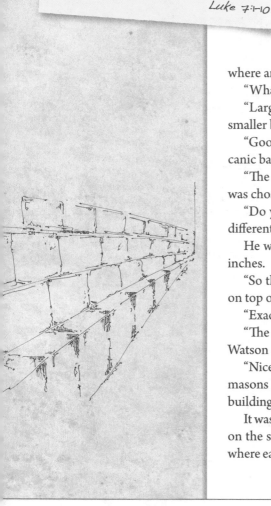

"*After Jesus had finished all his sayings in the hearing of the people, he entered Capernaum. A <u>centurion</u> there had a slave whom he valued highly, and who was ill and close to death. When he heard about Jesus, he sent some Jewish elders to him, asking him to come and heal his slave. When they came to Jesus, they appealed to him earnestly, saying, 'He is worthy of having you do this for him, for he loves our people, and <u>it is he who built our synagogue for us.</u>' ... When those who had been sent returned to the house, they found the slave in good health.*"

Luke 7:1-10

"A synagogue. The Franciscan excavators say it's fourth century. I say fifth. It was built as a Jewish response to the church that Christians built to honor St. Peter."

"Were the local Jews nervous about a Christian takeover of the village?"

"Could be. It was certainly built to impress— one of the largest, most well-built synagogues of the Byzantine period."

"Are those bleachers along the walls?"

"Exactly. Tiered seating."

I pictured the seats packed with villagers, while others filled the doorway to hear Jesus teach. "Have we found evidence of the synagogue from Jesus's day?"

"Good question. Follow me."

Jonathan took me to the west side of the synagogue, where an excavator's trench had exposed the foundations.

"What do you see?" he asked.

"Large white blocks of the synagogue resting on a wall of smaller black stones."

"Good. The white ashlars are limestone. The dark stone is volcanic basalt. What else?"

"The basalt wall isn't as well built. Makes you wonder why it was chosen as a foundation."

"Do you see how the upper limestone wall runs at a slightly different angle?"

He was right. At one end the white stones were inset several inches.

"So the Byzantine builders decided to build their synagogue on top of a basalt wall but didn't strictly follow its line."

"Exactly," said the professor. "What else?"

"The slopes of the two walls are different!" I said proudly, like Watson announcing something painfully obvious to Sherlock.

"Nice work. The lower wall slopes downward so the Byzantine masons had to taper their first course of limestone to keep their building level."

It was clear that the builders had gone out of their way to build on the site. My mind recalled the Bethesda pools in Jerusalem, where each layer of the site seemed to remember the one beneath.

"The Franciscan excavators believe the Byzantine synagogue rests on the foundations of a first-century synagogue," Jonathan explained.[36]

"The synagogue of the Gospels?"

"Not so fast. There's no evidence the earlier building was a synagogue. I want proof that Jews were building dedicated prayer houses in the homeland that early."[37]

"Don't the Gospels describe Jesus going to synagogue?"

"Absolutely. Jesus teaches and heals and casts out demons in the synagogue of Capernaum.[38] He gets himself in trouble in the synagogue of Nazareth."[39]

"And doesn't some gentile build the Jews a synagogue somewhere?"

Synagogues/Prayer-Houses in Jesus's Day

Josephus, *Life*, 277, 280 (cf. 293)—in **Tiberias**
The next day there was a general assembly in the Prayer-house, a huge building, capable of accommodating a large crowd. . . . Arriving there about the first hour next day, I found the people already assembling in the Prayer-house.

Josephus, *Jewish War*, 2:285, 289—in **Caesarea-on-the-Sea**
The Jews in Caesarea had a synagogue adjoining a plot of ground owned by a Greek of that city. . . . On the following day, which was a Sabbath, when the Jews assembled at the synagogue, they found that one of the Caesarean mischief-makers had placed beside the entrance a pot, turned bottom upwards, upon which he was sacrificing birds. This spectacle of what they considered . . . a desecration of the spot enraged the Jews.

Philo, *Every Good Man Is Free*, 81–82
Now these laws are taught at other times, indeed, but most especially on the seventh day . . . on which they . . . frequent the sacred places which are called synagogues, and there they sit according to their age in classes, the younger sitting under the elder, and listening with eager attention in becoming order. Then one, indeed, takes up the holy volume and reads it, and another of the men of the greatest experience comes forward and explains what is not very intelligible.

"*Somewhere?* How about Capernaum? It's in Luke 7. If you accept the Franciscans' theory about the basalt wall, we could be looking at the handiwork of laborers paid by the benevolent centurion whose slave Jesus healed!"

"How cool would that be?" I squinted at the wall, half hoping it would settle the debate for us.

"Very cool. But of the few first-century synagogues we've found in the Jewish homeland, most were buildings adapted for synagogue use during times of crisis.[40] The evidence that Galilean Jews had dedicated synagogue buildings in Jesus's day is scant."

"Shouldn't we count the Gospels as evidence?"

"Sometimes the word *synagogue* in the Gospels refers to a gathering—an assembly, not a building."

Something near the main gate had Jonathan's attention. I turned to see several men maneuvering a cartload of equipment: the film crew. In the Middle East an hour late is early.

"Wonder what they have in mind for today. We've been filming in the area for three days, but they like to keep me guessing."

More interesting to me than the architecture was what went on inside. Apparently the Jews of Jesus's day met weekly to sing, pray, hear Scripture, and have it explained. Sounds like church back home, except we've added PowerPoint and our pews face the same direction. Tiered seating around the walls would make it easy for many, including Jesus, to participate (Mark 6:1–5; Luke 4:16–30; cf. Acts 13:15–16). At some of those gatherings, he evidently made quite an impression.[41]

The Way That You See

"I didn't show you Peter's house!" Jonathan called over his shoulder. "Could be the *actual* house of the apostle Peter. It's there, under the alien spaceship!"

Jonathan disappeared around a corner, leaving me alone in the ruins. I followed his gesture toward a large octagonal structure that seemed to hover a few feet above the ground like a tourist center for extraterrestrials. The house of Peter? Beneath *that*?

I hesitated. Something about that synagogue wouldn't let me go. For the moment the building's threshold seemed like a portal to another time. Passing over it, I slumped into a shaded corner, dug out my Bible, and began to read the very first miracle story in the oldest Gospel (Mark 1:21–28).

What gave Jesus such an aura of authority? It had to be more than charisma and *chutzpah*. As I sat where I imagined Jesus once stood, I was struck by the fact that Mark's first demonic showdown (1:23–26) took place precisely where the people had gathered to hear Jesus's message. The demoniac couldn't bear what Jesus was *saying*. Demons were pushing away for the same reason crowds were drawing close: because of Jesus's audacious assertion that God was moving against the forces of evil (cf. 1:15). The same kingdom that announced good news to the poor (in spirit) heralded bad tidings for the unclean (spirits). When rebels stage a coup, the masses rejoice but the guardians of the old order protest. Sometimes violently.

Other episodes came to mind in which Jesus confronted demons. In Mark's Gospel alone there are five exorcism stories, not counting passing references. Mark also describes Jesus conferring authority over demons upon his disciples. And as if Satan's minions weren't challenge enough, Mark pits Jesus directly against Satan himself.

	Mark	Details	Words of Jesus
	1:32–34 (Matt. 8:16–17; Luke 4:40–41)	People brought many who were ill or demon possessed. He cast out many demons and did not permit the demons to speak because they knew who he was.	——
Summary Statements of Jesus's Exorcisms	1:39 (Matt. 4:23; Luke 4:44)	Jesus went into synagogues of Galilee, preaching and casting out demons.	——
	3:11–12	Whenever unclean spirits saw Jesus, they would fall down and cry out, "You are the Son of God!" Jesus warned them not to make him known.	——

	Mark	Details	Words of Jesus
Exorcism Episodes	1:23–28 (Luke 4:33–37)	A man with an unclean spirit challenges Jesus in Capernaum.	"Be silent, and come out of him!"
	5:1–20 (Matt. 8:28–34; Luke 8:26–39)	A demoniac calling himself "Legion" encounters Jesus across the Sea of Galilee in the country of the Gerasenes.	"Come out of the man, you unclean spirit!" "What is your name?" "Go home . . . and report what . . . the Lord has done." (NASB)
	7:24–30 (Matt. 15:21–28)	A Syrophoenician woman asks Jesus to cast a demon out of her daughter.	"Because of this answer go; the demon has gone out of your daughter." (NASB)
	9:14–29 (Matt. 17:14–21; Luke 9:37–43)	Jesus's disciples are unable to cast out a spirit that makes a boy deaf and mute. Jesus is able and does.	"You deaf and mute spirit, I command you, come out of him and do not enter him again." (NASB)
	16:9* (cf. Luke 8:2)	Jesus had cast out seven demons from Mary Magdalene.	——

	Mark	Details	Words of Jesus
	1:12–13 (Matt. 4:1–11; Luke 4:1–13)	Jesus, in the wilderness for forty days, is tempted by Satan.	——
Jesus Standing against Satan	3:22–30 (Matt. 12:22–37; Luke 11:14–23; 12:10)	Jerusalem scribes accuse Jesus of using Satan's power to exorcise demons.	"How can Satan cast out Satan?" "Whoever blasphemes against the Holy Spirit never has forgiveness." (NASB)
	4:15 (Matt. 13:19; Luke 8:12)	Satan is the birds who eat the seed (= Jesus's message) that falls beside the road (= people).	——
	3:14–15 (Matt. 10:1)	Jesus appoints twelve to be with him, to preach, and to have authority to cast out demons.	——
Jesus Confers Authority to Exorcise upon His Disciples	6:7, 13 (Luke 9:1)	Jesus sends out the twelve in pairs with authority over unclean spirits.	——
	9:14–29 (Matt. 17:14–21; Luke 9:37–43)	Disciples try but fail to cast out a demon. See above.	——
	16:17*		"By using my name [those who believe] will cast out demons."
Exorcisms in Jesus's Name	9:38–39 (Luke 9:49–50)	The disciples try to hinder someone casting out demons in Jesus's name.	"Do not hinder him, for there is no one who will perform a miracle in My name, and . . . soon afterward . . . speak evil of me." (NASB)

*Since Mark 16:9–20 is not in the best Greek manuscripts, scholars consider it secondary.

Peter's House

One conclusion was hard to escape: for Jesus, the world was a *cosmic* battleground. Jesus had no doubt about the final outcome of the war, but there could be no avoiding combat. With each exorcism another POW was released and sent home. This was why I couldn't let Guilder translate *demons* into "disorders." It wasn't enough to say that my esteemed professor had different words for the same reality. He saw a different reality. He inhabited a different universe.

It's like the standoff between Palestinians and Israelis. Each side lobs its ideological mortars across the divide; each group tells the world a different story. This is more than a war of words. Each side sees, each side inhabits, a different reality. Lyrics from an old song came to mind:

> Depends on what you look at obviously.
> Even more it depends on the way that you see.
> Bruce Cockburn,
> "Child of the Wind," on *Circles in the Stream*

The "house of Saint Peter" proved cooler than expected. A large sign offered images and commentary to decipher the ruins. Its title left no room for doubt.

The House of Saint Peter
Composite Plan of the Insula Sacra
from the second century BC
to the seventh century AD

Turns out the layers of the site, like chapters in a book, tell an intriguing story of veneration and pilgrimage. Archaeologists first exposed the fifth-century Byzantine church in the sixties. Oddly enough, the church's design consisted of concentric octagons. A century earlier, the same sacred area was enclosed by an eighty-by-eighty-foot square stone wall, with an arch supporting the roof over a central room. For several centuries before that, the floors and walls of that central room were coated, again and again, with plaster, on which hundreds of pilgrims etched crude invocations in Greek, Syriac, Hebrew, and Latin. Nowhere else in Galilee do we find anything like it. One conclusion seems inescapable: within a century or less of Jesus and Peter, a common courtyard house was thought to be of some significance. Evidently, second-century Christians thought this was the house of Peter. Many scholars today say the odds are good that they were right.

Here, then, was where Jesus restored Peter's mother-in-law (Mark 1:29–31), where a "whole city" once urged a holy man to tend to their sick and diseased and demonized (1:32–34). Here also was where Jesus exposed, and redirected, his disciples' passion for greatness, and where they learned that greatness in God's kingdom is measured by selfless service. Nothing could be more subversive to Roman social order, obsessed as it was with status and addicted to public recognition. And nothing could be a more apt description of what Jesus would do in a few months, years maybe, when he gave his life, a ransom for many.

As I approached Peter's house, I was initially annoyed by the modern memorial that, since 1990, has brooded over the ruins like a protective griffon over its nest. It made the ruins harder to see, which made no sense to me. But then I watched a pair of nuns ascend the stairs and disappear inside, which made me realize my attitude was painfully Protestant. Why was I eager to skip over centuries of Christian worship and memory, ready to clear away the layers, inclined to privilege dead stones over living faith? I was nothing if not one more in a long stream of pilgrims, each one on a quest for the grace it takes to remain faithful.

Lord of the Dance

For several days I wandered the Galilean countryside where Jesus preached and performed miracles. I wanted to sense the distances, the terrain, and the size of the towns where his message was first heard, to see where he enjoyed hospitality (Mark 6:10) and where he didn't (Mark 6:11; Matt. 8:34). I wanted to pass through grainfields, rub heads of grain, blow away the chaff, and eat the kernels (Luke 6:1). I wanted to follow the pathways along which Jesus's kingdom message moved, carried first in his own heart and then, when they were duly commissioned, in the hearts of his disciples.[42] But my plan to hike from Galilee through "Samaria" to Jerusalem hit a wall. Literally. The only checkpoint at the north end of the West Bank was closed. So much for rehearsing Jesus's pilgrimage ascent.[43] But that didn't stop me from exploring Galilee. I hitched a ride to

> "Then they came to <u>Capernaum</u>; and when <u>he was in the house</u> he asked them,' What were you arguing about on the way?' But they were silent, for on the way they had argued with one another who was the greatest. He sat down, called the twelve, and said to them,' Whoever wants to be first must be last of all and servant of all.'"
>
> Mark 9:33-35

> "So Jesus called them and said to them,' You know that among the Gentiles those whom they recognize as their rulers lord it over them, and their great ones are tyrants over them. But it is not so among you; but whoever wishes to become great among you must be your servant, and whoever wishes to be first among you must be slave of all. For the Son of Man came not to be served but to serve, and to give his life a ransom for many.'"
>
> Mark 10:42-45

Magdala and headed west on foot, passing beneath the cliffs of Arbela, whose caves, Guilder had told me, were once home to Jewish brigands and Christian monks. From there it was a sweaty eleven miles of grainfields and overgrown paths to Cana (*Khirbet Qana*), the hilltop village in the fertile Beth Netofa valley where Jesus turned water to wine (John 2:1–11) and healed from a distance an official's child (John 4:46–54).[44]

The wedding miracle at Cana (John 2:1–11) is to John's Gospel what the Capernaum exorcism is to Mark's: Jesus's first public display of power. In both the author supplies the lens through which we're to view the rest of the book. Mark's Jesus establishes God's rule by binding Satan. John's Jesus offers signs of divine glory.[45] As a sign, the wine-from-water miracle points, like many episodes in John, to Jesus's role as filler (pun alert) and fulfiller of Israel's hopes, institutions, and expectations. If Israel's temple was God's house, Jesus is more so (2:21); if Jacob's well once quenched thirst, Jesus now offers living water (4:14); if God's people had to survive on manna, their new sustenance is the Bread of Life (6:58). So also here at the beginning of the Gospel: Israel's laws of ritual purification, *signified* by six stone water pots, give way to the new wine of a new covenant. And surely the wedding, with its abundant provision of fine wine, is a foretaste (sorry) of the great Wedding Feast, when the messianic bridegroom finally arrives to take with him his spotless bride (3:29; cf. Rev. 19:7–8; Eph. 5:27).

I'd never understood why the early Christians imagined the end of the age as a wedding banquet.[46] But that was before I attended a traditional Arab wedding early during my time in Israel. It happened because a French grad student moved into my dorm at the Austrian Hospice. Marc was heading to a village in the northern West Bank for the wedding of a friend's brother. Did I want to come? Yes, yes I did.

Getting from Jerusalem to Yabad, up near Jenin, meant hailing a series of service taxis and negotiating a number of fixed and "flying" (= mobile) military checkpoints. The wedding party was well under way when we arrived late in the afternoon. Instantly we were guests of honor. Elders, young men, the groom himself—all were eager to meet us, to have their picture taken with the only foreigners in town.

Only a few guests spoke English. One of the groom's brothers, twenty-something but with older eyes, had just been released from prison. My mind went on alert. What had he done? Was I in danger? Inwardly I knew, and Marc quietly confirmed, that this was no time to be talking about wounds and warfare. This was a wedding!

Soon enough the men ascended to the roof, where long tables bent under the weight of the feast. Standing shoulder to shoulder, we ate with our hands from bowls of rice, pita, hummus with meat, chicken, soured yogurt, and salads. Then it was time to dance. The road, blocked off and lined with chairs, became our dance floor. Speakers pulsed Arabic techno. Everyone was there. Or, all the men. Women were again out of sight, leaving brothers, husbands, fathers, and sons to bond in solidarity, one after another taking his turn at the head of the *Dabkeh* procession—a synchronized, snaking chain of rhythm, energy, and laughter.

Several things about that day reminded me of the wedding at Cana. First was the absence of wine. "Good" Muslims don't drink. Had Jesus attended *this* wedding, I thought, he might have turned water into Arabic coffee or grain into flatbread. Second was the strong woman. She came and went discreetly—the mother of the groom, herself a widow—keeping her distance and speaking quietly. Her movements were quick, her eyes sharp, and, like Mary in Cana, she was first to notice when supplies ran low. Why did Mary expect Jesus to solve the problem? Did she see him and his band of thirsty disciples as partly responsible for the shortage? One thing was clear to me: for the host to run out of food or drink at a Middle Eastern wedding—ancient or modern—would be a major embarrassment.

The third link between the two weddings was joy. Here I was, twenty-five miles from ancient Cana, witnessing the exuberance of an entire community celebrating the wedding of two of their children. Some of them had spent years in prison for armed resistance. Most had known long periods of unemployment. But this was not a day for bitterness or conflict. Tomorrow would see the young bride arrive and the couple proceed to their new house. Tonight the world would dance. Where there is joy, there must be hope for better days.

Perhaps John's wedding story is not so different. Didn't Jesus and the other revelers hold out hope that Israel would see better days—days free from internal corruption and external oppres-

"For John came neither eating nor drinking, and they say, 'He has a demon'; the Son of Man came eating and drinking, and they say, 'Look, a glutton and a drunkard, a friend of tax collectors and sinners!' Yet wisdom is vindicated by her deeds."

Matt. 11:18–19

sion? Did not Jesus, like my dance partners, cherish the levity and the bounty of a good feast?

Images of that Arab wedding appeared and faded as I scanned the ruins of Cana. Arid winds whistled under a cloudless sky. I wondered where the wedding guests might have danced and drunk their fill. On the east slope, terraced houses would have crowded together with no courtyard space between them. Perhaps it happened on the gentler north slope, where houses had side courtyards and even ritual baths. I pictured Jesus raising a glass of very new wine to the very new bride and groom.

The wedding story of John 2 overflows with more than wine. It surges with symbol and mystery, with foreshadowing and premonition. Phrases like "on the third day" and "my hour has not yet come" preview the end of the story at its beginning.[47] The more I read the story, the more I could see John's theological fingerprints. Jesus's reluctance to get involved has John's smudge on it. So does the persistence of Jesus's mother. We see a third smudge in the epilogue about Jesus's *glory* and the disciples' *belief* (2:11).

Why is it, I've wondered, that after the wedding Mary disappears from sight and remains absent until we see her beneath the cross in chapter 19? At the wedding Jesus's "hour [had] not yet come." At the cross, it had. No sooner does Mary reappear (19:25–27) than we see Jesus's thirst quenched by *wine* drawn from a *jar* (19:28–30). Careful readers experience déjà vu.

To say that John's theological artistry is on display is not to say John meant to write fiction. Indeed, John is preoccupied with historical events and figures of recent memory. But I could no longer read his story as a courtroom transcript or official chronicle. He was a preacher, not a reporter; a storyteller, not a photocopier.

Has John gathered up historical recollections about a memorable wedding at Cana—one at which Jesus took particular interest in securing badly needed provisions—and transformed them, like water into wine, into a parable about Jesus's new-covenant glory?[48] This would explain why the puzzled remarks of the steward read like a veiled metaphor for Jesus's climactic role in Israel's story. And why Jesus's actions in John 2 find apt commentary in Jesus's teachings in Mark 2 and Luke 5.

Sayings of Jesus | Story about Jesus

Mark 2:19
Jesus said to them, "The wedding guests cannot fast while the bridegroom is with them, can they? As long as they have the bridegroom with them, they cannot fast."

Jesus as guest → Jesus . . . had . . . been invited to the wedding.

← Jesus as groom

Luke 5:36–39
He also told them a parable: . . . "And no one puts new wine into old wineskins; otherwise the new wine will burst the skins and will be spilled, and the skins will be destroyed. But new wine must be put into fresh wineskins. And no one after drinking old wine desires new wine, but says, 'The old is good.'"

the good wine has now come → When the steward tasted the water that had become wine, . . . the steward called the bridegroom and said to him, "Everyone serves the good wine first, and then the inferior wine after the guests have become drunk. But you have kept the good wine until now."

← the new wine has now come

new wine delayed →

← new wine rejected

As I took a sip of nearly hot water, a voice in my head cautioned against de-mythologizing the wedding at Cana, against turning miracle into parable. The marginal references of my Bible summoned me to Amos 9:13–14; Hosea 14:7; and Jeremiah 31:12, all of which (I discovered) picture Israel's future restoration as an age of outrageous bounty. Amos says the wine will flow so freely that the hills will dissolve. If Jesus believed the messianic age was dawning and if his imagination was fueled and fired by prophetic imagery, is it so unlikely that Jesus himself would ask God for the gift of new wine? Wouldn't such provision be, for Jesus as much as for John, a harbinger of Israel's restoration? Wasn't a wedding the ideal time for Jesus to test his calling by summoning from nature tangible signs of cosmic renewal?

Together with his mother, brothers, and disciples, Jesus set out from Cana toward Capernaum (John 2:12). The hike would have taken all day. I continued in the other direction, toward Sepphoris, five miles to the south.

Sepphoris was where I fell in love. Mom would want details. Among the ruins near the summit is the house of somebody important from the third century.

"Mona Lisa of the Galilee"

Archaeologists found the dining room floor about twenty years ago. Painstakingly preserved, the floor mosaics are breathtaking. One and a half million stones in twenty-eight colors, the sign says.

The floor depicts the life and times of Dionysus, a.k.a. Bacchus, the god of wine: happy peasants, drinking bouts, satyrs, nymphs, and trampled grapes. Guilder spoke of an old Dionysus legend that some have compared to the wedding at Cana. It's in one of Euripides' tragedies from the fifth century BCE. Female devotees of Dionysus miraculously bring wine out of the ground while some cowboy looks on in amazement. Not just wine: water, milk, and honey too. Were such legends popular enough in John's circle to influence the shape of his Gospel? Has John, in dialogue with paganism, cast Jesus in the role of Dionysus?[49]

Where was I? Right. Falling in love. I was at the far end of the mosaic floor when I saw her. She wore earrings and a laurel garland, her cheeks blushing slightly. One look and we were frozen in time. I was Westley to her Buttercup. *Sigh.* Who was this stone maiden? What was her life like? Did she ever find twoo wuv? *Sigh again.*

Since I couldn't time-travel, our relationship was short-lived. Another four-mile trek brought me, exhausted, to the bustling Arab-Israeli city of Nazareth, Jesus's boyhood home. In the heyday of Sepphoris's expansion (3 BCE to 17 CE), there would have been plenty of work for good tradesmen and their young apprentices. It wasn't hard to imagine Joseph and Jesus commuting daily between their home in Nazareth and bustling, lucrative Sepphoris, another city set on a hill.

History's ironies are hard to ignore. These days the once-noble Herodian capital, home to the girl of my dreams, lies in ruins, but the once-lowly hamlet of Nazareth is home to seventy-four thousand Arab Israelis, and a major destination for countless pilgrims. The first shall be last and the last first.

Looking for Abuna

From Nazareth, after a day of rest, I hitchhiked west. This was still Jesus's world, but now I was looking for someone in the modern Arab town of Ibillin. Ibillin straddles several hills with houses cascading down its slopes. Streets are steep and pitted. On arrival I kept asking questions and taking wrong turns until I finally found it: the Mar Elias Educational Institution. The only person in sight pointed me to his house next door to the large church.

Since 1965, a Galilean Elijah has been proclaiming the ludicrous message that Jews, Christians, Druze, and Muslims can live together in peace. After all I'd witnessed in Jerusalem and the West Bank—fear, suspicion, despair—reconciliation seemed as improbable as walking on water. Elias (Elijah) Chacour is a Melkite priest whose parish lies between Mount Carmel (where Elijah challenged the prophets of Baal) and the Mount of Transfiguration (where Elijah reappeared with the transfigured Jesus). The place was called, fittingly, Mar Elias. Elijah's Hill.

The church there is a remarkable monument to this man's tenacity and perseverance, and to God's blessing. To ascend its steps is to encounter one beatitude after another, incised in the stone risers in Arabic, Hebrew, English, and Latin. Blessed are those who bring peace. Pax. Shalom. Salaam. This was no sectarian enclave; the world was welcome, if it dared. When I entered the sanctuary, my eyes were drawn to huge murals. Icons and texts in several languages. Some scripts were Latin; most were Arabic. The interior space was vast—enough seats for sixteen hundred worshipers. This man has faith.

I approached the parsonage through a small gate. Suddenly, an Arab voice. I'd been caught trespassing, I thought. A short man emerged from behind a wall.

"Looking for Abuna?" he beamed.

"Yes!" I replied.

"He is there." The man pointed to a simple door that appeared to lead beneath the church. "Come."

I crossed the threshold and descended several steps. There he was, clad in a dark robe, a long, square white beard hanging from his chin. He was speaking quietly to a laborer who hovered over carpet and plywood. Fitting, I thought, to find a Galilean saint in the company of a lowly carpenter.

He turned easily, welcomed me, and asked about my journey. My family. My heart. I searched for something profound to say but to no avail.

"The church. The schools. So much good has happened here, Father," I finally blurted. "It's a miracle!"

The words sounded even sillier in the air than in my head. Abuna smiled but didn't offer an answer. Instead he told a story.[50]

"Back in 1967," he said, "weeks before the Six-Day War, the church here was splintered by factions and paralyzed by indifference. On Palm Sunday that year I could tell that most had come only to fulfill a holiday obligation. There was no peace. No joy. When they rose for the benediction, I did not dismiss them. Instead, I strode to the back, shut the doors, and locked them with a chain.

"I confronted my people about our divisions," he said. "I rebuked them for their arguments and hatred, their gossip and lies. I told them that Jesus was the only one who could unite them and give them power to forgive, and that if they wouldn't forgive each other, perhaps they should kill each other. I offered to conduct the funerals for free.

"I waited," Abuna continued, "for over ten minutes. Someone rose—the village policeman, a hard-bitten character whom many considered a sellout to the Israelis. Stretching out his arms, Abu asked forgiveness for hating his three brothers, for wanting to kill them. His brothers rushed to embrace him. That's when the walls of hostility came down. Repentance, reconciliation, and joy spilled from the church into the street."

Father Chacour's eyes swam as he relived the moment from forty years ago. "That was our resurrection," he said.

Abuna smiled. Somehow I knew that my time with the prophet was up. But instead of sending me on my way he led me back to his house, where he handed me a copy of his latest book. He would take no payment. Not until I had passed through the gate did I open it. Inside the cover, his signature in Arabic. Above that, four words scrawled in English: *God does not kill*. I closed the book, hoisted my pack, and began the descent from Elijah's hill.

CHAPTER 5

Time
Imagined

In which Norm survives the gates of hell but manages to get trapped in a corridor.

MONTY PYTHON'S LIFE OF BRIAN, SCENE 16

BRIAN: Consider the lilies . . . in the field.

ELSIE: Consider the lilies?

BRIAN: Uh, well, the birds, then.

Crossroads

Leaving the hardened paths and fertile plains of lower Galilee, I hitchhiked north into the forested hills of upper Galilee to explore the northern limits of Jesus's travels. As the Synoptics tell it, not long before his arrest in Jerusalem Jesus led his disciples on a twenty-five-mile trek, uphill, to a place called Caesarea Philippi. What took me a few hours would have taken them several days.

There on the northern edge of things was where Simon first declared Jesus to be the Christ, Israel's Messiah. According to Matthew's Gospel, Jesus returned the favor, calling Simon *Peter* ("Rocky") and promising him keys to the coming kingdom. There also was where Jesus broke the news that things were about to get ugly. To Jerusalem they would go, but not to stage a coup or seize a crown. As Israel's Christ, Jesus was destined to suffer, then die outside the city, then return to life on the third day. Impressed by none of this, Peter objects and earns himself a harsh rebuke.

Jesus is at a crossroads. Just when the disciples begin to grasp his significance (Matt. 16:17), Jesus declares that his death is inevitable (Matt. 16:21). The shadows on the horizon, he explains, are storm clouds (Mark 10:32–34). Why, I wondered, did Jesus pick this far-flung location to break the news? Did he announce the end of his ministry at the Jordan's source because it all began with his baptism at the river's mouth? Did Jesus have to travel far from the Holy City, like a comet from the sun, before its gravity would pull him back?[1] All three Synoptics include the same pivotal moment in their story.

Matthew 16:13–22 (RSV)	Mark 8:27–33 (RSV)	Luke 9:18–22 (RSV)
Now when Jesus came into the district of Caesarea Philippi, he asked his disciples,	And Jesus went on with his disciples, to the villages of Caesarea Philippi; and on the way he asked his disciples,	Now it happened that as he was praying alone the disciples were with him; and he asked them,
"Who do men say that the Son of man is?" And they said, "Some say John the Baptist, others say Elijah, and others Jeremiah or one of the prophets."	"Who do men say that I am?" And they told him, "John the Baptist; and others say, Elijah; and others one of the prophets."	"Who do the people say that I am?" And they answered, "John the Baptist; but others say, Elijah; and others, that one of the old prophets has risen."
He said to them, "But who do you say that I am?" Simon Peter replied, "You are the Christ, the Son of the living God."	And he asked them, "But who do you say that I am?" Peter answered him, "You are the Christ."	And he said to them, "But who do you say that I am?" And Peter answered, "The Christ of God."
And Jesus answered him, "Blessed are you, Simon Bar-Jona! For flesh and blood has not revealed this to you, but my Father who is in heaven. And I tell you, you are Peter, and on this rock I will build my church, and the powers of death shall not prevail against it. I will give you the keys of the kingdom of heaven, and whatever you bind on earth shall be bound in heaven, and whatever you loose on earth shall be loosed in heaven."		

Matthew 16:13–22 (RSV)	Mark 8:27–33 (RSV)	Luke 9:18–22 (RSV)
Then he strictly charged the disciples to tell no one that he was the Christ. From that time Jesus began to show his disciples that	And he charged them to tell no one about him. And he began to teach them that	But he charged and commanded them to tell this to no one, saying,
he must go to Jerusalem and suffer many things from the elders and chief priests and scribes, and be killed, and on the third day be raised.	the Son of man must suffer many things, and be rejected by the elders and the chief priests and the scribes, and be killed, and after three days rise again. And he said this plainly.	"The Son of man must suffer many things, and be rejected by the elders and chief priests and scribes, and be killed, and on the third day be raised."
And Peter took him and began to rebuke him, saying, "God forbid, Lord! This shall never happen to you." But he turned and said to Peter, "Get behind me, Satan! You are a hindrance to me; for you are not on the side of God, but of men."	And Peter took him, and began to rebuke him. But turning and seeing his disciples, he rebuked Peter, and said, "Get behind me, Satan! For you are not on the side of God, but of men."	

It looks like Matthew and Luke edit Mark in opposite directions. Luke abbreviates to avoid calling Peter *Satan*. Matthew elaborates by having Jesus bless Peter for his insight and designate him the *rock* on which the church will be built. All accounts agree that Jesus was widely thought to be a prophet, that it was appropriate (if risky) to call Jesus the *Christ*, and that Jesus somehow understood his messianic identity in terms of the suffering and vindicated Son of Man. Popular opinion at the time, Peter's included, seems to have pegged Jesus as a budding militant, poised to instigate another Maccabean revolt, a populist uprising against Roman occupation. Jesus, however, thought otherwise: before national deliverance could come, the nation's representative would have to suffer defeat, and only then vindication. Apparently the only suitable place for all this to occur was Jerusalem.[2]

More than once the Gospels depict Jesus displaying supernatural knowledge.

Mark 2:8	Jesus perceived in his spirit that they were discussing these questions among themselves
Mark 12:15–16	knowing their hypocrisy
John 1:47–48	Jesus answered, "I saw you under the fig tree before Philip called you."
John 2:24–25	But Jesus . . . knew all people and needed no one to testify about anyone; for he himself knew what was in everyone.
John 4:29	"Come and see a man who told me everything I have ever done!"
John 18:4	Jesus, knowing all that was to happen to him

Problem is, the Gospels also imply that Jesus's knowledge was sometimes limited.

Mark 5:9	Then Jesus asked him, "What is your name?"
Mark 5:30	Jesus turned about in the crowd and said, "Who touched my clothes?"
Mark 6:5	And he could do no deed of power there, except that he laid his hands on a few sick people and cured them.
Mark 6:38 (8:5)	And he said to them, "How many loaves have you?"
Mark 8:23	he asked him, "Can you see anything?"
Mark 8:27	"Who do people say that I am?"
Mark 13:32	"But about that day or hour *no one knows*, neither the angels in heaven, *nor the Son*, but only the Father."

I love the story Luke tells of young Jesus journeying with his family to Jerusalem. Already at age twelve Mary's son feels at home in the temple and senses a unique relationship to the God whose cause he feels compelled to take up. Many scholars regard this account as a blend of history and legend, if not a completely fictional tale. Luke wants to portray Jesus like other ancient heroes: as a precocious child whose destiny was clear from the beginning.[3] Perhaps, but I am struck by something else: how the story portrays Jesus having something to *learn*. There he is, listening and asking questions (Luke 2:46). Gifted and wise for his age, yes, but also yearning to study and to learn from the teachers of his day.

The evangelists describe Jesus having uncommon insight into human nature and prophetic clarity about God's will. They do not depict a gypsy Jesus touring

Galilee with a crystal ball, or a Superman-Jesus hiding an *S* under his robes. The Jesus of the Gospels doesn't have X-ray vision, nor does he know the periodic table or the cure for cancer or even—I speculate—the airspeed velocity of an unladen swallow. What the Gospels show us is a robustly human Jesus whose earliest disciples heard his labored breathing and watched him collapse after an endless day on his feet. This Jesus sheds tears, suffers hunger, meets with disappointment, burns with anger, needs space, and dislikes pain.[4] Which makes all the more remarkable Jesus's steadfast insistence on going up to Jerusalem to suffer and die.

Jesus predicts his death three times in the Synoptic Gospels. With each prediction Jesus moves physically closer to Jerusalem. The closer he gets to the cross, the larger looms its shadow. How much of the future did *this* Jesus really know?

1. **Caesarea Philippi** (Mark 8:31 RSV; cf. Matt. 16:21; Luke 9:22)
   And he began to teach them that the Son of man must suffer many things, and be rejected by the elders and the chief priests and the scribes, and be killed, and after three days rise again.
2. **Galilee** (Mark 9:30–32; cf. Matt. 17:22–23; Luke 9:43–45)
   They went on from there and passed through Galilee. He did not want anyone to know it; for he was teaching his disciples, saying to them, "The Son of Man is to be betrayed into human hands, and they will kill him, and three days after being killed, he will rise again." But they did not understand what he was saying and were afraid to ask him.
3. **Approaching Jerusalem** (Mark 10:32–34; cf. Matt. 20:17–19; Luke 18:31–34)
   They were on the road, going up to Jerusalem, and . . . those who followed were afraid. He took the twelve aside again and began to tell them what was to happen to him, saying, "See, we are going up to Jerusalem, and the Son of Man will be handed over to the chief priests and the scribes, and they will condemn him to death; then they will hand him over to the Gentiles; they will mock him, and spit upon him, and flog him, and kill him; and after three days he will rise again."

Some people think these sayings were composed after the fact to persuade doubters that Jesus's death was part of the plan. Others say Jesus may have sensed a shift in the political winds or maybe had a hunch he would share the fate of John the Baptist.[5] What I wanted to know was this: if Jesus did sense a call to suffer and die for his people, what did he think that death would accomplish?

As I studied these passages two things seemed odd. First, we read nothing about *why* Jesus had to die. If I were making this stuff up, I'd have Jesus assure us he was dying *for us* or *for our sins*, or I'd have Jesus promise that when he died he would *draw all people unto himself.*[6] All we get are bare bones:

Where: Jerusalem
What: Rejection, suffering, execution
Who: First priests and scribes, then the gentiles
What next: Resurrection three days later

The other odd thing was the reaction of the disciples. Even though the Gospels have Jesus repeatedly promise that the dead Son of Man will rise again, Peter can't keep from rebuking Jesus (Mark 8:32), nor do Jesus's words keep the disciples from being distressed (Matt. 17:23), confused (Mark 9:32), and afraid (Luke 9:45). Perhaps the deafening announcement of Jesus's death left their ringing ears unable to hear. Or maybe they assumed the resurrection of which he spoke wasn't scheduled until the end of history. Small comfort in the short term.[7]

Peter, Pan

The odds that I would settle the debate about Jesus's expectations were slim. I thought they might improve if I took my quest to the source, so I asked my last ride to drop me at the foot of Mount Hermon, Israel's northern tip, its highest, coldest peak, and the source for most of its water.

Mount Hermon is also in the political twilight zone. My guidebook explained that before 1967 Hermon's ridgeline separated Lebanon from Syria. During the Six-Day War in June of that year, Israel seized the Syrian side of the mountain, ostensibly in self-defense but also for guaranteed access to precious natural resources. Four decades later dozens of Israeli settlements dot a region that remains, at least in world opinion, part of Syria. One more loop in a twisted knot.

Back in Jesus's day, things were equally tangled. Rome drew and redrew its territorial boundaries at will. Halfway through the reign of Herod the Great, he annexed to his realm a town

> "Jesus, from the time of John's death, thought about his possible death. And what he seems to have thought about was that he would die prematurely, that it was part of God's plan, that he was like other martyrs and prophets and figures in the Tanakh, and, most especially, that his death would occur at the onset of the Final Ordeal."
>
> Scot McKnight, *Jesus and His Death*, 238

> "Jesus did not simply predict his own death and the dissolution of his movement. Surely he assumed that God would vindicate his cause notwithstanding the coming time of trouble. It would have been altogether natural for one who had faith in God's justice and power to look beyond present and expected troubles and hope for the Lord's favourable verdict."
>
> W. D. Davies and D. C. Allison, *Matthew*, 2:660

called Banyas (or Panias, after the god Pan) and passed it on to his son Philip. The new tetrarch made it his capital, renaming it, like my favorite salad, after Caesar Augustus. Philip's rule was stable enough. Unlike brother Antipas, who rashly executed John the Baptist, Philip had a steady hand and an even temper. If coins are any indication, his official loyalties were clearly with Rome and its emperor cult, not with his Jewish kin.

Did the Jewish minority in Philip's villages dream of independence? Would they welcome rumors that a prophet of God had made it this far north? When they saw Jesus, would some think of Elijah, who also journeyed up here to care for the poor and perform miracles?[8] Might they have hoped that Jesus, like Elijah, would pray on *their* mountain before wielding a sword in the name of Israel's God?[9]

That the Golan of Jesus's day was firmly in Rome's grip became clear when, a few decades later, after crushing the Jewish intifada in the south, General Titus came here to Philip's Caesarea to bask in his victory by executing prisoners of war.

Reaching my destination, I passed through a gate, skirted a shallow pool, and mounted an ancient stone terrace. It was immediately clear why Greeks and Romans thought the place was sacred. Dominating the center of a weathered limestone cliff, the dark mouth of a huge cave yawned. A menacing doorway to the underworld. The sign said snowmelt from Mount Hermon used to surge from the cave—no doubt adding to the mystique—until an earthquake rerouted the underground waterway.

Directly in front of the cave lies the footprint of a white marble temple that Herod the Great dedicated to Augustus. Along the cliff face to the east, hewn niches offered space for gods who were, these days, nowhere in sight. Several inscriptions honored Pan, god of woodlands and shepherds—mute testimony to ancient worship, and fear, of nature.

The strangeness of the place made my questions more urgent. What brought Jesus here? Did he venture close enough to see the cave and its temples, or did he find shelter nearby in less pagan villages? Had he come north to hide

"Titus . . . now passed to Caesarea Philippi so called, where he remained for a considerable time, exhibiting all kinds of spectacles. Here many of the prisoners perished, some being thrown to wild beasts, others compelled in opposing masses to engage one another in combat."

Josephus, _Jewish War_ 7.23-24

"At this spot a mountain rears its summit to an immense height aloft; at the base of the cliff is an opening into an overgrown cavern; within this, plunging down to an immeasurable depth, is a yawning chasm, enclosing a volume of still water, the bottom of which no sounding-line has been found long enough to reach. Outside and from beneath the cavern well up the springs from which, as some think, the Jordan takes its rise."

Josephus, _Jewish War_ 1.405-406

or to preach? Was this a spiritual retreat designed to prepare his disciples for what lay ahead? Or did he plan one final southward sweep through Galilee before mounting his final "assault" on Jerusalem? Was it coincidence that Mount Hermon was also the northern limit of an earlier campaign led by another "Jesus" (Josh. 12:1)?[10]

Pan's Cave

Since I could peer but not climb into the dark, I tried to make sense of the niches and holy remains a few steps to the east. I was clearly standing on (pagan) holy ground. Like the pool at Bethesda and the synagogue at Capernaum, this sacred site had long-term memory. I turned west along the spring-fed stream, pausing on a bridge that, I decided, both Pan and Jesus would have liked. Willow branches and tangled vines bent low for a drink. Waters churned and surged toward the Sea of Galilee as if eager to bring life to the Jordan Valley. What they could not know was that their death in the briny Dead Sea, like Jesus's death in Jerusalem, was foreordained.

In no *pan*ic (sorry) to leave the bridge's natural air-conditioning, I looked more closely at Matthew 16. This time one verse stood out: "On this rock I will build my church, and the powers of death shall not prevail against it." I knew from Greek class that "powers of death" was literally "gates of Hades." Three metaphors caught my eye.

> BUILDING Jesus intended to *build* something
> ROCK on a solid *foundation*
> ENDURANCE that would resist *the fury of the underworld.*

That pagan terrace—was *that* what inspired Jesus to announce his sacred building program? Did Pan's cave inspire Jesus's reference to the gates of Hades?[11] Like the air around me, the idea was cool. Cool but speculative. For all we knew, the exchange between Jesus and Peter was over before they rolled into town (Mark 8:27).

From the footbridge I continued downstream, passing under an ancient bridge of large hewn stones. Roman(tic), definitely. Note to self: bring girlfriend here. Supplemental note: get a girlfriend. Beyond the bridge, the path led past an old flour mill, where, to my delight, an aging woman offered me goat cheese and warm pita made with fresh-milled flour. I found a stone bench and lingered gratefully to watch and eat. In spite of the heat, the woman wore a long, heavy blue dress and tight white scarf—standard attire among the Druze, a religious community that broke away from Islam a thousand years ago and backed Israel in the 1948 Arab–Israeli war. Expertly she kneaded dough and rolled it onto a hot, domed plate. Bright eyes, flour-dusted hands, tireless pace—she was my mom in the kitchen. Home felt suddenly closer.

Strength renewed, I continued my trek, looping around impressive ruins said to be the basement of a massive palace belonging to Agrippa II,[12] Philip's great nephew. From there I followed the stream for thirty minutes to the Banyas waterfall. Mystery and moisture hung in the air. Something told me Jesus and his disciples spent quality time here. Sadly I could not, for the day was getting late and a stern-faced security guard was thrusting me along the path and away from the water.

Solomon Sequel

Someone in the parking lot offered a ride as far as Moshav She'ar Yashuv, where I decided to forgo hitchhiking and catch a bus. Which is how I met Ben, a thin, nervous man in his fifties who explained, as we waited for the bus, that a moshav is an agricultural community, like a kibbutz but not as radical and with more private property.

"We're not hippies," he said. Then he added, "This moshav is famous."

"Famous? I didn't . . ."

"Back in '97," he interrupted, "two Israeli helicopters bound for Lebanon collided over our heads. All seventy-three soldiers on board perished. Worst air disaster in Israeli history. Sparked a national debate and pressured the government to withdraw our troops from southern Lebanon."

He spoke earnestly, as if he had played a central role in the decision.

"Did you evacuate during the Israel-Lebanon war?"

"Many fled to escape the rockets," he rolled his eyes heavenward. "I stayed with family in Jerusalem for two weeks."

"What about the rest of the name? *She'ar Ya-shuv?*"

"That's from the Bible."

"The Bible?"

"The son of the prophet Isaiah. His name meant *a remnant shall return. She'ar Yashuv.* That's us. We have returned. Isaiah chapter 10, verse 21."

"So the ancient prophets predicted your return to the Holy Land?" I asked. "Is God fulfilling a promise and restoring his people?"

"You tell me," he replied with a shrug. "Something is keeping us Jews from drowning in a sea of Arabs. This close to Lebanon and Syria, I hope God is watching over us." He paused. "God and maybe a few F-16s."

The bus made stops in Galilee before turning toward Haifa on the Mediterranean coast. Looking out the window I imagined life during the recent Israel–Lebanon war, when Hezbollah was lobbing Katyusha rockets onto places like Haifa, forcing thousands to evacuate, and when Israeli air strikes were raining cluster bombs on Hezbollah strongholds and Beirut neighborhoods. Why is shalom so elusive here? Where was the God of peace?

At a kibbutz along the way two teenage boys came aboard. The younger one looked familiar. I kept glancing sideways until I had it: he was the kid I sat beside on the plane so long ago. So much had happened since that day. His return glance didn't signal recognition, so I left him alone, like on the plane. The older one, who promptly covered his head with a kippah, was eager to talk. Levy-from-New-Jersey had come to Israel to become a citizen.

"Making *aliyah*," we call it. "Going up."

He was living on a kibbutz only to learn Hebrew. Soon it would be time for his military service, after which would begin his new, observant life in Israel. His cousin Reuben—my seatmate on the plane—was visiting for a few months. Both were riding to Jerusalem to observe Shabbat with friends.

"When I first arrived at the kibbutz wearing my kippah, they made fun of me. They blamed *me* for what's wrong with Judaism!" he said in disgust.

Levy's dissatisfaction went well beyond the kibbutz. "The Israeli government doesn't respect God's law," he said.

I asked him to explain.

"There is one place on earth a Jew is required to pray. And Israeli law forbids it."

"The Temple Mount?"

"Yes of course. Har Ha-bayit."

"According to the Talmud," Levy continued, "Zion is where God gathered dust to form Adam. And where Adam offered his first sacrifice. And where Abraham came to offer Isaac. When the temple is rebuilt, it will rest again on the foundation stone. Then Messiah will come. Nothing will stop it."

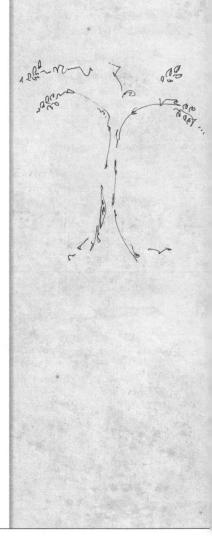

"When . . . you [David] lie down with your ancestors, I will raise up your offspring after you, . . . and I will establish his kingdom. <u>He shall build a house for my name</u>, and I will establish the throne of his kingdom forever. I will be a father to him, and <u>he shall be a son to me</u>."

2 Sam. 7:12–14

Levy's final words struck a chord, and, rather than fading, the sound grew. Suddenly I knew why. The cast of characters in Levy's Jewish vision of the future looked remarkably familiar: a Messiah, a stone, a holy building, and certitude.

"You are the CHRIST."
"I tell you, you are Peter,
and ON THIS ROCK I will build MY CHURCH,
and the powers of death shall NOT PREVAIL against it."

Was Matthew's Gospel saying that the job of the Messiah, the royal son of David, was to build the final temple? That Jesus was a second Solomon[13] but that the foundation for God's new house would not consist of limestone but of living stones?[14]

All the pieces fit, but moving beyond possible to probable was hard to do, as was separating Jesus from the Gospels. I recalled how Guilder followed the Jesus Seminar crowd in denying that Jesus ever promised to "build his church" upon Peter, "the rock." We owe that idea, he said, to Matthew, who embellished Mark to elevate Peter's stature among the early Christians. I didn't share Guilder's confidence. Whether or not Matthew left his fingerprints on the story, Jesus himself, way up here in Caesarea Philippi, had reason to think that God was behind his kingdom movement and that his followers were fulfilling God's plan for Israel's restoration. If Jesus believed that, wouldn't he also expect vindication after death?

Ascent

From Haifa, the bus turned south along the coast. After passing a string of tidy, planned seaside communities, I was tempted to hop down at the other Caesarea—Caesarea Maritima, the coastal capital of Roman Judea in Jesus's day—to explore what was left of Herod the Great's urban showpiece.

A palace, theater, aqueduct, and harbor all broadcast Herod's unparalleled confidence and ambition. I'd read that the harbor, now mostly shadows under the surface, was an utterly brilliant piece of engineering in Herod's day. According to Josephus, Herod constructed the breakwater on a foundation of massive stone blocks, 50 x 9 x 10 feet in size, resting 120 feet below the water surface.[15] You try it. Only recently have divers discovered Herod's little secret: he filled wooden forms with rubble and special volcanic sand that turns to mortar and hardens in water. The finished product was a harbor that stretched 800 feet out to sea and created 40 acres of safe haven. Think 40 American football fields.

Pilate's Palace

Herod's message to the world couldn't be clearer: no force on earth, not even a Mediterranean tempest, shall threaten Caesar's dominion. Anyone foolish enough to challenge Roman might—anyone, say, planning to inaugurate an alternative kingdom—should think again.

Such ambitious undertakings in Caesarea rivaled Herod's other major engineering project: the renovation and expansion of the Jewish temple in Jerusalem. Slippery guy, Herod. Like a major corporation that shamelessly donates to radically opposite political parties, Herod constructed monuments to Rome's emperor and, simultaneously, to the emperor's competition: the God of Israel.

When Herod's son Archelaus got himself fired in 6 CE, Rome seized the chance to assume direct control of Judea. Cutting out the middle man can be good for profits. So the palace-by-the-sea with rock-cut pool and adjacent horse track became the official residence for a string of Roman governors, including Pontius Pilate (26–36 CE), who did archaeologists a favor by having his name inscribed on a stone slab in the theater.

Later on, less famously, Caesarea was home to Cornelius the god-fearing centurion, who summoned Peter from Joppa and promptly burst into tongues during his sermon (Acts 10:44–46). Later still, the town played host to another charismatic convert: St. Paul. This was where Paul did two years of hard time (Acts 24:27) and where he finally appealed to Caesar and began his famous journey to Rome (Acts 25:11).

"You will rise up and have compassion on Zion, for it is time to favor it; the appointed time has come. For your servants hold its stones dear, and have pity on its dust. The nations will fear the name of the LORD, and all the kings of the earth your glory. For the LORD will build up Zion; he will appear in his glory."

Ps. 102:13-16

"How could we sing the LORD's song in a foreign land? If I forget you, O Jerusalem, let my right hand wither! Let my tongue cling to the roof of my mouth, if I do not remember you, if I do not set Jerusalem above my highest joy."

Ps. 137:4-6

As I said, I almost hopped down at Caesarea to sprint along the hippodrome and swim in the Med. But if the place was too pagan for Jesus, I would stay away too. Onward and up to the Holy City.

As the bus wended through the foothills, I felt a wave of anticipation. I was sensing Levy's zeal to be in Jerusalem for Shabbat, to exhale with a city taking its rest.[16] But there was more. Rising before me was a city that had won poets' hearts and prophets' rebukes. Ahead were stones worn smooth by trudging pilgrims, darkened by the blood of battle, and etched with the Crusaders' cross. The air around me echoed saints' prayers and warriors' cries. The sky had often been dark with the smoke of sacrifice or war. Could Jesus have made his ascent without sensing all this? Surely he did not ascend at Passover, like Levy for Shabbat, simply to celebrate a holy day in Jerusalem. He must have known that his ascent to Jerusalem was a climb into a much larger story.

When the wheels of the bus stopped, it was because police were blocking access to the terminal. The building had just been evacuated. Sniffer dogs and steel-eyed agents in blue sweatshirts were emerging from a white van. Someone had noticed a suspicious package, our driver remarked over shrugging shoulders. Probably laundry, he said. Maybe a bomb.

As I said good-bye to my two kibbutzniks, I asked Levy if he planned to visit the Temple Mount while in Jerusalem, even though he was not able to pray there. With images of Banyas's pagan shrines fresh in my mind, and with Jesus looking more and more like a Solomon wannabe, I was eager to explore the platform where Israel's temples once stood. Levy's answer caught me off guard.

"There's been a ruling."

"A ruling?"

"A halakhic ruling. The rabbis have forbidden us to enter any part of the Temple Mount."

"Why?" I blurted. "Are they worried about violence? An uprising?"

"No. They say we don't know for sure where the temple used to stand. We might accidentally enter the sanctified area of the temple and step on holy soil. We may enter the holy area only if we have been sanctified by the ashes of the red heifer."

I was at once impressed and suspicious. Impressed because these rabbis took holy space so seriously. Moses approached the burning bush in bare feet; these guys stayed away entirely. Suspicious because I knew that many religious Jews did visit the Temple Mount. Was this ruling meant to stem the number of Jews on the mount? Were there fears of a provocation? A clash with Muslims? I'd grown up in a land that works hard to separate religion from politics. One is private, I'd been told. The other public. They attempt no such exotic stunt here in the Middle East; a ruling about purity is also about politics.

Levy's comments got me thinking about Jesus's visit to the temple. Was Jesus motivated by politics as much as by religious zeal? Did he hope to provoke an uprising? Did he think the money changers had drawn too close to holy ground? Was it coincidence that Jesus was tried for and convicted of sedition less than a week after visiting the temple?

Navigating from the bus station to the Old City, I was a weary ship returning to port. Through Jaffa Gate I ran the gauntlet of eager merchants—*scuse-me-where-you-from?*—along David Street—*come, have a look*—turned up Christian Quarter Road, past Shaaban's money exchange, east, then north along Souq Khan al Zeit toward Damascus Gate. I'd decided to forgo the western familiarity of the Austrian Hospice for a room at the Hashimi, a Palestinian hotel in the heart of the Muslim Quarter. The price was right, the staff was kind—Muslims all, except for their French Jewish cook, who lived in a tent on the roof. I dumped my pack, made myself mint tea in the kitchen, and ascended to the hotel roof. A warm breeze welcomed me "home" as I gazed upon the charmed chaos of the Old City. In retreat behind me, the sun had gold enough for only the tips of the tallest domes and minarets. The Dome of the Rock, crown jewel of the city, seemed close enough to touch. I watched as dusk faded to black and a red crescent rose through a veil of clouds between the Dome of the Rock and Al Aqsa Mosque.

Since the seventh century the dome has graced the platform Arabs call *al Haram esh-Sharif*, the Noble Sanctuary. Jews like Levy call it *Har Ha-bayit*, the Mountain of the House (of

Old City Dome in Distance

God). Herein lieth the problem: for Muslims the dome marks the destination of Muhammad's magical Night Journey from Mecca. For Orthodox Jews the same dome is a bitter reminder of Islam's ascendancy and a desecration of the place Israel's God chose for his temple.

A few minutes on the roof and the Old City had once again cast its spell. No wonder this place drives people crazy. Jerusalem syndrome, they call it. Delusions. Fanatical urges to dress like Jesus. My feelings were less messianic than melancholy. From my perch I watched as four quarters settled for the night—Muslim, Jewish, Orthodox, Catholic—like weary boxers retreating to their corner stools. Gilded and shining like Jesus on the mountain, the transfigured city whispered of coming glory. Drawn into quarters like a sacrificial lamb, it bleated for something, someone, to inaugurate its restoration.

Kingdom Come

Jake's second cousin was a rabbi connected to The Temple Institute, an organization founded by Rabbi Yisrael Ariel. Rabbi Ariel was one of the paratroopers who helped Israel capture East Jerusalem, the Temple Mount, and the Western Wall back in 1967. These days The Temple Institute is directed by Rabbi Chaim Richman. As best I could tell, his small, devout group on the fringe of Israeli society believes not only that there will be a third temple where the Dome of the Rock now stands, but also that they can help make it happen. On their website they post an aerial photo of the modern mount, except it's been Photoshopped so the Dome of the Rock is replaced by a rebuilt temple! No separating religion and politics here. Under the picture is a quotation of Isaiah 56:7—the same verse Jesus quoted after he expelled the buyers and sellers in the temple and overturned the money changers' tables (Mark 11:17).

> FOR MY HOUSE SHALL BE CALLED A HOUSE OF PRAYER FOR ALL NATIONS.

Both Rabbi Jesus and Rabbi Chaim indict Israel for failing to fulfill Isaiah's vision. But whereas Jesus quoted Isaiah 56 to condemn the guardians of the second temple, the institute employs the same text to summon builders of the third.

Folks at the institute helped me contact Jake's cousin, Rabbi Feldman, who agreed to guide me on the Temple Mount, but not for three days. I was glad for the time to read and snooze at the École. By day two my head swirled with questions. I fired off another email to Guilder.

Dear Randall:

Back from Galilee and the Golan. Different world up there. More secular. More relaxed, except for the part about kids my age packing automatic weapons.

Nope—didn't eat "St. Peter's Fish" in Tiberias. I'm eating at street stalls and from grocery stores. Maybe someday I'll return to guide a rich tour group with a fat budget. ☺

Thanks for your treatise on miracles! I especially like the parallels you drew with Moses and Elisha. You convinced me that early Jewish readers of the Gospels would indeed experience déjà vu. Or is that déjà *lu*—already *read*? Or déjà entendu—already heard? (Guess French class was good for something.) But you seem to be saying more: that the Gospel writers or their sources looked at Jesus through Moses-Elisha goggles. You say:

> Moses and Elisha inspired the early Christian storytellers to remember a large-scale communal meal with Jesus as a miracle of feeding.

Would you object if someone (like, say, me) suggested that the influence also worked the other way? If Old Testament stories shaped the imagination of Jesus's storytellers, wouldn't those same storytellers be watching to see whether their memories of Jesus—of what *actually* happened—matched up with Scripture? Wouldn't they scout for symmetry between Jesus and the Old Testament? Wouldn't they listen for echoes?

You say collective memory of the Last Supper influenced the telling of the feeding miracle. Couldn't it work the other way as well? If one remembered seeing large crowds looking to Jesus for sustenance, wouldn't that memory shape the way one thought about the Eucharist?

But hey, miracles are so last week. Now that I've ascended to Jerusalem I'm thinking mostly about **the temple** and whether Jesus meant to challenge the religious system of his day and offer an alternative. Jesus's sparring partners in the Gospels are most often Pharisees because, as you argued in class, they had much in common. So the real chasm was between Jesus and the temple elites. They were the ones most threatened when he offered forgiveness without sacrifice. They were the ones who wanted to safeguard their stability, their good standing in the eyes of Rome. They were the ones who put him on trial and ultimately delivered him to Pilate.

Looks like I'm finally getting up on the Temple Mount. With a rabbi, no less. I hear security is tight up there. I want to figure out how Jesus's temple demonstration fits into the story. Assuming, of course, that there *is* a fit—that there are (theo-)logical connections between Jesus's self-understanding, his message, his outburst in the temple, and his death. As I recall, you said as much in class.

Hopefully you are cruising through term. Will you be attending the Society of Biblical Literature annual meeting? Where is it this year? Are you reading a paper or just hanging out with friends? Wish I could tag along.

Shalom/salaam
Norm

Jerusalem was enduring a heat wave from the gates of hell. Miraculously, the École stayed cool. I decided to tackle a question that had been asserting itself since Caesarea Philippi: WDJE. What Did Jesus Expect? What was Jesus's vision of the eschaton?

After Jesus calls Peter "Satan" (in Mark 8 and Matt. 16) he adds (in all three Synoptic Gospels) a haunting footnote about taking up one's cross and following. No empty cliché, this was a sober warning that Jesus-loyalists were in for a rough ride, maybe even tragedy. Of course the disciples don't get it. "No need to be so negative," they were thinking. "Lead this convoy to Jerusalem, O King, and you'll see how loyal we are."

Jesus's reply includes a jarring paradox—loss (of physical life) is gain (of spiritual life)—followed by a shocking disclosure: the Son of Man will appear during their lifetime.

Matthew 16:27–28	Mark 8:38–9:1	Luke 9:26–27
	"Those who are ashamed of me and of my words in this adulterous and sinful generation,	"Those who are ashamed of me and of my words,
	of them	of them
"For the Son of Man is to come with his angels	the Son of Man will also be ashamed when he comes	the Son of Man will be ashamed when he comes
in the glory of his Father,	in the glory of his Father with the holy angels."	in his glory and the glory of the Father and of the holy angels.
and then he will repay everyone for what has been done.		
	And he said to them,	
Truly I tell you, there are some standing here who will not taste death before they see the Son of Man coming in his kingdom."	"Truly I tell you, there are some standing here who will not taste death until they see that the kingdom of God has come with power."	But truly I tell you, there are some standing here who will not taste death before they see the kingdom of God."

Several other sayings are similarly urgent. One appears only in Matthew in a passage about the physical dangers that lay ahead for the twelve disciples.

Matthew 10:23 (RSV; no parallels)

When they persecute you in one town, flee to the next; for truly, I say to you, you will not have gone through all the towns of Israel, before the Son of man comes.

Another saying occurs within a warning of intense tribulation after which the Son of Man will appear.[17]

Matthew 24:34 (RSV)	Mark 13:30 (RSV)	Luke 21:32 (RSV)
"Truly, I say to you, this generation will not pass away till all these things take place."	"Truly, I say to you, this generation will not pass away before all these things take place."	"Truly, I say to you, this generation will not pass away till all has taken place."

As I flipped between these sayings, I noticed several shared elements: all three envision a coming time of distress (Mark 8:34–38; Matt. 10:16–23; Mark 13:11–23); all describe a coming of the *Son of Man* (Mark 8:38; Matt. 10:23; Mark 13:26); and all follow a similar logical sequence. No wonder some scholars think all three go back to the same original saying.[18]

Logic →	Announcement…	… of what won't happen…	before	what will happen.
Matthew 10:23 (RSV)	Truly, I say to you,	you will <u>not</u> have gone through all the towns of Israel	before	the Son of man comes.
Mark 9:1 (RSV)	Truly, I say to you,	there are some standing here who will <u>not</u> taste death	before	they see that the kingdom of God has come with power.
Mark 13:30 (RSV)	Truly, I say to you,	this generation will <u>not</u> pass away	before	all these things take place.

My trek into Jordan on the trail of John the Baptist had me convinced that the river prophet expected that divine intervention would vindicate him from his enemies. The fact that Jesus submitted to John's baptism and preached a similar kingdom message makes it likely that Jesus shared John's belief: they were both witnessing history at a turning point. So here are my questions: Did Jesus expect history's dramatic finale to occur immediately? Within, say, a generation? If so, weren't his expectations disappointed? Aren't we, twenty centuries later, still waiting for the curtain to fall? Still praying "thy kingdom come"?

I prowled the lonely stacks, dousing the lights behind me, until I'd tracked down tomes by a number of big-time Jesus scholars with names like Dunn, Ehrman, Allison, Crossan, Meier, and Wright. Perhaps the pile of books was my tower of Babel. Perhaps my quest to understand the coming of the Son of Man was one more audacious attempt to reach the heavens. After several hours of page turning and note taking, zeal surrendered to weariness. I laid my head in the narrow space between walls of books. Sleep came quickly. And with sleep, a dream.

The Corridor

I dreamed I was in a long, narrow corridor that continued in both directions as far as I could see. It was like the "long, low hall" in Alice's Wonderland, lit by a row of hanging lamps. Before me I noticed three doors and, fixed to each one, a wooden plank etched with some kind of riddle. I approached the closest one.

My fingers traced the cursive script before I knocked. Shuffling feet. A turning knob. Before me, suddenly, stood a man with dark, slicked-back hair, an equally dark suit, and a white clerical collar. It was John Paul Meier, except taller. Or maybe I was smaller. The smell of corn beef and cabbage followed him through the opening.

"*Say it he didn't*," he said, adjusting his glasses.

"Say *what who* didn't?" I asked.

"Jesus didn't say," he replied in a biblical voice, "*there are some standing here who will not taste death until they see that the kingdom of God has come with power.*"

He wheeled as if his job was done.

"Wait," I blurted. "Said enough you haven't."

"Mark 9:1 circulated as an independent saying before Mark inserted it into his Gospel. Did you not notice the verse's redundant introduction, '*And he said to them . . .*' ?"

"Umm."

"*Say it he didn't.*" Meier tapped the sign.

"Aren't there other sayings of Jesus along the same lines? Maybe Jesus said it on some other occasion."

"Unlikely. Jesus warned his followers to be watchful. He demanded an *immediate* response. *Let the dead bury the dead.* If Jesus had said that some disciples would not live to see the kingdom, he'd be assuming that years, decades would pass before kingdom come. So much for urgency. These words must have come from a Christian prophet who meant to encourage believers who were weary of waiting for Jesus to return."[19]

"Would Christians invent a saying that opened Jesus up to charges of false prophecy?"

"Ah, you invoke the criterion of *embarrassment*. I don't think Mark 9:1 would embarrass Jesus's followers, at least not until the end of the first century."

I didn't back down. "Mark 9 isn't the *only* place Jesus predicts the coming of the Son of Man. What about Mark 13:26 and 14:62, and Matthew 10:23?"

"Ah, the criterion of *multiple attestation* . . ."

"Jesus never said any of them," another voice, vaguely Irish, said from beyond the doorway.

Appearing behind Professor Meier was a short, suited figure with folded arms hidden by huge green mittens. Eyes flashed beneath dark brows and a full head of straight white hair. There was no mistaking the face and voice: it was John Dominic Crossan.

"The Gospels get it wrong," he continued. "Early in his career Jesus embraced the apocalyptic message and water rite of the Baptist. Over time Jesus abandoned John's apocalyptic framework to teach and heal in the hamlets of lower Galilee. That later Jesus assured peasants that God's rule was available here and now, in an egalitarian kingdom of nobodies."

"Pay no attention to the Irishman in the oven mitts," Meier said. "Dom doesn't think Jesus promised a *future* kingdom at all. He says that idea was invented by the early church."

Crossan smiled, shrugged, and excused himself before I could reply. Dom's night to cook, Meier explained, as he too retreated behind the door.

Maybe it was because the two of them interpreted the evidence in opposite directions that I didn't try to follow. Meier slid the bolt into place, the metal echoing along the corridor. Alone and hungry, I turned toward the next door, on which a plank posed a second riddle. It contradicted the first.

DOOR THE SECOND

SAY IT HE DID.

HAPPEN IT DID

Confused, I knocked several times and waited. The latch slid. Hinges complained. From the opening came a shaft of light and several billows of smoke through which emerged a middle-aged man, mostly bald, stocky, in gray tweeds, a waistcoat, and a black T-shirt. Wearing rimless glasses, rolling a lit cigar between his fingers, he extended a hand while exhaling a plume of smoke.

"*Say it he did. Happen it did.*"

"So, uh, you believe Jesus promised that the kingdom would come while some of the Twelve were still alive? And it came?"

The professor savored a long draw on his cigar. "*Happen it did,*" he nodded.

"*When?*" I exhaled. "*When* did the kingdom of God *come with power?*"

"Depends on whom you ask," he said with a smile, looking back through the door. "Some folks in here think the promise of Mark 9:1 refers to the Transfiguration in Mark 9:2. They say Jesus's radiant appearance was a preview of coming kingdom attractions. For Peter, James, and John, if not for the rest, the kingdom *did* come."

"Why would Jesus assure his disciples they would not taste death before an event that happened a week later?"

"It's a problem, I agree. Perhaps those folks would say that Jesus knew something was happening soon but not *how* soon. Speaking of *taste*, this is one fine Cuban. Cigar?"

His hand slid into his coat pocket.

"Speaking of tasting *death,*" I replied, "aren't those things bad for you?"

The professor ignored my comment and continued.

"Others think Jesus was predicting resurrection, ascension, or the arrival of the Spirit. In other words, the coming of the Son of Man occurred when Christ rose and approached the Ancient of Days to receive his kingdom."

"Like the *son of man* in Daniel 7?"

"Exactly. C. H. Dodd thought Mark 9:1 meant the same thing as Romans 1:4: the disciples came to recognize Jesus's power and glory only at the resurrection."

"So Jesus promised his disciples that some would live to see something that would happen a *few months* later. That's better than one week, but I'm still not buying in."

"What did you say your name was?"

"I didn't. It's Norm."

"Sure you don't want a smoke, Norm?"

"Not unless you have a hookah."

"A water pipe? This isn't Wonderland."

"Where exactly am I?"

"You're in Questers' Corridor."

"Alright," I said, "'answer me these questions three.'"

"You look nothing like the Keeper of the Bridge of Death."

Even in dreams I couldn't escape Monty Python.

"What . . . is your name?" I asked, in a British accent.

"Scot McKnight."

"What . . . is *my* quest?"

"*Your* quest? *Your* quest is to know when kingdom comes."

"When . . . does kingdom come?"

"I thought you might ask for the airspeed velocity of an unladen swallow. When does the kingdom of God arrive? Jesus said it would arrive within a generation."

"Did it?"

"Tell me what happened forty years after his crucifixion."

"Jerusalem fell. The temple was destroyed."

"Give the man a cigar."

"No thanks."

"Jesus believed some disciples would live to see him vindicated as God's true herald. And they did. Jesus's vindication took place when Jerusalem was sacked by Rome."[20]

Professor McKnight paused to take first a short, then a longer draw. I was glad for the time to think. His explanation fit the timetable perfectly; only a few followers lived to see *that* kingdom-come, precisely as Jesus predicted. Still, something didn't seem right.

"Let's see," I began, fanning smoke with my hand. "Jesus promised a dramatic display of God's power, but what happened was a Roman siege."

"The sack of Jerusalem was much more than the work of pagans," McKnight replied. "It was also Yahweh's judgment for unfaithfulness to Israel's covenant. Rome filled the role in God's plan that Babylon played centuries earlier."[21]

"But doesn't Mark refer to the *glorious coming of the Son of Man* and to the *powerful coming of the kingdom of God*? How can the "glorious appearance" of Jesus be code for flames, slaughter, and the destruction of Jerusalem?"[22]

"You've got it backward," said McKnight. "The fall of Jerusalem was the code. It was a crisis so cosmic in scope that it could be described only as falling stars and a darkening sun. Too bad Tom is asleep."

"Tom?"

"Tom Wright. *N. T.* Wright. Tom just finished his latest book, so he's taking a nap. He would say Jesus aligned

"As he came out of the temple, one of his disciples said to him, 'Look, Teacher, what large stones and what large buildings!' Then Jesus asked him, 'Do you see these great buildings? Not one stone will be left here upon another; all will be thrown down.'"

Mark 13:1-2

"As he came near and saw the city, he wept over it, saying, 'If you, even you, had only recognized on this day the things that make for peace! But now they are hidden from your eyes. Indeed, the days will come upon you, when your enemies will set up ramparts around you and surround you, and hem you in on every side. They will crush you to the ground, you and your children within you, and they will not leave within you one stone upon another; because you did not recognize the time of your visitation from God.'"

Luke 19:41-44

himself with the saints of the Most High—that Jesus saw himself as the *true* Israel and was convinced that the nation's destiny depended on him. Jesus was following in Jeremiah's footsteps, which is why he saw the temple leadership as a big part of Israel's problem, and why he foretold the temple's destruction."[23]

"That would explain why some people mistook him for Jeremiah," I replied.[24] "Wait. If Jesus said Jerusalem would suffer horrors before the Son of Man comes (in Mark 13), how can you say Jerusalem's destruction *is* the Son of Man's coming?"[25]

I remember thinking how smart I sounded. The professor was unimpressed.

"Your problem is that you still think that when Jesus spoke of the coming Son of Man he meant a Second Coming of Jesus *to earth*. Jesus was not picturing the vindicated Son of Man coming down to earth but into God's presence! Have you read Daniel 7 lately?"

Daniel 7:13–14	Daniel 7:27
Human Figure Receives Kingdom	**God's People Receive Kingdom**
As I watched in the night visions, I saw one like a human being coming with the clouds of heaven. And he came to the Ancient One and was presented before him. To him was given dominion and glory and kingship, that all peoples, nations, and languages should serve him. His dominion is an everlasting dominion that shall not pass away, and his kingship is one that shall never be destroyed.	The kingship and dominion and the greatness of the kingdoms under the whole heaven shall be given to the people of the holy ones of the Most High; their kingdom shall be an everlasting kingdom, and all dominions shall serve and obey them.

Dreams are curious. This one was getting curiouser. Suddenly the professor produced a shiny watch from his waistcoat and exclaimed, "Oh dear, I shall be late!" With that he was gone, and I was alone again in Questers' Corridor. The pocket watch got me wondering how long I had been there and whether I would ever escape. Which got me wondering whether ancient folk experienced time the way we do. I tried to imagine Jesus worrying about being late for anything. I couldn't even picture him making an appointment. When Mary and Martha told Jesus that Lazarus was sick, he didn't show up for two days (John 11:6). In Jesus's story of the farmer who wanted bigger barns, the guy is driven by a present surplus, not a ten-year business plan (Luke 12:17). Hunger was beginning to cloud my judgment. I moved toward the only other door in sight. Another sign, another riddle.

DOOR THE THIRD

SAY IT HE DID.
HAPPEN IT DIDN'T.

The idea that Jesus was mistaken about timing is not new. Ever since Albert Schweitzer a century ago, a procession of scholars has maintained that Jesus's apocalyptic expectation went unfulfilled. For Schweitzer, who coined the phrase "quest of the historical Jesus,"[26] Matthew 10:23 was the smoking gun—proof that Jesus's expectations were disappointed. In Matthew 10 Jesus sends the Twelve on a mission to the "house of Israel" (10:5–6), during which time, he warns, they should expect persecution, arrest, perhaps even death (10:16–23). According to Schweitzer, when the disciples set out, Jesus

> does not expect to see them back in the present age. The Parousia of the Son of Man, which is logically and temporally identical with the dawn of the Kingdom, will take place before they shall have completed a hasty journey through the cities of Israel to announce it. . . . This prediction was not fulfilled. The disciples returned to Him; and the appearing of the Son of Man had not taken place. . . . An event of supernatural history which must take place . . . at that particular point of time, failed to come about.[27]

In Schweitzer's thought, when the disciples returned safely from their little operation and the end hadn't come, Jesus took it on himself to accelerate God's timetable by heading, like Frodo to Mount Doom, straight toward Mount Zion, the stronghold of his opponents.

Schweitzer's particular spin on Matthew 10:23 hasn't fared well, partly because the sweep of Matthew 10 envisions a grand mission—reaching "all the towns of Israel"—that would hardly fit within the span of Jesus's brief campaign. His followers didn't face hostile "governors and kings" until *after* he was gone, when the young movement began to upset the status quo. Even if Jesus meant only that fleeing missionaries would never exhaust every hiding place, that feat alone would require several years.[28] My little "campaign" in Galilee was tiring and plenty dusty; the thought of a much longer, sweatier trek, all on foot, at risk of bandits and under threat by authorities, made my feet ache.

Okay, so Schweitzer was wrong on a key point: Jesus did not pin his hopes for vindication on a short-term Jewish mission. That said, more than a few scholars since Schweitzer have concluded that Jesus thought his disciples would live to see the culmination of the age, the consummation of the kingdom, the glorious coming of the Son of Man. Prominent members of the Jesus-was-wrong school of thought include Dale Allison and academic rock star (and *Daily Show* guest) Bart Ehrman.[29]

I wondered how Mom would react to the idea that Jesus envisioned a seismic apocalyptic shift in a matter of years, not centuries or millennia. That history has not unfolded the way Jesus imagined it would. If Jesus could confess ignorance—about who touched him in a crowd (Mark 5:30) or about whether a blind man could see (Mark 8:23)—could he also underestimate? If his knowledge of details could be fuzzy (Mark 13:32), could he also have misjudged the timescale?

"What else could he be wrong about?" I could hear Mom asking. Would faith in a mistaken Jesus be misplaced?

When I summoned the courage to knock, neither Ehrman nor Allison opened the door. A short man in his sixties, sleeves rolled up, tie loosened, greeted me over reading glasses.

"Stopping by for a cuppa?" he said in a clean Scottish brogue.

"James Dunn?"

"Call me Jimmy. Tea?"

"With mint?"

"Sorry, old man, but we do have scones."

I followed him happily into his study, where two wingback leather chairs were waiting. Walls of books rose to the ceiling. Must and smoke mixed in the air. A flickering fireplace provided our only light. Teapot, cups, saucers, and a mound of steaming scones beckoned from a low table. I took a bite and got down to business.

"So Jesus predicted that the age would end within a generation . . . but he was wrong?"

"People don't take Jesus seriously *as a Jewish prophet*," Dunn complained, eyeing me over reading glasses. "Israel's prophets held out hope—hope of redemption and return, of a temple restored—but they didn't always get the timing right. Sometimes they painted a picture that was only partially, or oddly, fulfilled. Sometimes their words had to be reinterpreted, renewed, and redirected. This didn't mean they were false prophets; it just meant they weren't time travelers. They didn't get a special screening of history before it got released to the rest of us! Hope partially fulfilled is hope preserved, not hope nullified. The sayings of the prophet Jesus say more about his assurance that God held the future than they reveal details of the 'end' itself."[30]

That was a lot to consider. I concentrated on the fire for several minutes. When I finally looked up, I realized a pale figure had materialized beside Professor Dunn. "It's the ghost of Ben Meyer," Dunn explained calmly, pointing with his tea cup as if at a book on the shelf. "May he rest in peace."

Meyer's ghost began to speak.

"It's not whether Jesus was authentically human but whether he was an authentic prophet," said the ghost. "Prophets claim to speak for God, and do so in symbols. What the symbol means is what God means. So the question is this: 'Did Jesus have determinate knowledge of what God intended by the symbolic scheme of things which Jesus himself was commissioned to announce?' The answer would appear to be 'No.'"[31]

According to Meyer, prophetic knowledge was always limited knowledge. Only history could decipher prophetic symbols, "translating image into event and symbolic time into real time."

The ghost began to glow.

"If a prophet of Israel warned that a coming event was imminent," the ghost continued, "but the prediction was not fulfilled immediately, Israel did not simply repudiate the prophecy."

I now had to squint.

"They had learned," he continued, "to expect fulfillment in the *kairos* of God's choosing."[32]

Silence, broken only by sipping and chewing. If Dunn and Casper were right, then maybe projecting into the future was less like time travel and more like following headlights in the fog or arranging fragments of a manuscript.

I ran cross-country for two years in high school (mostly because of a girl). Maybe Israel's prophets were time runners looking furtively backward to see approaching threats and soberly forward at the rising terrain. They couldn't see over even the nearest hill, but they still ran confident of ultimate victory.

By now Meyer's ghost was shining so brightly I had to shield my eyes. As it turns out, rays from the setting sun were angling through the library window and striking my face as I slept. Almost blinded me when I opened my eyes.

Pocket Watch

My quest to understand Jesus's vision of the future continued the next day and into the night. I was sure that when Jesus spoke of the coming of the kingdom (Mark 9:1) or the Son of Man (Mark 13:26; Matt. 10:23), he was not referring to his transfiguration. And I was doubtful Jesus had in mind his resurrection or ascension or the coming of the Spirit or the emergence of the church. As for the fall of Jerusalem in 70 CE, I was convinced that Jesus saw it coming but couldn't imagine him describing its horrors as the glorious coming and vindication of the Son of Man. Maybe I was missing something.

The problem was that *all these things* had to occur before *this generation* passes away (Mark 13:30). It would be convenient to limit *these things* to the woes of Mark 13:5–23 so they don't have to include the appearance of the Son of Man in verses 24–27.[33] That would remove the embarrassment of failed prophecy, but in a roundabout way, like the time my Palestinian service taxi went off-roading through olive groves to avoid an Israeli checkpoint.

I returned to the idea that prophecy was by definition indeterminate and that prophetic visions were always limited. What if prophetic imagery was abstract art? What if the ambiguities of prophecy became clear only as the story unfolded? Even the best mountain guide can mistake a near ridge for the summit, but that doesn't mean we shouldn't trust him with our lives.

What would life be like in a world without clocks? Bruce Malina is an anthropologist who claims that peasant cultures perceive time very differently than we do. He says mainstream America is future oriented, which is why we go to college and take out thirty-year mortgages and save for retirement. We keep Day-Timers, set goals, and make appointments. For us the present is a snapshot, a mile marker along the highway into the future.

By contrast, says Malina, peasant societies are present oriented. When they pray for daily bread, they are not using metaphors. According to Malina, the present imagined by peasants stretches from the recent past to the soon-anticipated (or "forthcoming") future. When a farmer welcomes winter rains after the dry season because they foreshadow a bountiful yield, it is because drought, rainfall, and harvest all belong to the present. I read that many Iraqi newlyweds are having children as soon as possible because they want their name to live on if they die in the conflict. For a people in crisis, name, pregnancy, and legacy mingle in the moment.

For such people to move "beyond the horizon of the present," Malina writes, would be to enter the realm of "imaginary time, the world of past and future." For present-dwellers, this realm belongs only to God. It is real, but it is like another dimension to which they have access only indirectly through God's prophets, and then, only through a glass darkly.[34]

"Present Orientation"

Matthew 6:34	So do not worry about tomorrow, for tomorrow will bring worries of its own. Today's trouble is enough for today.
Matthew 20:8	When evening came, the owner of the vineyard said to his manager, "Call the laborers and give them their pay, beginning with the last and then going to the first."
Mark 1:15	The time is fulfilled, and the kingdom of God has come near; repent, and believe in the good news.
Luke 3:9	Even now the ax is lying at the root of the trees; every tree therefore that does not bear good fruit is cut down and thrown into the fire.
Luke 11:3	Give us each day our daily bread.
Romans 15:23–25	But now . . . I desire, as I have for many years, to come to you when I go to Spain. For I do hope to see you on my journey and to be sent on by you, once I have enjoyed your company for a little while. At present, however, I am going to Jerusalem.

Revelation 1:7	Look! He is coming with the clouds;
	   every eye will see him,
	even those who pierced him;
	   and on his account all the tribes of the earth will wail.

Can an apocalyptic preacher like John the Baptist or Jesus live in the present? Apparently so. In the same way that the visionaries at Qumran could believe heaven was mobilizing (in their present) for imminent apocalypse, John could call for repentance and Jesus could announce the kingdom's arrival. Both figures believed the in-breaking of Israel's God had begun. The end of the ages had come. Apocalypse was now.

A voice in my head told me this might not play well back home. For one thing, my friends at church would concede that Jesus had physical limitations—he got hungry, thirsty, tired—but probably not mental ones. Jesus would never forget someone's name or need to stop for directions. His knowledge of the past must have been full; his window on the future, clear. The idea that Jesus's thoughts were constrained by time would make little sense to them. To suggest that Jesus's knowledge of the future was impressionistic and imaginary, and that he may well have expected the dawn of the messianic age within a generation, would border on blasphemy.

Besides, many folks back home had read the *Left Behind* novels. For author Tim Lahaye, Bible prophecy is literally world history written in advance. The earliest readers of Daniel or Revelation could only peer into the mist, but we who have witnessed Jews return to the land (1948) and capture the Temple Mount (1967) can now appreciate how far into the future the prophets were looking. This is why Lahaye connects the dots between biblical prophecies and today's headlines. Prophecy is a jigsaw puzzle; his books provide the box top. For Lahaye, the idea that the eyes of New Testament prophets were fixed on their own generation, and that Jesus may have expected the end to arrive shortly after the fall of Jerusalem, would mess up everything (and be extremely bad for sales).

What They Want to Hear

I was swimming in deep waters and couldn't see land, which I took as a good reason to abandon the books and set out across the Old City. I resolved to try to live in the present. Wending south through the chaotic choreography of the "triple souk" (avoiding the meat market), I emerged into the open spaces and chiseled symmetry of the Jewish Quarter. It was like tumbling out of a cramped wardrobe into a wintry forest. When Israeli fighters captured the Old City in 1967, parts of the Mughrabi Quarter next to the Western Wall were promptly leveled to make room for Jewish worshipers. Many Palestinian families lost their homes overnight.

At the end of the Jewish Quarter I exited through Dung Gate and descended into the Valley of Hinnom in the general direction of Akeldama, where, Acts tells us, Judas ended his life. After fifteen minutes of wandering, I pulled out a map to see how close I was.

"Do you need help?"

A young man holding a baby was peering over a gate.

"I'm a tour guide," he smiled. "You've come to the right place. I am Salah."

Salah offered directions and a drink in the same breath. In no time I was sitting in Salah's tiny front yard holding baby Muhammad while Salah's wife, careful to keep out of sight, passed grape punch through the open door. Conversation came easily. Salah

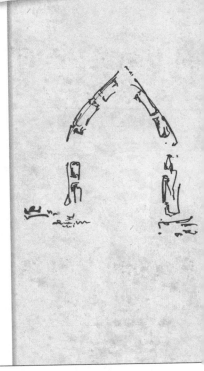

Dome of the Rock

worked freelance when he wasn't guiding groups for the British Embassy. His family received Israeli residency (but not citizenship) shortly after the 1967 war when his neighborhood was annexed by Israel. In guide school, he was the only Arab in a class of forty-nine students.

"What do you tell Christians when you guide on the Temple Mount . . . I mean, the Haram?" I asked cautiously.

"I tell Southern Baptists one thing and Indonesian Muslims something else," he answered wryly. "Whatever they want to hear."

"I want to hear what *you* think," I pressed. "Do you think the Dome of the Rock marks where the Jewish temple once stood?"

"If there was a temple, who knows where it stood? Where is the archaeological evidence that it stood on the Haram?"

"Have you read what Josephus says about Titus's siege of the city?"

"Of course. Most Muslims have never heard of Josephus. I own a copy of the *Jewish War*."

"And?"

"Josephus exaggerates."

I was not persuaded by Salah's sweeping dismissal of Josephus's agonized account—of warring Jewish factions storming the temple, slaughtering its priests, and refusing to surrender to Roman legions—but I decided not to challenge him while enjoying his gracious hospitality. Here was a vivid reminder that we all interpret history *from somewhere*; there is no neutral point of view. I wanted to ask Salah about Herod's massive retaining wall, but our conversation ended abruptly when a friend stopped by. Did Salah want to go horseback riding in Jericho? No, he couldn't. Swimming tomorrow in Jaffa, then? That wouldn't work either. Salah had to visit family up in Nazareth. The gap between Arab-Israelis living in Israel and Palestinians living in the West Bank is wide. Arab-Israelis like Salah live simply, but they have jobs, travel freely, and make plans with confidence. For Palestinians living behind checkpoints and walls, living is day to day. Unemployment hovers at 40 percent. Plans are always tentative and short-term.

Salah wouldn't let me leave before serving watermelon (which magically appeared at the door) and asking about my family. What mattered to him were kinship, honor, and hospitality, not schedules and efficiency. Inhabiting the present was effortless for Salah. By the time we said good-bye there wasn't light enough to explore Akeldama. That could wait. There would be time.

CHAPTER 6

Wall of Tears

MONTY PYTHON'S LIFE OF BRIAN, SCENE 2

GREGORY: What was that?

MAN #1: I think it was "Blessed are the cheesemakers."

MRS. GREGORY: Ahh, what's so special about the cheesemakers?

GREGORY: Well, obviously, this is not meant to be taken literally. It refers to any manufacturers of dairy products.

In which Norm shivers on a mountain, peers through glass, breaks the law, and interviews the dead.

The death of Jesus is a detective's nightmare. The evidence points to several suspects at once, all with motive and opportunity. Plus we don't have the body. Unanswered questions circle like a kettle of vultures over a Roman crucifixion.[1] What was Jesus implying by riding the donkey into Jerusalem? Why did he overturn tables in the temple? What turned Judas from disciple to collaborator? Did Jesus have a change of heart in the garden? What did he hope his death would accomplish? Did he expect to be vindicated? Why was he executed? And how reliable are the earliest reports of a resurrection?

Bound to these historical puzzlers, of course, are theological questions about the meaning of Jesus's death and resurrection. What could the execution of a Galilean rabbi accomplish? Was Jesus's death God's doing? Was God punishing one for the sins of many? Back when my trip was a dream, I pictured myself physically retracing Jesus's final week, from his entry into Jerusalem to his ascension. The answers to all my questions, I thought, would be strewn along the Via Dolorosa or inscribed in the Church of the Holy Sepulchre. Now, though I knew better, I remained eager to make that final ascent to the Holy City.

Sunshine and Shadow

I slept restlessly and rose before sunrise as the fajr echoed across the Muslim Quarter. I would surely miss the predawn call to prayer. I still found the muezzin's rhythm and quarter-tone scale impenetrable, but I loved waking to haunting refrains of "God is great" and "prayer is better than sleep." Determined to meet the rising sun on the Mount of Olives, I was soon padding along the cobbles of the Via Dolorosa, the route countless pilgrims traced to reenact their Lord's sufferings—except that I moved in the wrong direction. East I marched, then north and east again, following a route that skirted the northern end of the Temple Mount. Shops along the way, now secure behind heavy doors, would soon spill onto the street with olive wood carvings, Byzantine icons, and Christian kitsch. I made the gradual ascent toward the Ecce Homo arch, continued past the Monastery of the Flagellation and Church of St. Anne, and finally passed through Lion's Gate, relieved to abandon the narrow passages and anxious shadows of the Old City. Beyond the walls I turned south onto Jericho Way and east across the bridge spanning the Kidron Valley, where I began threading a narrow road up the famous hillside. With each step dawn banished more of night's secrets and painted pastels across the sky.

At the summit were a parking lot and several hillside amphitheaters. In a few hours busloads of pilgrims would be squinting across the valley; local boys with pouting faces would be waving postcards; and windy preachers would be holding forth on the place of the Holy City in God's grand plan. I found shelter from the icy breeze and curled up to await the sun.

The shaded western slope of the mount made me think about the east side, where the sun had already appeared. Over there in the warmth was Bethany— home to Mary, Martha, and Lazarus. Apparently Jesus commuted from Bethany to Jerusalem during the week of Passover (Mark 11:1, 11–12; Luke 21:37; John 12:1). No need for pricy accommodations in the city when you have a place with friends in a village less than two miles away.

Bethany in the Gospels

Luke 10:38–42; John 12:1–8	Jesus stays with Mary, Martha, and Lazarus.
Mark 14:3–9; Matthew 26:6–13	Jesus is anointed in the house of Simon the leper.
John 11:38–44	Jesus raises Lazarus.
Luke 24:50–51	Jesus ascends.

Lazarus is actually the third person Jesus brought back to life. Doubters might point out that the other two—a widow's son (Luke 7:11–15) and Jairus's daughter (Matt. 9:18–26; Mark 5:22–43; Luke 8:41–56)—had been dead for less than a day. About Lazarus's body temperature, however, there could be no question: he'd been in the grave for four days when Jesus arrived (11:17, 39)! So did Jesus actually resuscitate a corpse? Some say such things never happen. Others that the Gospels never speak in metaphors. Since I was persuaded neither by naturalism nor by fundamentalism, my quest for the historical Lazarus wasn't simple.

John says the raising of Lazarus was public enough to mobilize priests and Pharisees to plot Jesus's demise (11:46, 53, 57). Why, then, would three out of four evangelists omit such a momentous event?[2] Curiously, a Lazarus does appear in Luke, but he is a character in a parable—the tale of the rich man who implored Abraham to send poor Lazarus back from the grave to warn his brothers (Luke 16:19–31). Has Luke's fiction been rewritten as John's fact? If it has, most of Luke's parable has been utterly obscured. The figure in John is hardly poor, alone, and destitute. He has two sisters and a home with a table where guests are fed. And he has friends and money enough to be buried in a decent tomb.

Unlike when I left home, I was now thinking about history on several levels at once. It was clear to me that John's Gospel as a whole is not allegory; it is a historical narrative about a figure from Galilee (and from heaven) who spoke truth to power, offered bread to the hungry, and gave life to the dead. It was also increasingly clear that John's historical agenda did not require that his every detail be factual in the modern sense. John is too much of an artisan to be content chronicling the past. He doesn't want us simply to know; he wants us to understand, believe, and live (20:31). He doesn't want to unload facts on us; he wants to drive us forward toward the story's climax. How else can we understand

Jesus's word to a grieving Martha that he is resurrection and life for all who believe (11:25)?

John 11 flashes *forward*, much as the feeding miracles foreshadow the Last Supper, and Cana's new wine the bounty of the messianic age. When sunlight strikes Bethany, Jerusalem knows it will soon feel warmth. So when Lazarus emerges into the light, we witness a preview of God's kingdom and receive assurance that Jesus's death will not be the end. The symmetry between Lazarus and Jesus is striking:

- Jesus foresees both Lazarus's death and his own (11:11–13; cf. 10:11; 12:7, 32–33; 13:1; 18:4).
- A woman named Mary weeps in Jesus's presence (11:33; cf. 20:11–15).
- A stone must be moved to let Lazarus out (11:38–41; cf. 20:1).
- The story highlights Lazarus's grave clothes (11:44; cf. 19:40; 20:5). (Unlike Lazarus, Jesus needs no help removing his.)

At last the sun rose over the Mount of Olives, casting golden hues over the domes, towers, and minarets of the Old City. There on the edge of the Kidron, with Lazarus's tomb behind me and ten thousand more below, one thing was clear: if death's minions are ever to be routed, God must lead the charge.

Too often the Bible was more textbook than inspiration. More ancient script than Holy Scripture. Mom worried aloud about this occupational hazard and once read me the counsel C. S. Lewis offered a new believer who was thinking of abandoning history to study theology:

> I think there is a great deal to be said for having one's deepest spiritual interest distinct from one's ordinary duty as a student or professional man. St. Paul's *job* was tent-making. When the two coincide I shd. have thought there was a danger lest the natural interest in one's job and the pleasures of gratified ambition might be mistaken for spiritual progress and spiritual consolation. . . . Contrariwise, there is the danger that what is boring and repellent in the job may alienate one from the spiritual

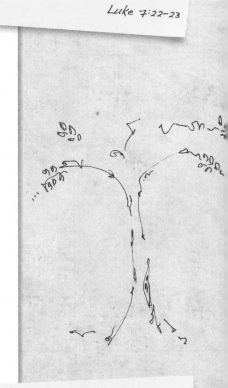

"Go and tell John what you have seen and heard: the blind receive their sight, the lame walk, the lepers are cleansed, the deaf hear, <u>the dead are raised</u>, the poor have good news brought to them. And blessed is anyone who takes no offense at me."

Luke 7:22-23

"<u>Your dead shall live, their corpses shall rise</u>. O dwellers in the dust, awake and sing for joy! For your dew is a radiant dew, and the earth will give birth to those long dead."

Isa. 26:19

life. And finally, someone has said "None are so unholy as those whose hands are cauterised with holy things": sacred things may become profane by becoming matters of the job. You *now* want spiritual truth for her own sake; how will it be when the same truth is also needed for an effective footnote in your thesis?[3]

Mom's fears were justified: my years in the religious academy had rendered more than a few sacred things profane. That day on the hilltop, however, things seemed inverted: domed rooftops, shaded tombs, morning chills—mundane things became holy. I held my Bible loosely, thumbing its pages, and opened to Isaiah 60, where the prophet imagines a sacred sunrise over Jerusalem.

> Arise, shine; for your light has come,
>   and the glory of the Lord has risen upon you.
> For darkness shall cover the earth,
>   and thick darkness the peoples;
> but the Lord will arise upon you,
>   and his glory will appear over you.
> Nations shall come to your light,
>   and kings to the brightness of your dawn.
> . . . .
> Violence shall no more be heard in your land,
>   devastation or destruction within your borders;
> you shall call your walls Salvation,
>   and your gates Praise.
> The sun shall no longer be your light by day,
>   nor for brightness shall the moon give light to you by night;
> but the Lord will be your everlasting light,
>   and your God will be your glory.
> The Lord will be your everlasting light,
>   and your days of mourning shall be ended.

Isa. 60:1–3, 18–20

Clear Glass

Out of nowhere a tour group materialized to profane *my* sunrise. Their guide identified the usual landmarks, giving special attention to the ridge that slopes south from the Old City toward the pool of Siloam. Discovered there in 2005, he explained, was a tenth-century BCE monumental building that some archaeologists believe was the palace of King David himself. (The guide mentioned 2 Sam. 5, which I decided I must look up.) What he neglected to mention was that several Jewish groups have been working to displace Palestinians from the neighborhood, known as Silwan, to make room for parking lots, Jewish residences, a national park, and more archaeo-logical digs aimed at strengthening the Jewish claim to the city. Not coincidentally, the Jerusalem municipality recently announced plans to demolish eighty-eight Silwan homes. Such is the dangerous politics of geography in this part of the world.

Luke's Gospel unfolds its own political geography, similarly fraught with danger. (*Fraught* is such a great word.) For Luke, Jesus's ascent to Jerusalem didn't begin in nearby Bethany. It began one hundred miles north in Galilee.

> When the days drew near for him to be taken up, he set his face to go to Jerusalem. And he sent messengers ahead of him. On their way they entered a village of the Samaritans to make ready for him; but they did not receive him, because his face was set toward Jerusalem.
>
> Luke 9:51–53

Along the way Jesus uttered a moving lament over the city.

> Jerusalem, Jerusalem, the city that kills the prophets and stones those who are sent to it! How often have I desired to gather your children together as a hen gathers her brood under her wings, and you were not willing! See, your house is left to you. And I tell you, you will not see me until the time comes when you say, "Blessed is the one who comes in the name of the Lord."
>
> Luke 13:34–35

And as Jerusalem drew near, Jesus told a story, "because he was near Jerusalem, and because they supposed that the kingdom of God was to appear immediately" (Luke 19:11). The story, about a returning king whose subjects rejected his rule, ends abruptly with the king sentencing the rebels to death. Luke immediately has Jesus complete the final leg of his journey.

> After he had said this, he went on ahead, going up to Jerusalem. When he had come near Bethphage and Bethany, at the place called the Mount of Olives, he sent two of the disciples, saying, "Go into the village ahead of you."
>
> Luke 19:28–30

Thus we arrive with Luke at our destination. Jerusalem rises before us behind a wall of Jesus's tears.

> As he came near and saw the city, he wept over it, saying, "If you, even you, had only recognized on this day the things that make for peace! But now they are hidden from your eyes. Indeed, the days will come upon you, when your enemies will set up ramparts around you and surround you, and hem you in on every side. They

will crush you to the ground, you and your children within you, and they will not leave within you one stone upon another; because you did not recognize the time of your visitation from God."

Luke 19:41–44

Even if this speech owes more to Luke than to Jesus, its somber tone conveys perfectly the burden Jesus must have carried as the city, and his death, loomed. Did Jesus's gaze turn northward to scan the horizon for Rome's legions? Did he squint west to imagine siege engines toppling Herod's marble towers? Did he look down where flames would soon engulf the temple? As Luke paints the scene, Jesus saw only two things: a people who had spurned his offer of peace and a city whose destruction was now assured.

The first time I felt the weight of Jesus's approach was when I encountered the travel diary of Mark Twain. Dry-eyed and self-composed, Samuel Clemens had an experience unlike Jesus's in almost every way.

At last, away in the middle of the day, ancient bits of wall and crumbling arches began to line the way—we toiled up one more hill, and every pilgrim and every sinner swung his hat on high! Jerusalem! Perched on its eternal hills, white and domed and solid, massed together and hooped with high gray walls, the venerable city gleamed in the sun. . . . We dismounted and looked, without speaking a dozen sentences, across the wide intervening valley for an hour or more. . . . I record it here as a notable but not discreditable fact that not even our pilgrims wept. I think there was no individual in the party whose brain was not teeming with thoughts and images and memories invoked by the grand history of the venerable city that lay before us, but still among them all was no "voice of them that wept." There was no call for tears. Tears would have been out of place. The thoughts Jerusalem suggests are full of poetry, sublimity, and more than all, dignity. Such thoughts do not find their appropriate expression in the emotions of the nursery.[4]

Mark Twain's Jerusalem was poetic and dignified; Jesus's was besieged and devastated. Twain fell respectfully silent, Jesus cried out with prophetic audacity.[5]

Hugging the slope of the Mount of Olives is a chapel that memorializes this poignant moment in Jesus's career. It is called *Dominus Flevit*: the Lord wept. A group of African pilgrims was filing out of the sanctuary as I arrived. Inside, my gaze was immediately drawn to the altar and the large arched window behind it. Strange, I thought: a shrine like this should feature an intricate leaded window full of colored glass. Visitors need to see Jesus, hands on face, weeping for Jerusalem. Yet the window's glass was perfectly clear. No image. No color. No Jesus.

Disappointed, I slumped onto a bench. Only then were my eyes opened. The "image" framed in the clear altar window was the city of Jerusalem itself. In the window's center was the Dome of the Rock, and behind it the Church of the Holy Sepulchre. Here, walls whispered, Jesus *still* weeps for Jerusalem. Not some Byzantine ideal, the city for which Jesus weeps is itself in mourning, fractured by faith and tinted by fear.

Dominus Flevit

> So do you wish us to be brothers? Father, help us
>   understand.
> Or will we each kill off the others to claim this same
>   piece of land?
>
>   David Wilcox, "Three Brothers,"
>   on *Airstream*

Beneath the window and the altar was a mosaic medallion. A haloed hen spread her wings over seven chicks. The text around the mosaic was from Luke 13:34: "How often have I desired to gather your children together as a hen gathers her brood under her wings, and you were not willing!"

Royal Theater

With the chapel to myself, I pulled out my Bible. Mark 11 pictures Jesus staging his entry into Jerusalem.

> He sent two of his disciples and said to them, "Go into the village ahead of you, and immediately as you enter it, you will find tied there a colt that has never been ridden; untie it and bring it. If anyone says to you, 'Why are you doing this?' just say this, 'The Lord needs it and will send it back here immediately.'"
>
>   Mark 11:1–3

Mark may want us to think that acquiring the donkey was a miniwonder, but the episode reads more like a spy novel than a miracle story. The detailed instructions and scripted dialogue may suggest that Jesus had sent prior word to a friend like Mary or Martha. One wonders whether Jesus was protecting the identity of the colt's owner because he knew the ride would be seen as political. Even subversive.[6]

The crowd, in any case, gave the rider a royal Passover welcome. Passover is the time to celebrate the exodus, to dream of freedom from foreign occupation, and to gossip about who might lead the charge. Parades of Galileans and desert people would ascend to the city as they have for centuries. Folks who spend their days plowing, harvesting, and herding would need little coaxing to drop their tools and join the palm-waving, garment-spreading throngs.

Each Gospel brings something unique to the celebration. Mark 10:32 implies that at least some in the parade were loyal disciples who had made the one-hundred-plus-mile trek with Jesus from the Galilee. Matthew emphasizes the impressive size of the procession and distinguishes carefully between the enthusiasm of Jesus's Galilean supporters and the curiosity of Jerusalem's residents (21:8–11). In Luke the "multitude," peppered with brooding Pharisees, swells as it gets closer to the city (19:37–39). In John, many pilgrims already on hand for the feast emerge from Jerusalem to welcome the approaching Jesus, encouraged by those who witnessed the raising of Lazarus (12:12, 17–18).

Why did Jesus choreograph his final approach to the city? Why not proceed on foot like everyone else? Did he crave attention? Was he campaigning for office? Creating a human shield against opponents? I recalled how Hermann Reimarus, one of my German ghosts, thought the ride was Jesus's last, bold attempt to win the city and the throne:

> Had the people in Jerusalem followed him and joined in proclaiming him king as the apostles did, he would have had all Judea on his side, the High Court of Justice would have been overthrown, and Jesus, together with his seventy chosen disciples, would have been placed in the Sanhedrin instead of the Pharisees and the learned scribes.[7]

Full points for drama, Hermann. Zero for plausibility.

Marcus Borg and John Dominic Crossan, still very much alive, propose an intriguing alternative: Jesus was staging a political demonstration.

> Jesus's procession deliberately countered what was happening on the other side of the city. Pilate's procession [from Caesarea, to reinforce the Antonia fortress during the festival] embodied the power, glory, and violence of the empire that ruled the world. Jesus's procession embodied an alternative vision, the kingdom of God.[8]

When I read Borg and Crossan for class, I liked their idea that Jesus's donkey ride was a parody of Pilate's military parade and a challenge to Roman imperial theology. I wanted them to be right, but as I sat there in Dominus Flevit, the idea seemed speculative and improbable. What could Jesus have known about Pilate's pompous procession? Would the people have joined so eagerly a march that was flagrantly seditious? If Jesus's ride was overtly anti-Roman, why wasn't he promptly arrested? And why don't they cite the ride as evidence in his trial?

Mark doesn't tell us why Jesus did what he did. Neither does Luke. Maybe neither of them knew. The other two Gospels, however, want it known that Jesus's actions were strictly by the Book. Jesus, say Matthew and John, entered Jerusalem to fulfill the Scriptures.

Matthew 21:4–5 (RSV)	Zechariah 9:9 (RSV)	John 12:14–16 (RSV)
This took place to fulfill what was spoken by the prophet, saying,		And Jesus found a young ass and sat upon it; as it is written,
"Tell the daughter of Zion,	Rejoice greatly, O daughter of Zion! Shout aloud, O daughter of Jerusalem!	"Fear not, daughter of Zion;
Behold, your king is coming to you,	Lo, your king comes to you;	behold, your king is coming,
humble, and mounted on an ass, and on a colt, the foal of an ass."	triumphant and victorious is he, humble and riding on an ass, on a colt, the foal of an ass.	sitting on an ass's colt!" His disciples did not understand this at first; but when Jesus was glorified, then they remembered that this had been written of him and had been done to him.

It is easy to see why Matthew and John turned to this verse to decode Jesus's cryptic ride: Zechariah's oracle has all the key elements.

> The inhabitants of Jerusalem . . .
> celebrate expectantly and . . .
> welcome a peaceful king . . .
> who approaches Jerusalem . . .
> on a donkey.

So striking are the parallels that if Jesus staged this ride himself, he surely took his cues from Zechariah. In which case Matthew and John simply say out loud what Jesus was thinking, and the ride becomes evidence that Jesus presented himself to Israel, in some sense, as her king.

A middle-aged couple suddenly entered the chapel, their accent and costume betraying them as Americans. Evidently, however, they knew almost nothing about the Gospels, let alone Jesus's tears. Their baritone Israeli guide recounted at length the story of Jesus's ride, though without the bit about Jews calling him the royal *Son of David*. The couple listened, snapped a single picture, and shuffled out.

The tourists' ignorance made me wonder how much the average out-of-town peasant would have known of Zechariah. Would ancient pilgrims know the prophets better than modern tourists know the Gospels? Could any of them have quoted what came next in Zechariah's oracle?

> He will cut off the chariot from Ephraim
>   and the war-horse from Jerusalem;
> and the battle bow shall be cut off,
>   and he shall command peace to the nations;
> his dominion shall be from sea to sea,
>   and from the River to the ends of the earth.
> As for you also, because of the blood of my covenant with you,
>   I will set your prisoners free from the waterless pit.
>
> Zech. 9:10–11

Those who knew Zechariah would know that his humble rider was not simply a celebrity engulfed in fans and paparazzi. He was a royal figure whose peaceful ride into the city came only after triumph in battle. This king's approach heralded conquest and liberation. Maybe Borg and Crossan weren't far off after all.

The other obvious Old Testament subtext comes from the Psalms. All four Gospels have the crowd reciting Psalm 118: *Blessed is the one who comes in the name of the Lord*. I wasn't sure whether this greeting originally extended to all pilgrims or was restricted to a certain "One." And each Gospel makes it clear that the psalm now applied specifically, preeminently, to Jesus, and that the people were welcoming Israel's next king.

Matthew 21:9 (RSV)	Mark 11:9–10 (RSV)	Luke 19:37–38 (RSV)	John 12:13 (RSV)
And the crowds that went before him	And those who went before	The whole multitude of the disciples began to rejoice and praise God with a loud voice for all the mighty works that they had seen, saying,	So they took branches of palm trees and went out to meet him, crying,
and that followed him shouted,	and those who followed cried out,		
"Hosanna to the Son of David!	"Hosanna!		"Hosanna!
Blessed is he who comes in the name of the Lord!	Blessed is he who comes in the name of the Lord!	"Blessed is the King who comes in the name of the Lord!	Blessed is he who comes in the name of the Lord,
	Blessed is the kingdom of our father David that is coming!		even the King of Israel!"
Hosanna in the highest!"	Hosanna in the highest!"	Peace in heaven and glory in the highest!"	

In case we missed it, Matthew repeats himself a few verses later:

> But when the chief priests and the scribes saw the wonderful things that he did, and the children crying out in the temple, "Hosanna to the Son of David!" they were indignant.
>
> 21:15 RSV

Although the title *king* is nothing if not political, the focus of the story seems to be less on Jesus's challenging the local ruler du jour and more on Jesus's fulfilling Israel's deepest yearning for restoration. As usual, Matthew and Luke are happy to explain Mark. Matthew has the people explicitly call Jesus *the Son of David*; in Luke they call him *the King*. John, meanwhile, saying nothing of David, calls Jesus the *King of Israel*. The list of titles Jesus appears to accept here is long: *Prophet, Coming One, Messiah, Davidic King,* and *Son of David.* We should perhaps add *Savior* ("Hosanna") and *Cornerstone* (Ps. 118:22). Religious officials who heard about the crowd's response would weigh the risks of Jesus's rapidly broadening base of support and worry about Roman retaliation. No wonder he was hanging on a Roman cross within the week.

As I crossed the courtyard to leave, a tall figure in a cowboy hat vaulted a barrier up ahead and disappeared from view. Drawing closer, I spied him in a pit examining several stone ossuaries. So much of the Mount of Olives is ancient cemetery. For some reason, I took his picture with my cell and departed.

I didn't know the route Jesus followed into Jerusalem, though I was betting he turned south along the valley floor so he could enter the temple from the main gates on the south side. A few hundred yards below Dominus Flevit, I found a foot path leading down to the valley floor. From there I hiked south, past countless graves, and then up a long stairway—no donkey, no crowd—to the southeast corner of the Temple Mount. Tired and hungry, I welcomed the sight of the snack shop outside Dung Gate. I bought a Magnum bar and found some shade.

Just then I saw an American group leaving the Old City. T-shirts, baseball caps, and New York accents gave them away. Their guide halted the parade within earshot.

"When you came through that gate," she said, "you exited the Old City, right? Wrong! We are still in the Old City. From the days of David and Solomon down to the Roman destruction of Herod's temple, this area was enclosed within the city. Where you are standing now was once home to Israel's greatest kings! David, Solomon, Hezekiah, Josiah—welcome to the City of David."

Several women feigned polite interest by looking around. Cameras clicked. A teenager near me nodded.

"This used to be a narrow ridge between two deep valleys: to the east the Kidron Valley separates us from the Mount of Olives."

She pointed. Everyone turned. Everyone except the teen who kept nodding. That's when I spied the ear buds for his iPod.

"To the west is the Cheesemakers' Valley. Today it is full of centuries of silt and debris so you'd never know it used to be a deep valley."

"Blessed are the cheesemakers," said the nodding kid to no one in particular.

"Obviously he didn't mean it to be taken *literally*," I said in response.

We traded glances of mutual respect. Against the odds two Monty Python aficionados had crossed paths.

". . . no choice but to expand uphill to the north." The guide was still talking. "Of course God's house had to be higher than the palace. Any questions?"

Awkward silence until a tour bus roared past.

"None? Okay, next stop: the Gihon spring, where Solomon was anointed king. When King David became frail, more than one of his sons thought he should inherit the throne. How would people know which son was the king's chosen successor? The answer might surprise you: a donkey ride. We press on."

My head jerked. Had I heard correctly? The chosen son of David . . . claimed the throne . . . by riding a donkey? The group shuffled off. I, ever hungry, headed into the Old City to find lunch and, on a full stomach, to compare two royal donkey rides.

Jesus rides up to Jerusalem (Mark 11; Matt. 21; Luke 19)	Solomon rides up to Jerusalem (1 Kings 1)
	1:30 David vows that Solomon will be king after him and sit on his throne that same day.
Mark 11:1–6 Jesus approaches Jerusalem from the Mount of Olives. He sends two disciples to get an unridden colt, telling them to say, "The Lord needs it."	**1:32–37** David commands three of his men to have Solomon ride on the king's own mule, down to the Gihon spring, where he will be anointed king.
Mark 11:7 They put garments on the colt; Jesus rides it up to Jerusalem.	**1:38–39, 44** Solomon rides the king's mule to Gihon, where he is anointed (*christos*), and then rides back up to the palace to sit on the throne.
Matthew 21:4–5 Events said to fulfill Scripture (Isa. 62:11; Zech. 9:9): "your king is coming to you, humble, and mounted on a donkey."	
Matthew 21:9 The crowds ahead of and behind Jesus shout. **Mark 11:8** Many spread garments and branches in the road. **Luke 19:37** The crowd of disciples praise God loudly.	**1:39–40, 45** A great public procession follows Solomon up to Jerusalem, with trumpet fanfare, flutes, and much rejoicing.

Jesus rides up to Jerusalem (Mark 11; Matt. 21; Luke 19)	Solomon rides up to Jerusalem (1 Kings 1)
Crowds cry out: **Matthew 21:9** "Hosanna to the Son of David!" **Mark 11:10** "Blessed is the coming kingdom of our ancestor David!" **Luke 21:38** "Blessed is the king who comes . . ."	**1:34, 39** David has the people say, "Long live King Solomon!" **1:43** "Our lord King David has made Solomon king." **1:48** The king says, "Blessed be the Lord, the God of Israel, who today has granted one of my offspring to sit on my throne."
Matthew 21:10–11 The people of Jerusalem ask: "Who is this?"	**1:41** Joab asks: "Why is the city in an uproar?"
Luke 19:39–40 Pharisees command disciples to stop.	**1:49** The guests of Adonijah, Solomon's opponent, are terrified when they hear that Solomon has been anointed and ridden the king's mule.
Mark 11:11 Jesus enters Jerusalem but departs quickly.	**1:46** Solomon sits on the throne of David but refuses to punish Adonijah.

Some of the parallels are subtle, and there are notable differences, but I couldn't deny the possibility that someone—Jesus? his earliest followers? Mark?—saw Jesus's donkey ride as a reenactment of Solomon's inaugural ascent.[9] Solomon's claim to fame, of course, was that he got to build the temple (1 Kings 5–6; 2 Chron. 2–7). He was the one of whom Nathan the prophet spoke to David:

> When your days are fulfilled and you lie down with your ancestors, I will raise up your offspring after you, who shall come forth from your body, and I will establish his kingdom. He shall build a house for my name, and I will establish the throne of his kingdom forever. I will be a father to him, and he shall be a son to me. When he commits iniquity, I will punish him with a rod such as mortals use, with blows inflicted by human beings. But I will not take my steadfast love from him, as I took it from Saul, whom I put away from before you. Your house and your kingdom shall be made sure forever before me; your throne shall be established forever.
>
> 2 Sam. 7:12–16

In fulfillment of Nathan's oracle, Zadok anointed Solomon at the Gihon spring (1 Kings 1:39), so that when Solomon approached Jerusalem on the royal mule, it was as the anointed one, Israel's messiah. Was it *as Solomon* that Jesus approached

Jerusalem, entered the temple, and staged his demonstration?

Steps to Dome

Holy Ground

I found Rabbi Feldman early the next day in the Western Wall plaza next to the wash basins. A wispy, graying beard with square corners supported a round, earnest face. Thick glasses kept his eyes at a distance. Wasting no time, he hustled me across the plaza to the security post at the bottom of a wooden ramp that led up to Mughrabi Gate. This was the only entrance open to non-Muslims, the rabbi explained, and the only gate whose keys are not held by the *Waqf*, the Islamic Authority. The damaged, forty-year-old ramp was the subject of an uproar recently when the city council voted to replace it. Opponents squared off. In one corner, archaeologists complained that the project would destroy priceless antiquities. In another, Muslim clerics accused Israel of undermining the foundations of the Al Aqsa Mosque. To restore calm, the project was scaled down and the ramp redesigned. Nothing is neutral or obvious here.

As we ascended we overlooked a pile of huge stones.

"They've lain there for two thousand years," the rabbi said, "ever since the Romans leveled the temple platform and a monumental staircase. Debris from the demolition completely buried the Roman street below. Look there. Burn marks from the devastation."

The chunks of masonry called to mind Jesus's stark announcement that every stone of the temple would be torn down. Guilder said Jesus's oracle against the temple ranked among the most authentic of his sayings. If so, I was looking down on "hard" evidence that Jesus's ominous prediction had been fulfilled.

"Do we know where pilgrims used to enter?" I asked, as we approached the gate. I was picturing Jesus's final approach on Palm Sunday.

"As Jesus came out of the temple and was going away, his disciples came to point out to him the buildings of the temple. Then he asked them, 'You see all these, do you not? Truly I tell you, not one stone will be left here upon another; all will be thrown down.'"

Matt. 24:1-2

Temple Mount Al Aqsa

"Most would ascend the monumental stairs on the south side and enter through the double and triple gates," he replied.

"Those arched gates on the south wall," I began. "Why have they been bricked in?"

"Those gates go back to Umayyad rule in the seventh century. The Crusaders blocked them in several centuries later when they used the south wall for the city's defenses."

"I'm confused," I admitted. "Aren't those arches far below the level of the inner platform?"

"Absolutely. If you could pass through one of those walled-up gates you would find yourself in a colonnaded tunnel at the end of which is a staircase that ascends up to the Court of the Gentiles, which is precisely where we're going right now."

"The tunnels are still there?"

"Definitely. They're beneath the Al Aqsa Mosque. Sadly, these days they're off limits to non-Muslims."

We crossed the threshold of the Mughrabi Gate. It pleased me that Jesus's tunnel entry would have been more grand and mysterious than mine. Israeli police at the entrance ignored me but eyed the rabbi suspiciously. I wondered if Jesus drew stares from the temple police in his day.

Inside the gate was a broad courtyard of polished stone testifying to millions of pilgrim feet, and to more than a few bloody confrontations. To our left trees spread shade over children, old men, and a dozen temple police. I had arrived at the most contested patch of real estate on earth—political and theological Ground Zero.

First impressions are important. My first impressions of the Herodian platform were two: vast and quiet. I'd read that the thirty-five-acre platform had room for twenty-six American football fields, including end zones. That's room for hundreds of thousands of Muslims during Ramadan. And for the same number of first-century Jews during Passover. Ahead of us the massive but unadorned Al Aqsa Mosque looked not a year older than thirteen hundred. Seven pointed arches on its north side channeled worshipers through doors whose thresholds I, as a non-Muslim, could not cross. As the third holiest site for the world's one billion Muslims, it was a daily reminder to ardent Zionists that the conquest of 1967 hadn't gone far enough.

Somewhere here Jesus overturned some tables, I thought.

"I've read that the money changers and dove sellers plied their trades in the Royal Portico," I began.[10]

"The Royal Portico was there," Rabbi Feldman said, waving his hand toward the south wall, where Al Aqsa stood. "Imagine four rows of massive columns supporting a wooden roof along most of that wall. Herod the Great spared no expense. Josephus says it took the outstretched arms of three men to reach around one column!"[11]

"Impressive."

"Impressive? It was *glorious*, I tell you. Not like today. Today there are piles of rubble desecrating the sanctity of this place!"

As we approached the southeast corner of the platform, an agitated Rabbi Feldman pointed to a broad stone stairway descending to several large arched doors. Though the steps were much newer than the cobbles under our feet, it was clear we would not be using them.

"Solomon's Stables," the rabbi began, with disdain. "For ten years they've been excavating and building down there without official authorization," he explained. "How many priceless artifacts have been destroyed? What evidence of Jewish presence have they stolen? Why must they constantly violate the sanctity of this place?"

We halted our march, but my mind would not slow down. There I was with a zealous rabbi brimming with righteous indignation because he believed God's sanctuary had become a robber's den and that the guardians of the Holy Place were promoting its pollution. Jesus's zeal for the temple suddenly acquired three dimensions. The rumble of an approaching tractor snapped me back to the present.

"Solomon's Stables," I said over the din. "Is that where the Knights Templar lived?" I gave no indication that the sole "scholarly" source for my question was *The Da Vinci Code*.

"You Christians love your legends. The Templars kept *horses* down there. The knights themselves lived up above in a wing of the Al Aqsa Mosque. This arrangement lasted about seventy years, until Saladin regained Muslim control of Jerusalem in 1187."

I pictured the portico of Jesus's day as a colonnaded, medieval cathedral pulsing with pilgrims buying doves and trading currency. What was it about all that commerce, I wondered, that Jesus found so scandalous? Didn't pilgrims need money changers and dove sellers? Weren't the merchants providing an essential service?

Turning tables in the temple

Mark 11:15–19

Then they came to Jerusalem. And he entered the temple and began to drive out those who were selling and those who were buying in the temple, and he overturned the tables of the money changers and the seats of those who sold doves; and he would not allow anyone to carry anything through the temple. He was teaching and saying, "Is it not written, 'My house shall be called a house of prayer for all the nations'? But you have made it a den of robbers." And when the chief priests and the scribes heard it, they kept looking for a way to kill him; for they were afraid of him, because the whole crowd was spellbound by his teaching. And when evening came, Jesus and his disciples went out of the city.

John 2:13–17

The Passover of the Jews was near, and Jesus went up to Jerusalem. In the temple he found people selling cattle, sheep, and doves, and the money changers seated at their tables. Making a whip of cords, he drove all of them out of the temple, both the sheep and the cattle. He also poured out the coins of the money changers and overturned their tables. He told those who were selling the doves, "Take these things out of here! Stop making my Father's house a marketplace!" His disciples remembered that it was written, "Zeal for your house will consume me." The Jews then said to him, "What sign can you show us for doing this?" Jesus answered them, "Destroy this temple, and in three days I will raise it up." The Jews then said, "This temple has been under construction for forty-six years, and will you raise it up in three days?" But he was speaking of the temple of his body.

If we go with Mark, Jesus did more than overturn a few tables. He blocked the movement of goods across the courtyard. I couldn't imagine anyone single-handedly shutting down traffic in so vast an area, though I could easily picture someone causing a commotion that would draw hordes of curious visitors and interfere with business. Jesus could not have expected to shut things down for long. It reminded me of the time I saw crowds converge on El Wad Street to watch an ultraorthodox Jew confront a Palestinian shopkeeper. No one could move until the police arrived to disperse the crowds.

In John's Gospel Jesus drives sheep and cattle out of the temple. Not just flocks but herds as well. Guilder didn't think large animals would have been kept on the mount itself. Too much noise, straw, and manure. People would buy them in shops on Western Wall Street, not up here.[12] Perhaps, but wouldn't there be less chaos and more calm if they brought sacrificial animals up here early, before the crowds, or in small herds as needed throughout the day? The merchants could assess the demand and dispatch young boys to replenish the supply.

All four Gospels locate the table turning "in the temple." Indeed, that seems to be a key detail in their story, which story is not about Jesus denouncing trade *per se* but about Jesus opposing those who exploit and defile holy space.

John's decision to locate this episode at the *beginning* of Jesus's ministry (John 2:13–22), rather than during Jesus's last week (as in the Synoptics), probably says more about John's Christology than Jesus's chronology. John wants us to see Jesus as the *new temple*—the place where God's glory was fully present (2:21; cf. 1:14; 17:22–24; 2 Chron. 7:1–3). But even if John relocated the story (and Photoshopped sheep and cattle into the picture), his independent testimony corroborates the Synoptic Gospels' claim that Jesus did something aggressive and controversial on the mount under the nervous gaze of authorities whose threat advisory would already be on high during Passover.

We found shade along the east wall and proceeded silently northward until we stood directly across from the Dome of the Rock. My orthodox rabbi was keeping his distance for fear of unwittingly crossing from the ancient court of the gentiles into the sanctified space once restricted to purified Jews. Without the ashes of the red heifer, he explained, even the strictest rabbi must remain in the outer court.[13]

To our west the golden dome hovered over an incandescent blue porcelain sanctuary. For a mystical minute I considered switching religions. Not so my rabbinic guide, who was glancing around furtively. Satisfied that we were not being watched, he turned toward the dome and began speaking Hebrew in low tones.

"What did you say?" I asked when his voice fell silent.

"The government won't allow Jews to pray here," he began. "But *here* is where I *want* God to see me. This is as close as I can get to the place God chose for his temple. The Holy of Holies was directly beneath that dome."

"Were you praying?" I pressed.

"Yes," he replied.

"What did you say?"

"I said, 'May it be your will, O my God and God of my fathers, that the temple be rebuilt speedily in our days,

"Proceeding across this towards the second court of the temple, one found it surrounded by a stone balustrade, three cubits high and of exquisite workmanship; in this at regular intervals stood slabs giving warning . . . of the law of purification, to wit that no foreigner was permitted to enter the holy place."

Josephus, *Jewish War* 5.194; cf. *Jewish Antiquities* 15.417

and give us our portion in your Torah, and there we will offer to you offerings as did our fathers in the days of old.'"

I let the words of his prayer sink in. There I was between a dome trumpeting the gilded glories of Islam and a rabbi praying fervently for a Jewish temple to arise in its place and inaugurate the apocalypse. There I was, follower of a scandalous Galilean whose provocations came six centuries *after* Solomon's temple and six centuries *before* Muhammad. Could a country preacher from Nazareth have been wiser than the wisest Jerusalem rabbi and greater than the greatest prophet? The idea that Israel's third temple had already come, that it was not built with human hands, and that its name was *Jesus*, seemed at once impossibly absurd and utterly compelling.

I suddenly remembered Levy on the bus telling me about the rebuilding of the temple.

"Why do you believe there will be a third temple?" I asked, in my most respectful tone.

"Read the prophets—it couldn't be more clear."

"And it has to be *here*," I continued cautiously, "where the Dome of the Rock is?"

"God used dust from this spot to create Adam. Abraham offered Isaac here. Jacob rested his head on that stone when he had his dream. The first and second temples were here. Yes, it will be built here. This is the center of creation."

"So will the Dome of the Rock be moved, destroyed, or left for God to deal with?"

Silence.

Hopes for a Restored Temple

Isaiah 2:2–4	In days to come the mountain of the LORD's house shall be established as the highest of the mountains, and shall be raised above the hills; all the nations shall stream to it. Many peoples shall come and say, "Come, let us go up to the mountain of the LORD, to the house of the God of Jacob; that he may teach us his ways and that we may walk in his paths." For out of Zion shall go forth instruction, and the word of the LORD from Jerusalem. He shall judge between the nations, and shall arbitrate for many peoples; they shall beat their swords into plowshares, and their spears into pruning hooks; nation shall not lift up sword against nation, neither shall they learn war any more.

Isaiah 56:6–8	And the foreigners who join themselves to the Lord, to minister to him, to love the name of the Lord, and to be his servants, all who keep the sabbath, and do not profane it, and hold fast my covenant—these I will bring to my holy mountain, and make them joyful in my house of prayer; their burnt offerings and their sacrifices will be accepted on my altar; for my house shall be called a house of prayer for all peoples. Thus says the Lord God, who gathers the outcasts of Israel, I will gather others to them besides those already gathered.
Ezekiel 37:26–28	I will make a covenant of peace with them; it shall be an everlasting covenant with them; and I will bless them and multiply them, and will set my sanctuary among them forevermore. My dwelling place shall be with them; and I will be their God, and they shall be my people. Then the nations shall know that I the Lord sanctify Israel, when my sanctuary is among them forevermore.
Ezekiel 43:6–7a, 10–12	While the man was standing beside me, I heard someone speaking to me out of the temple. He said to me: Mortal, this is the place of my throne and the place for the soles of my feet, where I will reside among the people of Israel forever. . . . As for you, mortal, describe the temple to the house of Israel, and let them measure the pattern; and let them be ashamed of their iniquities. When they are ashamed of all that they have done, make known to them the plan of the temple, its arrangement, its exits and its entrances, and its whole form—all its ordinances and its entire plan and all its laws; and write it down in their sight, so that they may observe and follow the entire plan and all its ordinances. This is the law of the temple: the whole territory on the top of the mountain all around shall be most holy. This is the law of the temple.
Zechariah 14:16–17	Then all who survive of the nations that have come against Jerusalem shall go up year after year to worship the King, the Lord of hosts, and to keep the festival of booths. If any of the families of the earth do not go up to Jerusalem to worship the King, the Lord of hosts, there will be no rain upon them.

Presuming on Grace

"Can I ask you," I continued, "about the offerings you mentioned in your prayer?"

"What about them?"

"In the New Testament it says Jesus overturned the tables of the money changers. Why would he do that?"

"Jesus was a rabbi from Galilee. Maybe he thought the city priests were corrupt. Maybe he didn't like the coins they were using for the temple tax."

"Coins?"

"Tyrian shekels."

"Tyrian? Like, from the city of Tyre?"

"Yes. The temple tax had to be paid in silver, but Rome didn't permit us to mint silver coins, so we had to get them from elsewhere."

"Why Tyre?"

"Perhaps because Tyrian shekels were so pure. Or because they weren't stamped with images of Roman emperors and phrases like *deified Caesar*."

"What was on the Tyrian shekel?"

"On one side, an eagle. On the other, the head of Tyre's god, Melkart."

"So there were thousands of tiny images of a pagan god in the temple. I see why Jesus might object."

I asked no more questions as we completed our loop, passing first the impressive but walled-up Golden Gate, which once opened toward the Mount of Olives, and then the foundation wall of the Antonia Fortress along the north side. The area was vast. A minor protest along the south wall—someone upending a few tables, say, or chasing a few merchants—would go completely unnoticed by soldiers patrolling near the Antonia barracks at the opposite end of the platform.

As soon as we completed our loop, the rabbi was eager to depart. Dismissing my offer of payment, he offered a quick blessing for me and my roommate, "Jacob," and then disappeared through one of the gates on the edge of the platform, leaving me in the shade of an olive tree. Truth is, I was glad to see him go—I was still tired from yesterday and glad for the solitude.

It hadn't always been that way. At first my solo escapades had been painful. As weeks became months, I learned how solitude could foster inner dialogue. And I learned to trade away my tidy system for an unfinished, mystery-laden story—a story in which I was, happily, only a minor character. As I looked back I realized that questions had become friends and doubt my sparring partner.

A gust summoned the dust at my feet to dance. Somewhere across the courtyard a child squealed. Farther away a tractor chugged. I closed my eyes and pictured a vast crowd of worshipers together in the plaza—Muslims, Jews, Christians. Some lay prostrate, some rocked back and forth, some raised their hands. Men stood with women, young with old. Could this place ever become a house of prayer for all the nations?

A solitary, middle-aged Palestinian in Western dress interrupted my reverie. His cautious smile separated a graying beard from a dark mustache. With guide credentials on display, Salim offered me a *special* tour of the *Noble Sanctuary*. I declined several price reductions before he withdrew in defeat. What would Jesus think, I mused, of a businessman working deals on the holy mount? Of tourist dollars trading hands at the site God chose for worship and sacrifice? Did Salim rank among the "money changers" whose commercialism turned this "house of prayer" into a "den of robbers"? As I watched him approach another customer, I couldn't picture Jesus rebuking him for corruption and contempt. Small-time merchants like Salim yearned to feed their families, not to desecrate holy space. If Jesus were here, I thought, surely he would speak kindly to this man; his rage would not target peasants but their overlords. He would, I decided, rebuke Israeli and Palestinian bureaucrats alike, for the way they play the mount like a pawn in their power games.

What drove Jesus to lash out (literally, according to John 2:15) against the merchants? I leaned against a gnarled olive trunk and pulled out my Bible—my little act of defiance against a political establishment that prohibited religious acts by non-Muslims. Part of me wanted to get arrested; most of me was glad the Bible was pocket sized.

In all three Synoptics Jesus invokes Isaiah's vision of the temple as a house of prayer[14] and then delivers a scathing rebuke: "you have made it a den of robbers" (Mark 11:17). Who was robbing whom? Was Jesus protesting unjust exchange rates? Were poor worshipers being exploited? Was the bustle of commerce making it impossible to pray? The cross-reference in Mark 11 pointed to Jeremiah 7. I glanced around—coast clear—and flipped back to the prophets.

Jeremiah 7 describes God sending the prophet to stand in the temple and call worshipers to repentance. The charges against Israel are damning: injustice; oppressing aliens, orphans, widows; shedding innocent blood; theft; murder; adultery; deception; following other gods; ignoring the prophets. God's response was clear: without faithfulness and justice in the streets, there would be no sacrifice in the temple. Those who presume they are safe from judgment by taking refuge in the temple are deceived.

Sacrifice without Justice

What to me is the multitude of your sacrifices?
    says the LORD;
I have had enough of burnt offerings of rams
    and the fat of fed beasts;
I do not delight in the blood of bulls,
    or of lambs, or of goats.

When you come to appear before me,
     who asked this from your hand?
     Trample my courts no more;
bringing offerings is futile;
     incense is an abomination to me.

. . . .

I cannot endure solemn assemblies with iniquity.

. . . .

When you stretch out your hands,
     I will hide my eyes from you;
even though you make many prayers,
     I will not listen;
     your hands are full of blood.
Wash yourselves; make yourselves clean;
     remove the evil of your doings
     from before my eyes;
cease to do evil,
     learn to do good;
seek justice,
     rescue the oppressed,
defend the orphan,
     plead for the widow.

Come now, let us argue it out,
     says the LORD:
though your sins are like scarlet,
     they shall be like snow;
though they are red like crimson,
     they shall become like wool.
If you are willing and obedient,
     you shall eat the good of the land;
but if you refuse and rebel,
     you shall be devoured by the sword;
     for the mouth of the LORD has spoken.

How the faithful city
     has become a whore!
     She that was full of justice,
righteousness lodged in her—
     but now murderers!

. . . .

Your princes are rebels
and companions of thieves.
Everyone loves a bribe
and runs after gifts.
They do not defend the orphan,
and the widow's cause does not come before them.

Therefore says the Sovereign, the LORD of hosts, the Mighty One of Israel:
Ah, I will pour out my wrath on my enemies,
and avenge myself on my foes!

Isaiah 1:11–24

Hear this, you rulers of the house of Jacob
and chiefs of the house of Israel,
who abhor justice
and pervert all equity,
who build Zion with blood
and Jerusalem with wrong!
Its rulers give judgment for a bribe,
its priests teach for a price,
its prophets give oracles for money;
yet they lean upon the LORD and say,
"Surely the LORD is with us!
No harm shall come upon us."
Therefore because of you
Zion shall be plowed as a field;
Jerusalem shall become a heap of ruins,
and the mountain of the house a wooded height.

Micah 3:9–12

The more I read Jeremiah, the more it seemed that the doomsday prophet held the key to Jesus's action in the temple. Jesus was repeating Jeremiah's call for national repentance in the face of imminent judgment. "Den of robbers" was no sound byte; Jesus was rebuking his people for presuming on grace. The second temple was no less vulnerable to judgment than the first.

Jeremiah 7, 11, 15, 18

Location	temple gate (7:2)
Sins	injustice; oppression of aliens, orphans, and widows; shedding innocent blood; idolatry (7:5–6, 9, 17–18, 30–31)
Threat	God will cause the temple's destruction (7:12, 14, 20) and send the people into exile (7:15, 34).
"Den of robbers"	A haven for villains, a hideout for bandits (7:11); a sinful people thinks the temple will keep them safe (7:4, 8, 10, 14).
Plots against Jeremiah	God tells Jeremiah that plots were devised against him (11:18); Jeremiah prays that God would take vengeance on his persecutors (15:15); Jeremiah's enemies devise plans against him (18:18).

Even Jesus's decision to upend tables had Jeremiah's imprint on it. Jeremiah once bought a clay jar only to smash it, while elders and priests looked on, to dramatize the pending destruction of Jerusalem (Jer. 19:1–15). In the light of Jeremiah, Jesus's move in the temple was provocatively prophetic, which explains his feisty reply to religious officials and the comparison to John the Baptist, a man whose *prophetic* credentials were widely respected (Mark 11:27–33).

No wonder, then, that "the chief priests and scribes" began scheming to destroy Jesus (Mark 11:18; Luke 19:47). If the temple was Israel's pride and refuge, anyone who threatened its destruction—as Jesus did on more than one occasion—would automatically be an enemy of the state. Jesus's arrest was not only inevitable. It was imminent.

Jesus foretells the temple's destruction

Luke 13:34–35	"Jerusalem, Jerusalem, the city that kills the prophets and stones those who are sent to it! How often have I desired to gather your children together as a hen gathers her brood under her wings, and you were not willing! See, your house is left to you."
Luke 19:43–44	"Indeed, the days will come upon you, when your enemies will set up ramparts around you and surround you, and hem you in on every side. They will crush you to the ground, you and your children within you, and they will not leave within you one stone upon another; because you did not recognize the time of your visitation from God."

Jesus foretells the temple's destruction

Mark 13:2 (Matt. 24:1–2; Luke 21:5–6)	Then Jesus asked him, "Do you see these great buildings? Not one stone will be left here upon another; all will be thrown down."
Acts 6:13–14	They set up false witnesses who said, "This man never stops saying things against this holy place and the law; for we have heard him say that this Jesus of Nazareth will destroy this place and will change the customs that Moses handed on to us."
Gospel of Thomas 71	Jesus said, "I shall destroy [this] house, and no one will be able to rebuild it."

Sayings and rumors about another temple

Mark 14:58 (Matt. 26:61)	"We heard him say, 'I will destroy this temple that is made with hands, and in three days I will build another, not made with hands.'"
Mark 15:29 (Matt. 27:39–40)	Those who passed by derided him, shaking their heads and saying, "Aha! You who would destroy the temple and build it in three days . . ."
John 2:18–22	The Jews then said to him, "What sign can you show us for doing this?" Jesus answered them, "Destroy this temple, and in three days I will raise it up." The Jews then said, "This temple has been under construction for forty-six years, and will you raise it up in three days?" But he was speaking of the temple of his body. After he was raised from the dead, his disciples remembered that he had said this; and they believed the scripture and the word that Jesus had spoken.

I looked up to see two armed policemen moving in my direction, making imminent my arrest for the crime of Bible study. Mark 11:11 says Jesus looked around at the temple and promptly departed. I felt the urge to follow his example.

Dialogue with a Traitor

Israeli security forces depend heavily on Palestinian collaborators to locate militants and thwart attacks. According to Gershom Gorenberg, "eighty percent of all attempted terror attacks . . . are prevented on the basis of intelligence. Much of it comes from informers."[15] Some become informers for money or business contracts; some to obtain permissions (e.g., for a Jordanian wife to join her husband in the West Bank); some are blackmailed or threatened; some are disillusioned. How-

Akeldama

ever they are recruited—willingly or under duress—Palestinian collaborators are crucial to the success of Israel's covert operations against their enemies—enemies like Sheikh Ahmed Yassin, spiritual leader of Hamas, who was killed in 2004 in Gaza by a missile from a helicopter.

Judas Iscariot is the poster boy for collaborators. The Jerusalem establishment wanted Jesus out of the way, but his popularity was on the rise and Passover was a bad time to cause a disturbance (Mark 11:18, 32; 12:12; 14:1–2, 10; Matt. 26:3–5). What they needed was intelligence. What they got was Judas, an insider, offering to lead a late-night sortie when the adoring crowds would be sleeping (John 18:3; Luke 22:6). Collaborators make things so much easier (Matt. 26:47–50).

Akeldama, where Judas's life came to an end (Acts 1:18–19), is below the Old City where the Hinnom Valley collides with the Kidron. We can thank Eusebius for identifying the spot. Whether or not he got it right, if you go you'll agree that if Judas's tragedy didn't happen there it should have. The rugged hillside is a mosaic of olive trees, dry grasses, and weathered limestone, pocked with eerie tombs, some of which would have been magnificent in Judas's day. I entered several, my flashlight illuminating arched burial shelves and body niches for some wealthy Jerusalem family. Charred walls testified to secondary use as dwellings; the stench of urine seemed appropriate, since Hinnom was the garbage dump of ancient Jerusalem. For generations the perpetual smoke and flames of this valley, Gehenna, served as a metaphor for hell. What better place, I thought, to ponder the mysterious death of a notorious sinner than in an ancient cemetery on the edge of hell itself?

As I wandered the tombs, my imagination informed me that the ghost of Judas still hovered. This was most convenient, since I was burning with questions. I sat down on a stone bench and informed the ghost that I would limit my questions to two. I interpreted its silence as consent.

First, Judas, *why* did you betray Jesus? Was your act calculated or impulsive? Were you *eager* to lead the troops to Gethsemane that night, like Saul hastening to Damascus, convinced in your soul that to eliminate a false prophet was to do God's work? Or were you simply jealous of Peter, James, and John? Did you hope the shock of arrest would nudge Jesus in a more militant direction? Or did you only want him safely out of the way before a riot broke out? Did you know his arrest would lead to condemnation and death? Or was it clear that Jesus was a marked man who would take you down with him if he wasn't removed from the scene?

Even though the Gospels are mute about your ambitions and motivations, we want to know. I doubt that you sold Jesus strictly for cash. Mark and Luke don't even mention payment until after you offer to betray Jesus (Mark 14:10–11; Luke 22:4–5).[16] Besides, thirty pieces of silver (Matt. 26:15; 27:3, 9) would amount to little more than a month's pay—hardly enough to turn a disciple into a traitor.[17] That you returned the money when you realized he was innocent (Matt. 27:3) means there must have been other motivations at work. All this I said to Judas.

The Gospel of John especially, but also Luke, is sure that behind you lurked the Evil One (John 6:70; 13:2, 27; 17:12; Luke 22:3; cf. Acts of Thomas 32). Judas, were you possessed by a demon, or was this their way of saying that your betrayal brought a truly cosmic battle to its climax?

"It means," said Aslan, "that though the Witch knew the Deep Magic, there is a magic deeper still which she did not know. Her knowledge goes back only to the dawn of time. But if she could have looked a little further back, into the stillness and darkness before Time dawned, she would have read there a different incantation. She would have known that when a willing victim who had committed no treachery was killed in a traitor's stead, the Table would crack and Death itself would start working backward."[18]

Did you expect to co-rule over a restored Israel? Were you a fervent nationalist—like Judas Maccabeus before you—who became disillusioned when Jesus failed to recruit others like yourself to help wage jihad against the foreign occupiers? Did you want insurgency training but get a nonviolence seminar instead? Were you upset because Jesus intended to delegate all combat to heavenly warriors? Or had Jesus's promises of the kingdom's imminent arrival begun to ring hollow? Was Jesus not the type of Messiah you expected? Is it ironic to you now that an anti-Roman agitator (if that's what you were) helped to preserve Roman social order? I think the wind picked up in response but I can't be sure.

My second question—all that was my first question—is this: Judas, how exactly did you die? Your death is one of those puzzlers that Bible-debunkers love, since Matthew and Acts describe it so differently. It's not a particularly important historical detail—no offense—but it does qualify as a nice test case on the matter of historicity. If both Matthew and Luke describe the same death—yours—then it's worth asking, isn't it, whether one or both or neither got it right?

Matthew 27:5–10	Acts 1:18–20
Throwing down the pieces of silver in the temple, he departed; and he went and hanged himself. But the chief priests, taking the pieces of silver, said, "It is not lawful to put them into the treasury, since they are blood money." After conferring together, they used them to buy the potter's field as a place to bury foreigners. For this reason that field has been called the Field of Blood to this day. Then was fulfilled what had been spoken through the prophet Jeremiah, "And they took the thirty pieces of silver, the price of the one on whom a price had been set, on whom some of the people of Israel had set a price, and they gave them for the potter's field, as the Lord commanded me."	(Now this man acquired a field with the reward of his wickedness; and falling headlong, he burst open in the middle and all his bowels gushed out. This became known to all the residents of Jerusalem, so that the field was called in their language Hakeldama, that is, Field of Blood.) "For[, Peter said,] it is written in the book of Psalms, 'Let his homestead become desolate, and let there be no one to live in it'; and 'Let another take his position of overseer.'"

Judas's ghost offered little advice as I compared the two accounts. I looked first for common ground, the shared elements that would likely point to an earlier stage of the tradition. Here's my list, Judas.[19]

- You died close to the time of Jesus's death.
- Your death was sudden and violent.
- The money you received for betraying Jesus was used to purchase land.
- The purchased land was called the Field of Blood.
- Your death was in some way tied to Scripture.

About those differences.

- You died by hanging in Matthew (27:5). You burst open in Acts (1:18).
- Priests bought the field in Matthew (27:7). You did in Acts (1:18).
- "Field of Blood" comes from the "blood money" you were paid in Matthew (27:8). In Acts it names the location of your death (1:19).

One could definitely hang oneself at Akeldama. That olive tree over there with the branch overhanging the ledge would do nicely. It was harder to imagine someone falling to his death. Should we combine the two accounts and have the hangman's rope (Matthew) snap and the body fall and burst open (Luke)? I heard a preacher suggest as much, but it felt more like hermeneutical gymnastics than fair reading.

Judas, we are stuck, I think, with two conflicting accounts of your demise. What if the surviving disciples didn't know how you died? What if they knew only that you died suddenly, shortly before or shortly after Jesus's crucifixion? If the earliest Christians needed Scripture to make sense of the betrayal—how Jesus's handpicked disciple could become a traitor—might they not also look to Scripture for the details?

	Appeals to Scripture	Details from Scripture
Matthew 27:9	Then was fulfilled what had been spoken through the prophet Jeremiah,	"And they took the thirty pieces of silver, the price of the one on whom a price had been set . . . and they gave them for the potter's field . . ." (Zech. 11:12–13)
John 13:18	But it is to fulfill the scripture,	"The one who ate my bread has lifted his heel against me." (Ps. 41:9)
John 17:12	"not one of them was lost except the one destined to be lost, so that the scripture might be fulfilled."	
Acts 1:16	"Friends, the scripture had to be fulfilled, which the Holy Spirit through David foretold concerning Judas, who became a guide for those who arrested Jesus—"	
Acts 1:20	"For it is written in the book of Psalms,"	"Let his homestead become desolate, and let there be no one to live in it"; and "Let another take his position of overseer." (Pss. 69:25; 109:8)

For Matthew, the Scriptures that make sense of Judas come mostly from Zechariah and Jeremiah.

The Judas narrative in Matthew		Inspiration and parallels in the Prophets	
26:15a (Mark 14:11)	Judas requests money in exchange for helping the chief priests.	An individual requests wages from a group.	Zechariah 11:12a
26:15b; 27:3, 9	The chief priests agree to pay thirty pieces of silver for Judas's help.	The payment is thirty pieces of silver.	Zechariah 11:12b
27:4	Judas confesses that he has betrayed innocent blood.	God condemns Jerusalem for shedding innocent blood.	Jeremiah 19:4
27:5a	Judas throws money into the sanctuary and departs.	The payment is thrown into the sanctuary.	Zechariah 11:13
27:5b	Judas, betrayer of the Son of David, departs and hangs himself.	Ahithopel, betrayer of King David, hangs himself.	2 Samuel 17:23
27:6, 8	The Field of Blood is traditionally located in the Hinnom Valley.	The prophet is told to go to the Ben-Hinnom Valley.	Jeremiah 19:2
27:7	The silver shekels buy a field.	Jeremiah buys a field (in Anathoth) for seventeen silver shekels.	Jeremiah 32:7–9
27:7, 9	Priests use the blood money to buy "the potter's field" as a burial place for foreign Jews.	Money is thrown to the potter.	Zechariah 11:13 (NIV)
		Prophet sent to the potter's house.	Jeremiah 18:2
		Prophet told to buy a potter's jar.	Jeremiah 19:1

Something drew me to the story of Ahithopel (2 Sam. 15–17), a counselor in David's court who backed Absalom's attempted coup. When the tide turned against Absalom, Ahithopel committed suicide. The parallels were striking. Did the earliest Christians see their traitor's death as a reenactment of the demise of Ahithopel? The idea gained further traction when I traced the passage Jesus recites in John 13:18 to its source. Psalm 41 expresses (what I think is) David's anguish when his life was in danger because, get this, a close friend had turned on him.

My enemies wonder in malice
>> when I will die, and my name perish.
And when they come to see me, they utter empty words,
>> while their hearts gather mischief;
>> when they go out, they tell it abroad.
All who hate me whisper together about me;
>> they imagine the worst for me.

They think that a deadly thing has fastened on me,
>> that I will not rise again from where I lie.
Even my bosom friend in whom I trusted,
>> *who ate of my bread, has lifted the heel against me.*
But you, O Lord, be gracious to me,
>> and *raise me up*, that I may repay them.

By this I know that you are pleased with me;
>> because my enemy has not triumphed over me.
But you have upheld me because of my integrity,
>> and *set me in your presence forever.*

Ps. 41:5–12

I wasn't clear whether the "bosom friend" of Psalm 41 was originally the treacherous Ahithophel or not, but by the time we get to John 13, the "friend" has clearly become Judas, the one who shared Jesus's bread before his traitorous rendezvous with soldiers. The line of the psalm after Jesus's citation made me smile: David asks God to *raise him up* to vindicate him before his enemies. Even if the poet hoped only to rise *from a bed of sickness*, the phrase was waiting to be read as a preview of Jesus's resurrection. All things considered, between Samuel, Psalms, and the prophets, Israel's Scriptures offered ample resources for any early Christian storyteller who needed help scripting the downfall of the archtraitor.

As I bade farewell to Judas's ghost and began the climb toward the Old City, it occurred to me that my two questions—why did you betray Jesus and how did you die?—were less about Judas than I thought. (Again, Judas, no offense.) My first question was actually about Jesus; the second was about Scripture. Judas's betrayal shows that Jesus's message provoked wildly diverse reactions even among his intimates. The Jesus of my quest looked increasingly provocative. His message could comfort but also afflict. Not everyone would embrace the kingdom he proclaimed; some, Judas among them perhaps, reacted with an impatience that led to rejection and, in the end, treachery.

As for how Judas died—it looked more and more like we have caught the evangelists in the act of interpreting history through the lens of Scripture. They

could not bring themselves simply to compile facts without offering interpretation. Sometimes that meant taking what they knew—memories, testimonies—and "scripturizing" it, in keeping with their conviction that every detail of Jesus's suffering was part of God's plan (1 Cor. 15:3). The only way they could grasp how a close friend could betray their Lord was to embed that tragedy in a larger story and show that Judas's isolated act fit perfectly the ancient pattern.

I feel sorry for collaborators. It's all but impossible to go back once they cross that line—once they accept money, say, or give information that leads to an arrest or assassination. The high priests of espionage never take back the shekels. If the identity of a Palestinian collaborator becomes known, his life expectancy (even at home) is brutally short.

I feel sorry for Judas too. Perhaps because, like Judas, I am desperate for kingdom come and feel the temptation to bolt from Jesus's ranks.

Judas is no longer a name; it's an epithet. *Judas* means archvillain, crazed demoniac, vile traitor. When Bob Dylan used an electric guitar to "betray" folk music, someone called him Judas. For Dante, Judas is consigned to the lowest circle of hell, where he spends eternity in the jaws of Satan.

All this even though Matthew tells us Judas tried to go back. We can ask whether Judas's remorse was genuine, whether his attempt to undo Jesus's betrayal was as desperate and presumptuous as the betrayal itself. I'm inclined to think—given that Judas not only declared Jesus's innocence, but also confessed his own sin, returned the money, *and* killed himself—that the remorse ran deep. Farewell, Judas. For your soul I shall hold out hope.

First Supper

Back on the roof of the Hashimi I was watching the sun set, waiting. My Bible lay open to Mark's story of the Last Supper. The Gospels agree that Jesus ascended to Jerusalem to celebrate Passover (Matt. 26:17; Mark 14:12; Luke 22:1; John 13:1). They also affirm that Jesus shared a solemn farewell meal with his disciples shortly before his arrest, a meal the Synoptics imply was Passover.

Mark 14:12 (cf. 14:1, 14, 16): His disciples said to him, "Where do you want us to go and make the preparations for you to eat the Passover?"

Matt. 26:18: The Teacher says, My time is near; I will keep the Passover at your house with my disciples.

Luke 22:7: Then came the day of Unleavened Bread, on which the Passover lamb had to be sacrificed.

Luke 22:8: "Go and prepare the Passover meal for us."

Luke 22:11: "Where is the guest room, where I may eat the Passover?"

Luke 22:13: . . . and they prepared the Passover meal.

Luke 22:15: "I have eagerly desired to eat this Passover with you."

Several details in John's Gospel, however, appear to suggest that Jesus was crucified *before* the feast of Passover began.

1. At some point during the "supper" (13:2, 4) Jesus dismisses Judas, a departure some disciples think is to allow Judas to fetch provisions for the feast (13:29).
2. When Jesus appears before Pilate, the priests will not enter the praetorium in order to remain pure for Passover (18:28).
3. Jesus is sentenced to death around noon on the *day of preparation* for Passover (19:14).

Which version is correct? Was the Last Supper a Passover meal, or did Passover not begin until after Jesus was crucified? Did he eat roast lamb with his disciples, or was he hanging on the cross when the lambs were being slaughtered?[20] When Guilder first flagged the different passion chronologies, I was bothered enough to spend an unsatisfying weekend scouring the commentaries. Now, however, I felt more curiosity than anxiety. It wasn't that I'd abandoned hope in the Gospels' reliability; my confidence in them had actually grown. Rather, I'd come to think about them differently. For me the evangelists were no longer courthouse lawyers glaring over reading glasses at one another's witnesses. They had become nimble musicians trading riffs on a well-loved classic. Sometimes we show the Gospels more respect by letting tensions stand or by suspending judgment than by hiding behind sketchy harmonization.

Finally my wait was over. There, between Al Aqsa and the Dome of the Rock, another full moon had begun its climb. From a nearby rooftop Bob Marley supplied the soundtrack. I recalled an equally haunting scene in Madaba—a full moonrise over the Jordanian village where a tiled Jerusalem covered the floor of a Byzantine church. The city before me was no mosaic; its stones were alive, cemented by memories, eroded by fear.

A full moon is what marks the beginning of Passover, the annual feast that recalls Israel's exodus from Egypt. The Bob Marley song "Exodus," like so many Marley tunes, is peppered with biblical images of liberation from captivity:

> We know where we're going, We know where we're from.
> We're leaving Babylon, We're going to our Father land.
> Jah come to break downpression, Rule equality,
> Wipe away transgression, Set the captives free.

Marley's promised land is not Canaan but Ethiopia, but any song that conjures images of Exodus will resonate in this part of the world. My favorite exodus allusion comes in the sermon Martin Luther King Jr. preached the night before his assassination.

> Well, I don't know what will happen now. We've got difficult days ahead. But it doesn't matter with me now. Because *I've been to the mountaintop*. And I don't mind. Like anybody, I would like to live a long life. Longevity has its place. But I'm not concerned about that now. *I just want to do God's will. And He's allowed me to go up to the mountain. And I've looked over. And I've seen the promised land. I may not get there with you.* But I want you to know tonight, that *we, as a people, will get to the promised land.* So I'm happy, tonight. I'm not worried about anything. I'm not fearing any man. Mine eyes have seen the glory of the coming of the Lord.[21]

When I mentioned the exodus to an elderly man on Ben Yehuda Street in West Jerusalem, he wanted to talk about his father. A Holocaust survivor, he was an original passenger on the *Exodus 1947*, a decrepit steamer conscripted to ferry Jewish refugees from Europe to Palestine in the chaotic aftermath of World War II. The British navy intercepted the ship and forcibly returned its forty five hundred refugees to Germany, where they were held in displaced persons camps, prompting an international outcry that may have tipped the balance in the UN and ensured the partition of Palestine. In less than a year David Ben-Gurion was proclaiming the existence of the State of Israel. So history repeats: after the exodus a state is born.

Christian Zionists speak of a different exodus. Texan megapastor John Hagee has raised enough money to help ten thousand Jews immigrate to Israel, a project he modestly calls Exodus II. Every Jew who returns to the land, Hagee assures donors, brings the last days closer.

The Upper Room

"Go into the city, and a man carrying a jar of water will meet you; follow him, and wherever he enters, say to the owner of the house, 'The Teacher asks, Where is my guest room where I may eat the Passover with my disciples?' He will show you a large room upstairs, furnished and ready. Make preparations for us there." So the disciples set out and went to the city, and found everything as he had told them; and they prepared the Passover meal. (Mark 14:13–16)

When they had entered the city, they went to the room upstairs where they were staying, Peter, and John, and James, and Andrew, Philip and Thomas, Bartholomew and Matthew, James son of Alphaeus, and Simon the Zealot, and Judas son of James. All these were constantly devoting themselves to prayer, together with certain women, including Mary the mother of Jesus, as well as his brothers. (Acts 1:13–14)

When the day of Pentecost had come, they were all together in one place. (Acts 2:1)

As soon as he realized this, he went to the house of Mary, the mother of John whose other name was Mark, where many had gathered and were praying. (Acts 12:12)

It occurred to me that all these exoduses weren't simply exits; they were also arrivals. The story doesn't end with escape from captivity but with entrance into freedom, whether Rastafarian bliss, racial equality, Israeli citizenship, or something else. Nor was the original exodus over when Pharaoh freed the Hebrew slaves. It flowed from emancipation to pilgrimage to entrance into the land (Exod. 12:25–27; 13:5–16). As Bob Marley puts it: "We know where we're going, we know where we're from."

Next morning after breakfast I cut across the Old City to exit through Zion Gate onto the slope called Mount Zion, where I easily found the cobbled alley that led to a chamber known as the Cenacle. As with so many places over here, the site had memory. Franciscans in the fourteenth century restored a twelfth-century Crusader church, itself built on a fourth-century Byzantine basilica known as the Upper Church of the Apostles. Deeper still is evidence of a second- or third-century building that some scholars say was used by Jewish Christians. Indeed, the site seems to have been holy already in the first century; the Cenacle may mark not only the house where Jerusalem's earliest Christians met to worship but also the place where Jesus and his disciples gathered for the Last Supper (Mark 14:15).[22] I removed my shoes as I crossed the threshold.

My eyes had to adjust before I could tell that the room I was in was thoroughly gothic, with three monolithic columns supporting ribbed vaults that spread toward the four winds. There beneath the stone canopy two familiar questions returned: why did Jesus believe he had to die and what did he think his death would accomplish?

Given the Passover connection, we can safely assume that as the disciples prepared and ate the meal together they would have recalled the time the Israelites smeared lamb's blood on their doorposts so that God would not strike down their firstborn. To eat the meal was to reenact a compelling drama full of haste, blood, death, and rescue.

The Gospels, however, suggest that Jesus ate this meal with another death on his mind.[23]

> Mark 14:21 (Matt. 26:24; Luke 22:22): For the Son of Man goes as it is written of him, but woe to that one by whom the Son of Man is betrayed!

> Mark 14:24 (Matt. 26:28; Luke 22:20): This is my blood of the covenant, which is poured out for many.

> Mark 14:27 (Matt. 26:31): You will all become deserters; for it is written, "I will strike the shepherd, and the sheep will be scattered."

> Luke 22:15: I have eagerly desired to eat this Passover with you before I suffer.

> John 13:1: Jesus knew that his hour had come to depart from this world and go to the Father.

We might wonder if Jesus saw himself as the new Passover Lamb, whose spilled blood protects, redeems, and saves.[24] Thing is, even though Jesus's remarks about the bread and wine suggest he foresaw an imminent, unnatural death, there is little encouragement here for us to recall the slaughtered lamb.

Matthew 26:26–29	Mark 14:22–24, 29	Luke 22:19–20	1 Corinthians 11:23–26
While they were eating,	While they were eating,	Then	The Lord Jesus . . .
Jesus took a loaf of bread, and after blessing it he broke it, gave it to the disciples, and said,	he took a loaf of bread, and after blessing it he broke it, gave it to them, and said,	he took a loaf of bread, and when he had given thanks, he broke it and gave it to them, saying,	took a loaf of bread, and when he had given thanks, he broke it and said,
"Take, eat; this is my body."	"Take; this is my body."	"This is my body, which is given for you.	"This is my body that is for you.
		Do this in remembrance of me."	Do this in remembrance of me."
Then he took a cup, and after giving thanks he gave it to them,	Then he took a cup, and after giving thanks he gave it to them,	And he did the same with the cup after supper,	In the same way he took the cup also, after supper,
	And all of them drank from it.		
saying,	He said to them,	saying,	saying,
"Drink from it, all of you; for			
this is my blood of the covenant, which is poured out for many for the forgiveness of sins.	"This is my blood of the covenant, which is poured out for many.	"This cup that is poured out for you is the new covenant in my blood.	"This cup is the new covenant in my blood.

see Exod. 24:4-8; Lev. 4:3, 7

Matthew 26:26–29	Mark 14:22–24, 29	Luke 22:19–20	1 Corinthians 11:23–26
			Do this, as often as you drink it, in remembrance of me." For as often as you eat this bread and drink the cup, you proclaim the Lord's death
I tell you, I will never again drink of this fruit of the vine until that day when I drink it new with you in my Father's kingdom."	Truly I tell you, I will never again drink of the fruit of the vine until that day when I drink it new in the kingdom of God."		until he comes.

How did Jesus understand his death? Our sources tell us that Jesus saw himself dying *for others* and that he expected his blood would inaugurate *a covenant*. What would his disciples, crumbs in beard, wine on lips, have done with such cryptic testimony? Were they too fearful to ask for elaboration? Too distracted by private pipe dreams? Or did some of them sense in those remarks a flicker of sacredness, a flash of cosmic singularity, like when the moon rises full over the Temple Mount?

As I reread the story of the Last Supper I took notes:

- Mark's Jesus has them drink the wine *before* he tells them it was his blood. Did Jesus know how utterly offensive his remarks would sound?
- All three Synoptics refer to blood *poured out*. That sounds like sacrifice, not crucifixion.
- "Forgiveness" language appears only in Matthew (26:28). The others say nothing about Jesus's death as an offering *for sin*. This matches the feast of Passover, which isn't so much about sin as emancipation. The blood of the lamb didn't cover the Israelites' transgressions; it shielded them from imminent death and guaranteed passage out of Egypt. Eating the lamb did not supply

I hate the sight of blood. I can't even watch when the doctor sticks me with a needle. I don't like thinking about the bloody hands of the priests or about knives slitting throats of lambs and bulls. Truth is, I don't understand why God would ordain the (bloody) death of Jesus.

For nine years of my life, we attended a church that took Jesus's *blood* very seriously. *There's power in the blood of the lamb*, we would sing. *Nothing but the blood of Jesus.* The most disturbing image I can recall was: *There is a fountain filled with blood drawn from Emmanuel's veins.* In that spiritual universe, the death of Jesus was about atonement—payment for sin—and there was a direct correlation between the sinfulness of humanity and the intensity of Jesus's pain. As we passed the bread and sipped the wine, we conjured images, sensations of Jesus's suffering on our behalf. I got pretty good at it. Every week, in my head, I directed a passion play that rivaled *The Passion of the Christ*.

As I pondered my blood-soaked childhood, a group of noisy teens spilled into the Cenacle. Clearly tired and hungry, they were unimpressed to be visiting one more holy site. Some of them found walls to lean against; others formed gossipy circles. One could be heard whining to a pair of middle-aged women—evidently chaperones—who feigned concern.

"Father Dan!" someone squealed.

In the doorway a tall man was removing a brown leather Stetson. His weathered face was half-hidden behind a white beard. Unkempt gray hair was beginning to thin. Except for the clerical collar, he could have been a founding member of the Grateful Dead.

Father Dan surveyed the scene, flashed a smile, strode toward a column, and dropped to the floor. In seconds the frazzled group was reborn. Like moths to flame, two dozen teens moved unbidden toward their master. Out of his shoulder bag Cowboy-Priest produced a loaf of French bread, which was passed quickly among grateful followers as he began to converse. These sheep didn't need a sermon.

Father Dan uttered no reprimand to the snobs, nor did he extend forgiveness to the whiners. He simply came among them and offered himself.

For me the kids became Jesus's weary band, worn down by travel and fear, plagued by petty conflict and self-absorption. Jesus's disciples didn't need another warning about the road ahead or a capstone lecture on Passover. They weren't even seeking his forgiveness. What they needed was simply Jesus, whose bread they ate and wine they drank. Broken bread is not only a symbol of death; it is sustenance. Life.

Father Dan produced a harmonica and suddenly everyone was singing. Together. In harmony. Mark's Gospel says Jesus and the disciples sang a hymn before they left for the Mount of Olives. I waited until their song was done and slipped out.

CHAPTER 7

This Side of the Tomb

In which Norm mourns a death wish, rides a bus to nowhere, and startles a tomb raider.

MONTY PYTHON'S LIFE
OF BRIAN, SCENE 31

REG: I should point out first, Brian,
. . . that we are not in fact the rescue committee.
However, I have been asked to read the following
prepared statement on behalf of the Movement. . . .
"Your death will stand as a landmark in the
continuing struggle to liberate the parent land from
the hands of the Roman Imperialist aggressors.
. . . Signed on behalf of the P.F.J., et cetera."
And I'd just like to add, on a personal note, my own
admiration for what you are doing for us, Brian, at
what must be, after all, for you, a very difficult time.

Slouching toward Gethsemane

Up ahead was a commotion. I was returning to the Mount of Olives to relive Jesus's final night with his disciples. Lion's Gate, the Old City's only eastern exit, was blocked by Israeli security. Guns, barricades, a jeep with light spinning. Three teens huddled off to the side, detained for questioning or perhaps caught with invalid IDs. Security is usually tighter on Fridays, but today was Wednesday.

An officer beckoned me forward and spoke in perfect English.

"There's been a terror attack in Jerusalem," he said, reading the confusion on my face.

"Was anyone killed?"

"Three, I think. Dozens wounded."

"A suicide bomber?"

"An Arab from East Jerusalem drove a damn bulldozer down Jaffa Street."

"A bulldozer?"

"I think he was working construction near the Central Bus Station. Plowed his shovel into a bus, crushed a van, some cars. Finally someone shot him."

"Damn," I said. No other words came to mind.

"Be careful today," he said ominously. "There may be more violence."

> The blood-dimmed tide is loosed, and everywhere
> The ceremony of innocence is drowned.
>
> Yeats, "The Second Coming"

I slouched toward Gethsemane under the weight of three senseless Israeli deaths and the summary execution of their attacker. Each side of the conflict would fit today's tragedy into its own narrative, offer its own commentary, and promote its own agenda. In West Jerusalem there would be calls for restrictions on Arab-Israeli movement and for the destruction of the man's home. In the West Bank and Gaza some were sure to declare the vigilante a hero. Unlike the lamb's blood smeared on the Israelites' lintels, the tide of blood that today flooded Jerusalem's streets wouldn't protect anyone.

I crossed the bridge and slipped into the grounds of the Church of All Nations, where Christian tourists hop off the bus to file around a square of gnarly olive trees while recalling Jesus's prayer, "Not my will but thine be done."

Gethsemane is surely one of the most dramatic moments in the Gospels. Cool night, full moon, unconscious disciples, anguished master, clubs, swords, lanterns, a traitor's kiss, an arrest—it's all there. The glimpse we get of Jesus in prayer is painful. Almost voyeuristic. Whether or not the location was exactly right, I found myself praying for the Israeli and Palestinian families now mourning their dead.

According to Guilder, it is almost certain that Jesus came to this hillside with his disciples and prayed shortly before his arrest. Guilder made his case in class by appealing first to *multiple attestation*: differing versions of this tradition appear in all four Gospels as well as Hebrews (5:7–8), so we can assume they (or their sources) were drawing on historical memory. Guilder next invoked the criterion of *embarrassment*: early Christians would hardly invent a scene in which Jesus's closest disciples dozed off at his greatest hour of need. Nor were they likely to paint Jesus as fearful and frail.

Guilder also thought the episode goes "against the grain" of the Gospels: the anguished Jesus in this story contrasts sharply with the evangelists' standard depiction of him calmly foreseeing death and embracing it as part of his calling. So the evangelists didn't make this up; something memorable happened here that night—something that revealed a side of Jesus normally hidden from view.

Both Luke and John say Jesus came here often, but neither explains why. Was it to escape the crowds? To enjoy the view? John says they *entered into* a *garden*, perhaps a walled orchard or cultivated plantation. Matthew and Mark call it *Gethsemane*, a word that means "oil press." Looking around, I had no doubt that the oil in question came from olives.

Matthew 26:30, 36	Mark 14:26, 32	Luke 22:39–40a	John 18:1–2
they went out to the Mount of Olives	they went out to the Mount of Olives	went, as was his custom, to the Mount of Olives	He went out with his disciples across the Kidron valley . . .
Jesus went with them	They went	when he reached	where there was a garden, which he and his disciples entered.
to a place called Gethsemane	to a place called Gethsemane	the place	Now Judas . . . also knew the place, because Jesus often met there with the disciples.

Everything I knew about olives I had learned from a remarkable man I met in the northern West Bank town of Jenin. When I visited Nasser, he proudly drove me to a hill outside Jenin to show me the large hole in the ground where a new plant would soon be processing olives from eight hundred local farmers. The hole was deep, he said, because they planned to store the oil underground to keep it cool.

If Gethsemane was an oil press, I reasoned, wouldn't there be a storage cave in the vicinity? I remembered the large cavern a few yards down the hill and across the road where pilgrims visit the traditional Tomb of the Virgin. When I arrived, the large door was locked tight. The heightened security today must be keeping pilgrims away, I thought. Scanning the scene, my eye caught sight of a narrow alley lined by high stone walls. The open door at the end of the alley was what got my attention. Over the lintel a single word was chiseled into the stone:

GETHSEMANI

Above that was a second word, not chiseled but painted:

GROTTA

The cave of Gethsemane? Entering eagerly, I almost collided with an old man, who spoke but one word in a thick Italian accent.

"Clo-sèd."

"Closed?" I tried to look devastated. "Can I have a quick look?"

"No possible. Polizia."

In the Middle East "not possible" is merely the starting point for negotiations.

"This is *Gethsemane*?" I pressed, switching to my earnest face.

"You not see sign?"

"I thought Gethsemane was up the hill at the church."

"This what everyone think."

"Was this cave used for storing olive oil?" I asked.

It worked. He hesitated. Then beckoned. "Come."

I followed him down the stairs into the cave. It measured maybe thirty by sixty feet. In a niche at one end was an altar.

"See," he commanded. He was pointing at a gutter near the entrance. "Drain for water." Then, pointing at a steel grate in the floor: "Big cistern down."

He hurried me across the room. I thought he wanted to sell me an icon.

"See hole?"

There was a square recess in the side wall near the altar.

"For olive press. Come."

He led me next to a table loaded with icons and religious jewelry, where he pointed at a picture—a sketch of an ancient press. A horizontal beam, braced at one end, was loaded with weights to crush the olives and release the oil. Nasser would love this, I thought, and bought the picture for a few shekels.

"Go now," he said, nudging me toward the exit.

Beam Olive Press

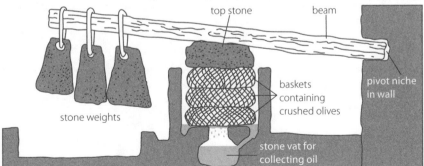

I left the grotto wearing a smile. Had I stumbled into the place where Jesus and his disciples spent their last night?[1] Did the disciples nod off in the dry warmth of this cave while Jesus, unable to sleep, needing to pray, left the lamplight to venture alone into the chilly dark?

Uphill from the grotto and past the garden was a tiny snack shop with a great view across the valley. I bought a Coke, found shade, and returned to the story. The margin of my Bible pointed me to 2 Samuel 15. As I'd learned down in Akeldama, this chapter tells of David's hasty escape from Jerusalem during his son's attempted coup. David, we read, crossed the "Wadi Kidron" (15:23) and then headed "up the ascent of the Mount of Olives," weeping as he went (15:30). Before he ascends, however, the distraught King David pauses long enough to talk about the will of God:

> If I find favor in the eyes of the Lord, he will bring me back and let me see both [the Ark] and the place where it stays. But if he says, "I take no pleasure in you," here I am, let him do to me what seems good to him.
>
> 2 Sam. 15:25–26

The parallels were impressive: a grieving king, within a Frisbee throw of Gethsemane, asks God to remove his humiliation and restore him to the throne. You can almost hear him say, "Not my will but thine be done."[2] Suddenly the praying Jesus was a second David.

Martyr in Palestine

Guilder says we know that the evangelists found the Gethsemane episode difficult because three of them turn from the stark agony depicted in the fourth. Compared to Mark, Matthew and Luke use progressively softer tones. John's Jesus challenges directly the very idea that he desired to avoid the cross. [3]

Mark 14:32–36	Matthew 26:36–39	Luke 22:40–42	John 12:27–28, 30; 18:11[4]
said to his disciples, "Sit here while I pray."	said to his disciples, "Sit here while I go over there and pray."	said to them, "Pray that you may not come into the time of trial."	
began to be distressed and agitated	began to be grieved and agitated		
"I am deeply grieved, even to death"	"I am deeply grieved, even to death;		"Now my soul is troubled.
threw himself on the ground	threw himself on the ground	knelt down	
prayed that, if it were possible, the hour might pass from him.	and prayed	prayed	And what should I say—
"Abba, Father, for you all things are possible;	"My Father, if it is possible,	"Father, if you are willing,	'Father, save me from this hour'? No, it is for this reason that I have come to this hour. Father, glorify your name." Then a voice came from heaven, "I have glorified it, and I will glorify it again." . . . Jesus answered, "This voice has come for your sake, not for mine." . . . "Put your sword back into its sheath.

Handwritten annotations:
- *Jesus isn't distressed. His concern is for the disciples.*
- *Jesus doesn't fall on his face, he kneels.*
- *Jesus's request becomes a polite condition.*
- *Jesus does not refer to what is possible but to what God wills.*
- *Jesus refuses to ask for deliverance.*

Mark 14:32–36	Matthew 26:36–39	Luke 22:40–42	John 12:27–28, 30; 18:11[4]
remove this cup from me; yet, not what I want, but what you want."	let this cup pass from me; yet not what I want but what you want." ...second time and prayed, "My Father, if this cannot pass unless I drink it, your will be done."	remove this cup from me; yet, not my will but yours be done."	Am I not to drink the cup that the Father has given me?"

Jesus makes a direct request.

Jesus's statement about the cup answers the Synoptic question.

Mark, then, is the Gospel most willing to paint Jesus as troubled, grief stricken, even terrified. Not only does Jesus ask God to remove the cup, but he reminds God that it lies entirely within the realm of possibility to do so: "for you all things are possible; remove this cup from me" (Mark 14:36). Since Mark never says outright that God sent Jesus *to* die, Jesus's prayer sounds more like a simple plea for rescue than an attempt to change the divine mind.[5] Either way, one has to wonder how this remarkable request came about. Was Jesus buckling under the weight of his mission? Was he doubting his calling? After telling others to take up their crosses, was he now reluctant to bear his own?

> I only want to say, If there is a way
> Take this cup away from me for I don't want to taste its poison
> Feel it burn me, I have changed I'm not as sure as when we started.
>
> *Jesus Christ Superstar*

> Abba, Father, we've been together a long time. I never asked to be chosen, but, I always obeyed. You've done many miracles for others.... Now you ask me to be crucified. Can I ask you one last time? Do I have to die? Is there any other way? Do I have to drink from this cup? Can't you take it away from me?
>
> *The Last Temptation of Christ*

What would it be like for Jesus's prayer to be answered affirmatively? He knew that the vocation of a prophet routinely included death, and he may have seen his own death as a required ordeal—the night before the dawn of a new age. Was he now proposing an alternative ending? One in which the king claims the throne without a struggle?

Given the intersecting trajectories of Jesus and the temple authorities, I could imagine for Jesus only one alternative to dying. Killing. To avoid the cross Jesus would need a crusade. He would have to trade in the cup for a coup. His disciples, after sufficient training, could be Jihadis for Jesus.[6] Zechariah promised, after all, that God would one day stand on the Mount of Olives. Why not invite God (along with, say, twelve legions of angels; Matt. 26:53) to drive out the foreign occupiers, purify Israel's worship, and install Jesus as her righteous king?[7]

Like the phantom who refused to tell Ebenezer Scrooge whether his vision was of "things that Will be," or "things that May be only," God does not tell Jesus whether his sufferings were written in stone or sand. God's response only becomes clear when the police arrive: there will be no rescue. Salvation will be through, not from, death.[8] However fleeting was Jesus's plea for rescue, the Gospels contend that Jesus never wavered in his resolve to accept God's will. Jesus trusted his life not to fate but to his Father.

The sad irony sank in that I was discovering Jesus's zeal for life on a day when another man from Jerusalem had shown himself zealous for death. Did the Jaffa Street attacker spend his final hours torn, like Jesus, between fulfilling his mission and saving his life? Did he too summon friends for support? Did he secretly hope they would rescue him from himself, or only that they would honor his memory? Was he seeking to avenge someone else's death, or only hoping that God would reward his?

The vast majority of martyrs in Palestine are not suicide bombers, let alone suicide bulldozer drivers. The attacker's mother would cry *shahid* ("martyr") from her rooftop, but so would the mother of a Palestinian fighter killed in battle, a pedestrian felled by cross fire, or a sick person whose ambulance was held too long at a checkpoint. In cities like Nablus and Jenin, martyr posters go up quickly after a deadly shootout or civilian casualty. They blanket the walls of public buildings, new martyrs hiding the tatters of older ones, with only wind and rain permitted to remove them. Which means many children walk daily to school eye-to-eye with gun-clutching fighters whispering for others to take their place. Three of the students I met in Nablus wore the image of a fallen brother or cousin around their necks. In the bowels of the conflict violent death is part of life. And voluntary-death-in-the-cause-of-liberation wins great honor.

Muslims are not alone in embracing martyrs and celebrating voluntary death. Christians honor their martyrs as well. *The Martyrdom of Polycarp*, required reading in my church history class, recounts the death of a second-century bishop.

At length the lawless men, seeing that his body could not be consumed by the fire, commanded an executioner to go up and stab him with a dagger, and when he did this there came out a dove, and much blood, so that the fire was quenched and all the crowd marveled that there was such a difference between the unbelievers and the elect.[9]

The striking thing about Polycarp's story is how much it parallels Jesus's.

- God tells Polycarp how he will die.
- A traitor discloses his whereabouts to the Romans.
- He is found in a large upper room.
- Polycarp refuses to escape, saying, "God's will be done."
- He prays for two hours before being taken away.
- He is arrested by an officer named Herod.
- He is transported to the city on an ass.
- Crowds demand his execution.
- He prays again just before they light the pyre.
- He is stabbed with a dagger and much blood comes out.

Even though the writer has clearly embellished history to present old Polycarp as a Christ figure, this Polycarp never asks God to let the cup pass. Indeed, he is eerily eager to drink from it.[10] For Polycarp, following Jesus meant *wanting* to die.

Jews, likewise, celebrate their fallen heroes, chief among them the Maccabean martyrs. According to 4 Maccabees, Eleazar and his band of brothers neither shrunk from torture nor pled for deliverance:

> You do not have a fire hot enough to make me play the coward.
>
> 4 Macc. 10:14[11]

Like Polycarp, they were eager to die for God:

> Tyrant, they are splendid favors that you grant us against your will, because through these noble sufferings you give us an opportunity to show our endurance for the law.
>
> 4 Macc. 11:12[12]

Some even hoped that their holy deaths would bring atonement and reconciliation to their people. Inspired by Isaiah 53:11–12, they believed that one innocent victim could save many:

You know, O God, that though I might have saved myself, I am dying in burning torments for the sake of the law. Be merciful to your people, and let our punishment suffice for them. Make my blood their purification, and take my life in exchange for theirs.

4 Macc. 6:27–29[13]

So how should we define *martyr*? Is it a victim whose cause is noble? Someone who repudiates violence? Must a martyr die so that others may live? May they be driven by hopes of vindication in the next life, or does self-interest diminish the value of their death?

However we define martyrdom, Jesus's death seems to qualify. Like the Maccabees, Jesus saw his death as a willful act of resistance and believed it was essential for Israel's redemption. Jesus may have followed them in believing his death would deflect wrath and summon mercy. And like them Jesus expected God would respond with vindication. Unlike the legendary Maccabees, however, Jesus did not die defending Jewish law, nor did he scoff at pain or suppress his desire to avoid it.

Like Polycarp and the early Christian martyrs, Jesus identified with the persecuted prophets before him. Instead of fleeing the authorities, Jesus confronted them. But unlike Polycarp, Jesus was not mentally detached from his flesh. He accepted death but did not seek it.

Like many Muslim *shuhada*,[14] Jesus saw himself locked in cosmic combat on the side of God. Unlike them, he refused to wield swords, bombs, or bulldozers, and he likewise forbade his followers from violence (John 18:10–11; Matt. 26:52). His martyrdom consisted not only in dying for what he knew but also in choosing not to fight for it. When Jesus told Peter to sheathe his sword, he was rejecting not only the disciple's fledgling crusade but every crusade since that has sought to advance righteousness through violence.

As I finished my Coke and rose to leave, I nodded a farewell to the shop owner.

"*Ma'asalaama*," came the response.

"What does *ma'asalaama* mean?" I asked.

"Go in peace, without fear," he replied.

"*Ma'asalaama*," I said and waved.

This city needs more *peace* and less *fear*, I thought on my descent. I wondered whether Jesus, as he descended in police custody, bore his distress and grief with him, or whether peace and clarity had returned. One thing was sure: he drew no strength from his band of disciples; all had fled in fear. The same ones who drank eagerly from the cup of blessing at dinner refused to sip from the cup of sorrows in the garden, not realizing that the two cups were the same.[15]

Lion's Gate was stilled clogged with barricades and a queue of Palestinians. As an officer waved me through, beneath the quartet of stone lions that gives the gate its name, I imagined Jesus entering the city under police escort. Not until I was almost back at my hotel did I remember the name this gate had among local Christians: St. Stephen's—in honor of the first Jerusalem martyr to die in Jesus's name.

Two Triangles

The invitation came out of the blue. Almost literally. I was up on the roof of the Hashimi sipping mint tea and watching a rare cloud approach from the Mediterranean when a group of Europeans burst through the door. They spoke Italian but greeted me in near-perfect English. Turns out they were lawyers and journalists investigating the Israel–Palestine conflict. In the morning they were touring Hebron. Would I like to join them? After four days in the École library basement I had become Lazarus in his tomb. Both of us required only one invitation to come forth.

I should back up to explain what had been keeping me off the streets. I was pursuing two questions:

1. Why did the religious leaders want Jesus dead?
2. Why did the Roman government sentence him to death?

Jewish Hearing

Beneath the Jewish Quarter of the Old City, not far from the Temple Mount, archaeologists have unearthed several palatial estates that may have belonged to priestly families in the time of Jesus. One residence covers sixty-five hundred square feet. I'll just say that if Jesus's night hearing before the Sanhedrin (Mark 14:53–65; 15:1) didn't happen there, it should have.

The initial allegation seems to be that Jesus had spoken against the temple (Mark 14:58; cf. 13:2; 15:29), a charge that grew in plausibility after his provocative act of overturning the tables (Mark 11:18; Luke 19:47). But this was not the only reason for Jesus's opponents to sound the alarm. According to John's Gospel, the main topic of the Jewish hearing was Jesus's surging popularity.

> So the chief priests and the Pharisees called a meeting of the council, and said, "What are we to do? This man is performing many signs. If we let him go on like this, everyone will believe in him, and the Romans will come and destroy both our holy place and our nation."
>
> John 11:47–48

Were Jesus to spark a popular uprising, the entire nation would suffer from Roman reprisals. Furthermore, the priests and elders presumably felt responsible to protect their people from false prophets. They saw Jesus's beguiling stories and wondrous deeds as the seductions of a deceiver (John 5:18; 16:2; 19:7)[16] and believed, no doubt sincerely, that such evil should be purged from their midst before more people were led astray.

> If prophets or those who divine by dreams appear among you and promise you omens or portents, and the omens or the portents declared by them take place, and they say, "Let us follow other gods" (whom you have not known) "and let us serve them," you must not heed the words of those prophets or those who divine by dreams; for the LORD your God is testing you. . . . But *those prophets or those who divine by dreams shall be put to death for having spoken treason against the LORD your God*—who brought you out of the land of Egypt and redeemed you from the house of slavery—to turn you from the way in which the LORD your God commanded you to walk. *So you shall purge the evil from your midst.*
>
> Deut. 13:1–5

Before this trip I didn't think one could mount a *biblical* case against Jesus. I assumed that his priestly opponents were insincere, consumed by professional jealousy, and corrupted by power politics. Now, in a land of holy books and religious zealots, I realized that the burden would have been on Jesus to prove he wasn't dangerous.

According to Matthew and Mark, the focus of the interrogation shifted abruptly from Jesus's speech about the temple (Mark 14:58–60) to Jesus's claims about himself (Mark 14:61). At first I couldn't see the logical connection. Then I read Nathan's prophecy in 2 Samuel 7.

> I will raise up your offspring after you . . . , and I will establish his kingdom. He shall build a *house* for my name, and I will establish the *throne* of his kingdom forever. I will be a *father* to him, and he shall be a *son* to me.
>
> 2 Sam. 7:12–14

David learns that his heir will not only reign as king but also build God's house as God's beloved son. It looks like the High

Priest wanted to know if Jesus's posture toward the temple was his way of posing as God's Anointed.[17] At which point Jesus decides to up the ante. Using thoroughly biblical language, Jesus predicts his own vindication as the *Son of Man*.[18] Today you may be my judge, he says, but soon I will be yours.[19] No wonder the high priest tore his robe and cried blasphemy.

Matthew 26:63–65	Mark 14:61–63	Luke 22:67–71
Then the high priest said to him, "I put you under oath before the living God,	Again the high priest asked him,	They said,
tell us if you are the Messiah, the Son of God."	"Are you the Messiah, the Son of the Blessed One?"	"If you are the Messiah, tell us."
Jesus said to him, "You have said so.	Jesus said, "I am;	He replied, "If I tell you, you will not believe; and if I question you, you will not answer.
But I tell you,	and	
From now on		But from now on
you will see the Son of Man **seated at the right hand of Power**	'you will see the Son of Man **seated at the right hand of the Power**,'	the Son of Man will be **seated at the right hand of the power of God**."
and coming on the clouds of heaven."	and 'coming with the clouds of heaven.'"	
		All of them asked, "Are you, then, the Son of God?" He said to them, "You say that I am."
Then the high priest tore his clothes and said, "He has blasphemed!	Then the high priest tore his clothes and said,	Then they said,
Why do we still need witnesses?"	"Why do we still need witnesses?"	"What further testimony do we need? We have heard it ourselves from his own lips!"

Daniel 7:13–14

As I watched in the night visions, I saw one like a human being coming with the clouds of heaven. And he came to the Ancient One and was presented before him. To him was given dominion and glory and kingship, that all peoples, nations, and languages should serve him. His dominion is an everlasting dominion that shall not pass away, and his kingship is one that shall never be destroyed.

Psalm 110:1–2

The Lord says to my lord, "**Sit at my right hand** until I make your enemies your footstool." The Lord sends out from Zion your mighty scepter. Rule in the midst of your foes.

As for what Jesus meant by the coming of the Son of Man, the Gospels seem to offer several options.[20] In Matthew Jesus says that "from now on" his opponents will witness his exaltation. A day later it begins to happen when they "see" the sky darken (Matt. 27:45), the temple curtain tear (Matt. 27:51), the earth shake, and the tombs open (Matt. 27:51–52; cf. 28:2–4, 11–15). In Luke, meanwhile, Jesus before the Sanhedrin does not promise to "come on the clouds" at all. Jesus's vindication takes place when he sits down at God's right hand. Whatever Jesus may have meant, the high priest heard Jesus's cryptic remarks as an audacious affront to God's honor and, I suspect, as a direct assault on his role as God's representative.

Pilate's Verdict

The Gospels tell us that Pilate dismissed the charges brought against Jesus (Mark 15:14; Luke 23:4; John 19:4) but nevertheless ordered his execution. Why? Did the governor regard Jesus as a treacherous insurgent, or simply a preacher whose provocations diminished the emperor's dignity? Was this Galilean a genuine threat, or an annoyance—like a mosquito in the dark—whose elimination would appease Jerusalem's agitated leaders? Sadly, our hardest (literally) piece of evidence—the placard hanging on the cross—doesn't tell us whether Pilate's verdict was sincere or cynical.

Matthew 27:37	Mark 15:26	Luke 23:38	John 19:19, 21–22
Over his head they put the charge against him, which read,	The inscription of the charge against him read,	There was also an inscription over him,	Pilate also had an inscription written and put on the cross. It read,
"This is Jesus, the King of the Jews."	"The King of the Jews."	"This is the King of the Jews."	"Jesus of Nazareth, the King of the Jews." . . . Then the chief priests of the Jews said to Pilate, "Do not write, 'The King of the Jews,' but, 'This man said, I am King of the Jews.'" Pilate answered, "What I have written I have written."

I decided that Jesus was innocent but not innocuous. He was not seditious but was subversive. He was not a rebel but was a revolutionary. One might say he was good but he wasn't safe. Maybe Pilate drew a similar conclusion.

> "Ooh!" said Susan, "I'd thought he was a man. Is he—quite safe? I shall feel rather nervous about meeting a lion."
>
> "That you will dearie, and no mistake," said Mrs. Beaver, "if there's anyone who can appear before Aslan without their knees knocking, they're either braver than most or else just silly."
>
> "Then he isn't safe?" said Lucy.
>
> "Safe?" said Mr. Beaver. "Don't you hear what Mrs. Beaver tells you? Who said anything about safe? 'Course he isn't safe. But he's good. He's the King, I tell you."[21]

I was making progress but still found the scene confusing. Why would Jews denounce a fellow Jew to their enemy? Why would Pilate allow silly threats to force his hand (Luke 23:23)? Why did he appease the very group he despised (John 19:12–15)? And why would a world-class military do the bidding of a few religious zealots? For the answers to these questions, it turned out, I had to peer not into a book but out a window.

I departed with the Italians after an early breakfast. The Old City was still yawning when we arrived at Jaffa Gate, where I announced abruptly that I had to make a brief side trip. I promised the group I would meet them at the central bus station in time for the tour. Some of them looked dubious.

South of Jaffa Gate are the remains of King Herod's magnificent palace. When Rome took control of Judea in 6 CE, the palace became a Roman mansion where the governor would stay when in town, say, for Passover. This, then, was Pilate's praetorium, the place where a shackled Jesus was brought for interrogation and sentencing.

> Then the soldiers led him into the courtyard of the palace (that is, the governor's headquarters); and they called together the whole cohort. And they clothed him in a purple cloak; and after twisting some thorns into a crown, they put it on him. And they began saluting him, "Hail, King of the Jews!"
>
> Mark 15:16–18

> Then they took Jesus from Caiaphas to Pilate's headquarters. It was early in the morning. They themselves did not enter the headquarters, so as to avoid ritual defilement and to be able to eat the Passover. So Pilate went out to them and said, "What accusation do you bring against this man?"
>
> John 18:28–29

I walked south along the outer edge of the Turkish wall, looking for the ruins of three ancient steps. Though partly hidden by grass and wildflowers, they weren't hard to find. Several scholars have argued recently that these steps once ascended to a platform where Pilate sat to render judgments, in which case I was standing near where Jesus stood when his death sentence was announced.

> When Pilate heard these words, he brought Jesus outside and sat on the judge's bench at a place called The Stone Pavement, or in Hebrew Gabbatha. Now it was the day of Preparation for the Passover; and it was about noon. He said to the Jews, "Here is your King!" They cried out, "Away with him! Away with him! Crucify him!" Pilate asked them, "Shall I crucify your King?" The chief priests answered, "We have no king but the emperor." Then he handed him over to them to be crucified.
>
> John 19:13–16

> So Pilate, wishing to satisfy the crowd, released Barabbas for them; and after flogging Jesus, he handed him over to be crucified.
>
> Mark 15:15

I sat on the highest stair and pictured Jesus, exhausted after a sleepless night and destroyed by a Roman scourging. Was his mind lucid? Was he able to pray? I looked up a pair of psalms, 2 and 22, read both aloud, and then set out for the bus.

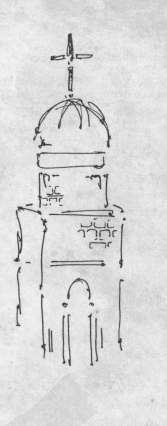

Turns out the Hebron tour was organized by veteran Israeli soldiers who'd been stationed there during the Second Intifada, the recent Palestinian uprising. After completing their military service they began collecting testimonies of fellow soldiers who had participated in acts of unnecessary violence and abuse. They called their group Breaking the Silence. In the cool of the tour bus, I had no idea how hot and contentious our trip to Hebron would be.

En route Mikhael rehearsed several chapters of Hebron's remarkable story. Genesis 23 details how Abraham paid for the cave of Machpelah, where he would later bury his wife. Abraham himself was later buried in the same cave (Gen. 25:9). Ditto for Isaac, Rebekah, Leah (49:31), and Jacob (50:13), which is why the burial site in downtown Hebron is sacred to both Muslims and Jews, and why Hebron has had more than its share of religious wars.

Hebron today bears the scars of two modern tragedies. In 1929, riots in Jerusalem spread to Hebron, where sixty-seven Jews were brutally killed and fifty more wounded. The small Jewish community in the city was evacuated. In 1994, after Hebron had passed from British rule to Jordanian to Israeli, an American-born Jewish settler, Baruch Goldstein, entered the shrine of the patriarchs with his M16, gunned down twenty nine Palestinians, and wounded one hundred fifty before he was subdued. Ever since, the site has been militarized, partitioned, and strictly controlled.

Hebron Settlers

Goldstein was part of a settler movement that, since 1968, has established a number of settlements near the tomb. Nowhere else in the West Bank do Jews and Arabs live so close together, nowhere else are settler tactics more extreme, and nowhere else are so many Israeli soldiers charged to protect so few (armed) Israeli citizens from the (largely unarmed) Palestinian population.

Breaking the Silence is facing growing opposition from the settler community. To prevent violence (settler against tourist), the police have blocked the tours, forcing BTS to take the dispute to Israel's High Court, which ruled that the tours should be allowed to resume. Our tour was the first since the ruling.

We approached Hebron through Kiriath Arba, a large settlement in the hills east of the city. When we reached the western gate, the boundary between the settlement and Palestinian Hebron, settlers were waiting. Old men and young, women and children, babies in arms and in strollers. A line of children and women, one pregnant, staked out positions in front of our bus. Some guy on a megaphone circled like Joshua around Jericho. Police jeeps and military vehicles descended.

While Mikhael worked his phone our other guide, Yehuda, in sandals and cowboy hat, stepped down to press his case with the authorities and film the settlers who were taunting him. Meanwhile the journalists among us recorded the story in ink and image—synoptic evangelists scribing an improbable gospel—as the rest of us, voyeurs all, peered out windows and tested the fit of our new, unsought identities as "restless provocateurs."

Hebron Boy

Midway through the standoff a young settler caught my eye. Maybe fourteen years old, he paced beside the bus like a caged ferret. When he spotted me, he stared back briefly, then drew several fingers across his throat. My first ever death threat.

The bitter choreography continued for two hours. The officers in uniform, although initially sympathetic to Yehuda's appeals, became, under pressure from settlers, increasingly restrictive. At first they said we could enter Hebron to visit a Palestinian family. Then only if we stayed on the bus. Then the bus could advance only a few hundred feet. These local authorities were caught between the law of the land and the tactics of settlers, between secular judges and religious zealots. The settlers were flagrantly ignoring Israeli law, but they had influential backers in Jerusalem—friends who could not be ignored without political consequence.

With the bus window framing the dispute between zealots, soldiers, and a sandal-clad prophet, another triangular spectacle—the one between the high priest, Pilate, and Jesus—came sharply into focus. Like modern Hebron, first-century Judea was under military occupation. Both the modern IDF and Pilate's Roman legions were trained to combat any uprising.[22]

Like Hebron's settlers, the priests of Jesus's day were nothing if not zealous for God and certain of God's will. Both wore tassels. Both quoted Scripture. Both called for violence against any who threatened their cause. Both won political victories even though the people at large rejected their agenda. And both groups charged their opponents with disturbing the peace and fomenting chaos, language intended to pressure the military into silencing dissident voices.

Like the IDF on the wild West Bank, Pilate's forces on Rome's eastern frontier had good reason to appease the local religious establishment and thus to reject the provocative claims of a sandaled Jew who rode audaciously down from the north with a band of odd-accented, unsuspecting followers. Both Yehuda now and Yeshua[23] then spoke out against injustice and rejected violence, and both clearly posed no physical threat to the security of the realm. The official representatives of God and Caesar decided, nevertheless, that the prophets' agenda of truth telling and reconciliation was too provocative, too dangerous. For Yehuda the result was a canceled tour; for Yeshua a death sentence. If each one was gracious in defeat, it was because he was convinced that one day a judge would vindicate his cause.

Instead of riding back to Jerusalem, I left the group at the turnoff on Hebron's north side, where service taxis shuttled Palestinians into the city. Traveling by myself without fanfare, I was soon wandering the market, sipping date juice and inflicting my Arabic on shopkeepers. I passed easily through the military check-point, ascended the stairs to the Tomb of the Patriarchs, and then, past more soldiers, out onto Shohada Street, the ethnically cleansed road that had been off-limits to our tour bus. Hebrew graffiti branded burned-out buildings. Razor wire hung from rooftops. Concrete barricades blocked alleys.

A lone boy moved toward me. Long side curls hanging below his blue knit cap identified him as a settler. I didn't understand his Hebrew, but the blow he delivered to my shoulder required no translation. Thankfully he was alone and about thirty pounds lighter than I. Not pleased to be threatened twice in one day, I took his picture with my cell and turned away.

That encounter put a new face on the tragedy. The boy's orange T-shirt read *NEVER AGAIN*, clear reference to the obscene horrors of the Holocaust, when Jewish property was seized or destroyed and when millions of Jews were imprisoned, gassed, and incinerated behind the barbed perimeters of Nazi death camps. As I glanced back to make sure he wasn't following, I noticed three words painted in English on a metal door that rusted nearby: *GAS THE ARABS*.

What shall we say when walls utter death threats, children become warriors, fear becomes hate, and violence valor? As a harmless foreigner I could inhabit both worlds, but it was obvious I was *of* neither. I sighed a prayer to the God of Abraham and set my face toward Jerusalem.

Cross and Chaos

Every Friday afternoon in Jerusalem a handful of monks in rough brown robes lead the local nuns and a hundred or so tourists on a pilgrimage across the Old

City. The men in earth tones are Franciscans. The route they follow is the Via Dolorosa, which Jesus followed on his sorrowful journey from Pilate's tribunal to the cross to the grave. More or less.

Actually, less. The present path goes back only to the fourteenth century, and today's fourteen stations weren't fully in place until the eighteenth. A more "historical" walk would begin on the west side of town at those stairs I sat on near the governor's palace. And it might have to drop the five stations that have no basis in history whatsoever.

Fourteen stations	Biblical ties
1. Pilate condemns Christ to death.	Mark 15:6–20
2. Soldiers lay the cross on Jesus.	John 19:17
3. Jesus falls for the first time.	——
4. Jesus meets his mother, who collapses in shock.	——
5. Soldiers force Simon of Cyrene to carry the cross.	Mark 15:21
6. Veronica wipes the face of Jesus.	—— (cf. Mark 5:25–34)
7. Jesus falls for the second time.	——
8. Jesus meets the women of Jerusalem.	Luke 23:27–31
9. Jesus falls for the third time.	——
10. Soldiers remove Jesus's garments.	Mark 15:24
11. Soldiers nail Jesus to the cross.	Mark 15:24
12. Jesus dies.	Mark 15:37
13. Jesus's body is taken down.	Mark 15:46
14. Jesus's body is laid in the tomb.	Mark 15:46

There was a time when I would sound the alarm whenever I smelled legend posing as history. I was the laborer in Jesus's parable who wanted to pull up the weeds that the enemy planted among the wheat (Matt. 13:28). How dare we allow Veronica, the mythical woman who wiped Jesus's face, to grow up alongside Simon of Cyrene, the historical figure Rome conscripted to carry Jesus's cross?[24] If Christianity is a *historical* religion founded on the *historical* death and resurrection of the *historical* Jesus, then Christians should avoid fictional embellishment like Superman avoids Kryptonite.

That was then, when my world was tidy. Back then answers were more interesting than questions. *Ah, but I was so much older then. I'm younger than that now.* I now understood that every historical account is someone's, that every story has a teller, and that ancient storytellers, like modern preachers, rarely announce when they slide from history into explanation into embellishment. Remembered history, like Dylan's harmonica, always bends, but the bent notes can convey just as much truth, sometimes more.

> . . . abstract threats too noble to neglect
> deceived me into thinking I had something to protect
> Good and bad, I define these terms . . . clear . . . somehow.
> . . . I was . . . much older then, I'm younger than that now.
>
> Bob Dylan, "My Back Pages,"
> on *Another Side of Bob Dylan*

I wasn't ready to venerate Veronica, but I was ready to walk with the Franciscans and to witness the passion through the eyes of tradition. The following Friday afternoon I made my way to the Umariyya Boys' School, where the weekly trek begins. Although I was early, the usually locked steel doors stood ajar, which I took as an invitation to explore. I crossed the threshold and padded quietly over the empty school courtyard. Then, voices. To avoid detection, I bounded up a flight of steps and ducked into a dark recess in the wall, an alcove lit at one end by two odd-sized openings. Instead of glass, each window framed a grid of iron bars. To my delight they opened directly on to the Temple Mount. Below was an olive grove. Farther south a row of towering cypress. Beyond these shades of green the Dome of the Rock glowed gold in the afternoon sun.

Temple Mount from Fortress

My guidebook told me that I had stumbled into more than just a room with a view. Murphy-O'Connor thinks this recess and these windows had been cut into the wall of the Antonia Fortress itself—or what remained of it after General Titus had the fifth and twelfth legions pull most of it down. I sat on the window ledge, kicked the stone, and closed my eyes. Were they stationed here—the soldiers who scourged Jesus, draped his bloody body in purple, and pressed a thorny crown onto his head? What crude jokes made the rounds about the one they crassly hailed as king? Did the legionnaire who drove in the nails sleep soundly in his barracks that night?

A crowd had assembled in the courtyard. I climbed out of my window seat and emerged from the shadows. The Franciscans, polished and choreographed, moved us like slow-motion dancers from one station to the next, and from Italian to English to Latin. One hundred thirty years of practice was showing. In a bizarre carryover from Ottoman rule, a man in a fez carrying a whip acted as our bodyguard.

Moving west along the Via Dolorosa, we remembered Jesus's condemnation and pictured the moment he took up his cross. Turning left onto El Wad, we reached the spot where it is said Jesus met his mother. Around another corner to the right, we stopped to honor (the "historical") Simon and (the "imaginary") Veronica, along with the grieving daughters of Jerusalem. I tried to stay focused on the story, but distractions were many. Shopkeepers offered batteries. Children waved postcards. Oblivious tourists obstructed our procession. Everywhere cameras created precise digital replicas of our imprecise replica of Jesus's journey. Halfway through our march the Muslim call to prayer sounded forth, drenching our Latin friars in a wave of Arabic.

By station seven, when we entered the *souq*, or marketplace, it finally occurred to me that irreverence and confusion were precisely what this walk needed. Jesus's own journey from Pilate's tribunal to Golgotha might have been more crude and frenzied than this, but it could not have been less. As I surveyed the chaos of the market, scales fell from my eyes. There was Jesus in that withered, weathered nun whose formless habit cloaked a body bent by a lifetime of faithful service. There too in the little boy with flashing eyes and missing teeth, holding out a fist of cross necklaces in hope of a sale. And somehow even there, in the burly man with the bulging fanny pack— poster boy for the affluent, accessorized church of the West. We shared little, he and I, except a cobbled path and a desire to know what following Jesus means when it is not metaphor. In the features of all these faces, and more, Christ was at play.

> for Christ plays in ten thousand places,
> Lovely in limbs, and lovely in eyes not his
> To the Father through the features of men's faces.
> Gerard Manley Hopkins, "As Kingfishers Catch Fire"

The last five stations all occur within the Church of the Holy Sepulchre. If anyone had hoped that by moving indoors we would find space for contemplation, harsh reality descended quickly. Inside the dark entryway hordes of visitors swarmed and pressed. Several tour guides held umbrellas high, like lighthouse beacons over a rolling sea of pilgrim faces. A handful of nuns bravely held vigil at the slab where tradition says Jesus's body was laid for anointing. Our guy in the fez tried vainly, sternly, to part the waters. Finally we managed to ascend the narrow steps to where two chapels, Latin alongside Greek, balance uneasily atop the hill known as Golgotha, Skull Place.

Matthew 27:35	And when they had crucified him . . .
Mark 15:24	And they crucified him
Luke 23:33	there they crucified him
John 19:18	There they crucified him

It was here "they crucified him." That's all it says. No hammer, nails, sounds, or smells.[25] Nothing about the shape of the cross or how they fixed Jesus to it.[26] Our best Gospel window on the horrors of crucifixion may be Jesus's simple "I thirst" (John 19:28), a remark that may signal severe dehydration. When the Gospels finally arrive at the climax of their story, they seem to hurry past, like the priest and Levite in the parable of the good Samaritan. It seems none can bear to look.

Paul's language of the cross is equally sparse. "We preach Christ crucified," he reminds the Corinthians (1 Cor. 1:23 RSV; cf. Gal. 3:1). Jesus was obedient unto death, "even death on a cross," he tells the Philippians (Phil. 2:8). That's it. The early Christians, Paul among them, had lots to say about the meaning of Jesus's death—it was sacrifice, example, conquest, reconciliation, revelation of love, hinge of history (2 Cor. 5:19; Col. 2:15; Heb. 9:22, 28; 1 Pet. 2:21–24; Rev. 5:6; 7:14)—but they refused to detail the physical brutality. Why was that? Was crucifixion too familiar to warrant commentary? Too distasteful? Too embarrassing?

The gore-free Gospels stand out starkly against the church of my childhood, where we sang weekly about Jesus's punctured side and bloodied head. Nor do the Gospels explain Mel Gibson's blood fixation in *The Passion of the Christ*. For all our zeal to catalog the physical sufferings of Jesus, in my low-Protestant world and in Mel's high-Catholic one, we may have overlooked a huge piece of the story the Gospels tell.

Every legionnaire knew that Roman crucifixion was at least as much about shame as it was about pain (cf. Heb. 6:6; 12:2). "They . . . mocked him . . . [and] led him away," we read (Matt. 27:29, 31; Mark 15:20), but do we cringe at the public humiliation of him and his family? They brought him to "Golgotha," it says (Mark 15:22;

"Whenever we crucify the guilty, the most crowded roads are chosen, where most people can see and be moved by this fear. For penalties relate not so much to retribution as to their exemplary effect."

Quintilian (35–95 CE), *Lesser Declamations* 274

Matt. 27:33; Luke 23:33; John 19:17), but do we remember that Rome liked to execute in public places—at a crossroads, a hilltop—to provide maximum exposure (cf. Mark 15:29)? "They divided his garments," we're told (Mark 15:24 RSV; Matt. 27:35; Luke 23:34; John 19:23), but do we blush to think of his nakedness? The cross was perversely cruel, yes, but it was also unimaginably degrading, all the more so in a culture obsessed with honor.

Americans understand guilt and avoid pain, but we don't know what to do with shame. Indeed, the premise of shows like *Jerry Springer*, *Cops*, and *Girls Gone Wild* is our collective infatuation with shame*less*ness. Here in the Middle East many would choose death over dishonor and pain over shame. What might this mean for those who dare take up their cross and follow? Perhaps bearing one's cross has as much to do with embracing insignificance and losing face as it has with the prospect of persecution.

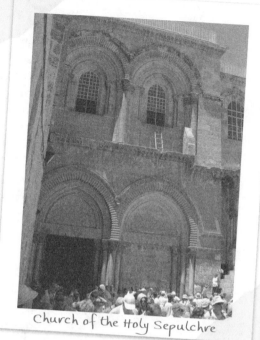

Church of the Holy Sepulchre

Since I came from a church back home that was devoid of smells, bells, candles, and robes, my first instinct on arrival at Golgotha was to look behind the sacred edifices and holy traditions for historical bedrock. The Franciscans intoned prayers, read Scripture, and swung the censer; I imagined the rocky scarp beneath my feet. Somewhere down there was an ancient limestone quarry that had become, in Jesus's day, an orchard and burial ground.

> Now there was a garden in the place where he was crucified, and in the garden there was a new tomb in which no one had ever been laid.
>
> John 19:41

At the time of the crucifixion, the site was outside Jerusalem's city walls, if not by much.

> Many of the Jews read this inscription, because the place where Jesus was crucified was near the city.
>
> John 19:20

> Therefore Jesus also suffered outside the city gate in order to sanctify the people by his own blood. Let us then go to him outside the camp and bear the abuse he endured.
>
> Heb. 13:12–13

After crushing the Jewish revolt in the second century, Emperor Hadrian constructed earthworks and terraces on the site to support a pagan temple, all of which was removed two centuries later after Helena's visit so her son, Constantine, could build a rotunda, garden, and basilica: the first Church of the Holy Sepulchre.

The perplexing state of today's church—it's a labyrinth of passageways, chapels, arches, and columns—attests to successive layers of destruction, fire, earthquake, conquest, and reconstruction. Constantine's church survived a fire during the Persian invasion of 614 CE, but it was almost completely destroyed and then partially rebuilt in the eleventh century. The Crusaders of the twelfth century are largely responsible for the building we enter today.

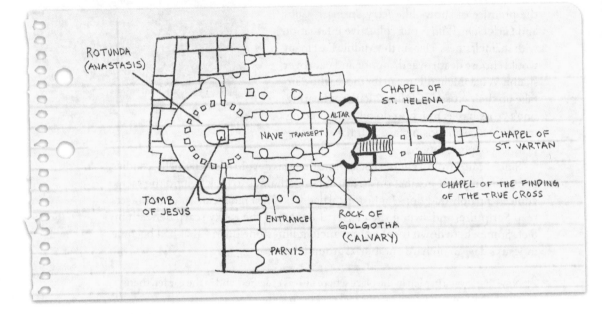

If an ancient place of shame is today highly exalted, it is also a place about which, sadly, Christians fight. The latest brawl was between the Armenians and the Greeks. (Or was it the Copts and the Ethiopians?) Typically it starts when one group charges another with violating the status quo—the precise distribution of duties and territory within the church. Tensions mount. Someone gets pushed. Israeli police must intervene.

From the heights of Calvary, I looked out over the throng of visitors. The scene was as chaotic as it was irreverent. Lamps jostled with pilgrims for space, icons posed for cameras, tapestries shimmered, and tourists shoved. Marble and mosaics ensured that nothing now visible was as it was long ago. Somewhere behind it all was the site of an innocent man's death—the sacrifice that Christians say redeemed captives and conquered violence. Somewhere here Jesus Christ became a curse so that a much older one might be broken.

I descended the steep stairs looking naïvely for a quiet corner. On my right a guide and his flock huddled around a glass case that offered a side view of the bedrock beneath the Golgotha chapels. The guide was pointing to a deep crack in the stone.

"Scripture says that when our Lord breathed his last, the earth shook and the rocks split."

The guide went on to explain that this crack, directly beneath the site of the crucifixion, was hard proof that Christ's was no ordinary death. Pilgrims took turns pressing against the glass as if to verify his claim. I thought of Susan and Lucy marveling at the stone table that cracked when Aslan, willing victim, was killed in place of treacherous Edmund. Predictably, biblical scholars see things differently: the natural fissure may explain why ancient quarrymen chose not to harvest this part of the quarry and how they inadvertently created an outcropping that served nicely for at least one public execution. So these pilgrims: were they looking at a miracle or a fault line?

The Gospels report a number of strange goings-on at the time of Jesus's death. The Synoptics describe unnatural darkness at high noon.

Matthew 27:45	Mark 15:33	Luke 23:44–45
From noon on, darkness came over the whole land until three in the afternoon.	When it was noon, darkness came over the whole land until three in the afternoon.	It was now about noon, and darkness came over the whole land until three in the afternoon, while the sun's light failed;

Matthew describes an earthquake and more:

Then Jesus cried again with a loud voice and breathed his last. At that moment the curtain of the temple was torn in two, from top to bottom. The earth shook, and the rocks were split. The tombs also were opened, and many bodies of the saints who had fallen asleep were raised.

Matt. 27:50–52[27]

Did the midday sun really go dark for three hours, and did the temple veil really tear? Was there a literal earthquake at precisely the moment of Jesus's expiration, and did it open tombs and awaken sleeping saints? Having to choose between belief and skepticism was like being trapped between somber nuns and snoozing tourists. If the Gospels are neither unedited footage nor historical fiction, their stories will always resist our attempts to classify them. It won't do to appeal to an untimely dust storm, say, or a thundercloud to explain the problem away. The point of the story is not that the Romans killed Jesus on a blustery day, but that God was actively weighing in on the side of Jesus.

Whether these events happened exactly as described or whether cosmic portents were added in the telling, you don't have to be a rabbi to hear the voice of Israel's Scriptures in the background. Matthew's earthquake seems to recall images from Ezekiel.

> As I prophesied, *suddenly there was a noise, a rattling*, and the bones came together, bone to its bone. . . .
>
> Therefore prophesy, and say to them, Thus says the Lord GOD: *I am going to open your graves, and bring you up from your graves*, O my people; and I will bring you back to the land of Israel. And you shall know that I am the LORD, *when I open your graves, and bring you up from your graves*, O my people.
>
> Ezek. 37:7, 12–13 (cf. Zech. 14:4–5; Joel 2:10)

And the noonday darkness could be an echo of Amos.

> On that day, says the Lord GOD, *I will make the sun go down at noon, and darken the earth in broad daylight*. I will turn your feasts into mourning, and all your songs into lamentation; I will bring sackcloth on all loins, and baldness on every head; *I will make it like the mourning for an only son*, and the end of it like a bitter day.
>
> Amos 8:9–10 (cf. Exod. 10:21–23; Jer. 15:9; Zeph. 1:15; Joel 2:2, 31)

For those with ears to hear, then and now, the earth groaned beneath the weight of the cross. For those with eyes to see, the skies went dark from divine abandonment (Mark 15:34; Rom. 8:32).

I was standing at the foot of the cross where unbelieving bystanders once hurled insult and ridicule, and where Bunyan's "Christian" felt a burden fall from his shoulders.

> Up this way, therefore, did burdened Christian run, but not without great difficulty, because of the load on his back. He ran thus till he came at a place somewhat ascending; and upon that place stood a cross, and a little below, in the bottom, a sepulchre. So I saw in my dream, that just as Christian came up with the cross, his burden loosed from off his shoulders, and fell from off his back, and began to tumble, and so continued to do till it came to the mouth of the sepulchre, where it fell in, and I saw it no more. Then was Christian glad and lightsome, and said with a merry heart, "He hath given me rest by his sorrow, and life by his death."[28]

My burden—my need for certitude—hadn't fallen away like Christian's, all at once. It loosened over time, as I came to accept that we never see with clarity but always through glass, that we arrive at conviction by crossing fields of probability and by placing cautious trust in testimony and tradition.

Sleeping in Church

I noticed that the Franciscans were descending to lead their motley entourage toward the rotunda, the domed shrine containing the tomb of Jesus—or what's left of it after laborers, attackers, fires, and earthquakes reduced the catacomb to a burial bench. The bench has been encased in marble and enclosed in a boxy *edicule* that is held together by scaffolding. Here, or close by, was where they laid Jesus's body. And here is where the monks halted to mark the final station of the cross.

I listened and watched the liturgy unfold but decided to find a quieter time to enter the tomb. Backing away from the crowd, I circled the edicule and spied an unguarded doorway. Inside was a small chapel, battered and smoke-charred, that I would later learn belonged to the Syrians. Low along the wall was a dark opening. Entering on all fours, I found myself in what were clearly the remains of an ancient rock-cut tomb. Radiating from the small chamber where I was crouching were several body-length niches. I slid feet first into one of them and extinguished my Maglite, my body filling the space once occupied by a shrouded, anointed, and, er, rotting corpse. I closed my eyes, glad to be horizontal after hours of standing. The death slab was smooth and cool. . . .

Voices brought me back to life. It took me a moment to remember I was lying in a tomb. A shadow was blocking the light outside the entrance. A man's arm was pointing directly at me.

"Look here," said a raspy voice.

I braced for a reprimand, but it never came. Evidently I was cloaked in darkness. The figure made no move to approach the chamber, so I remained still, hoping to stay hidden until they departed. The voice continued in American English.

"These tombs go back to the early first century. They must have been carved and used before the borders of Jerusalem expanded

to include this quarry. Jews would never build a cemetery within city walls."

"When did the city expand to include the cemetery?" The second speaker was from somewhere in the UK.

"A decade or so after Jesus's death, in the days of Agrippa the first," the American replied.

"So somewhere around here Joseph of Arimathea offered space in his family tomb to ensure Jesus had an honorable burial."

"Rental space."

"What do you mean?"

"I think the burial of Jesus was a temporary arrangement. They borrowed space in Joseph's tomb because it was handy and because the Sabbath was about to begin."

"I guess it wouldn't matter much either way if, come Easter, it was empty."

"But what if before Sunday morning someone moved Jesus's body away from Joseph's tomb and reburied it somewhere else?"

"Then one might say that although the tomb was *empty*, Jesus *didn't* rise from the dead."

"Exactly."

"Is that what you think happened?"

"I think the dead stay dead."

Suddenly from the open tomb before them came a sound that could only be a suppressed sneeze.

"My God! Someone's in there!" said the chap from Britain.

"What's going on?" said the American, his voice wavering noticeably. "Who's there?"

"Sorry," I said from the darkness. "Didn't mean to scare you."

I slid out of my niche, emerged into the light, and drew myself up under the suspicious gaze of a pair of middle-aged men.

"Guess I fell asleep in there," I said, using my sanest, most casual voice. "Mind if I listen in? You were speaking about how tombs don't give up their dead."

The Englishman wore a wool vest and cap. He threw back his head and howled. "That'll fix you, Mitch, for denying the resurrection in the Church of the Holy Sepulchre!"

Mitch clearly did not appreciate getting pranked. I couldn't see his eyes under his Stetson, but the voice was surly.

"I can't believe in a bodily resurrection anymore," he stated flatly. "This life is all there is. For me the story of the resurrection is a summons to take hold of life daily and to ignore the looming shadow of death."

"Do you think the earliest Christians saw the resurrection as a metaphor?" I asked. I wanted to follow up by asking if he still considered himself a "Christian," but Mitch ignored me completely and turned to his friend.

"Did you see the documentary *The Lost Tomb of Jesus*, Mr. Creedy?[29] The film's producers suggest that we have unearthed Jesus's family tomb. The discovery took place, they say, back in 1980 in Talpiot, a suburb of Jerusalem. The idea is that Jesus's burial *here* on Friday was a temporary arrangement. On Saturday night, say, or early Sunday morning someone moved the body. Now, thanks to a bulldozer and a journalist, we know where they took it. In fact, we even have the bone box—the ossuary—that held Jesus's bones!"

"Jesus's bones?"

"Scrawled in Aramaic on the side of one of the cave's bone boxes are the words *Jesus son of Joseph*."

"That explains all the excitement," said the one called Creedy.

"Exciting, yes, but few scholars found it persuasive. It asks us to believe too many things," said Mitch.

"Like what?"

"Like that Jesus's Galilean family owned an impressive, rock-cut tomb south of Jerusalem. Like that they would store Jesus's bones in a plain, no-frills ossuary and scratch his name in graffiti rather than legible script. Like that Jesus was married to a woman named Mariamne whose name is inscribed on another one of the ossuaries. Like that she was actually Mary Magdalene and that Jesus and Mary had a son named Judah."

My mind drifted back to when the documentary first aired. Professor Guilder invited his advisees over to watch it. Discussion afterward was tense. One student said the film dealt a death blow to Christianity as we knew it. Others pushed back. Guilder listened and then diffused the crisis by quipping that the film made Indiana Jones look like a serious archaeologist. Responsible scholars, he assured us, would say only what the evidence demanded. Not more.

Fair enough, but what if producer Simcha Jacobovici was onto something? What if Jesus's grave was empty on Easter morning because someone had already transferred his body to the family tomb?

In the weeks following the broadcast, the blogosphere went nuts, the reading of which gave me a respectable excuse to ignore homework. To me the striking thing was not the predictably hostile response of the right wing. I was more intrigued by the academic mainstream, many of whom had abandoned long ago any belief in Jesus's resurrection. Although a handful of academics liked the Jesus tomb hypothesis, most hurried to point out the speculative nature of the project, to kick at its central pillars, and to accuse its producers of disguising tabloid journalism as responsible archaeology.

The crux of the issue, for me, was whether or not the names found in the Talpiot tomb—Jesus-son-of-Joseph, Maria, Jose, Mariamene, Matya, and Judah-son-of-Jesus—were close enough to names associated with Jesus's extended family, and improbable enough as a cluster, that the only reasonable explanation would be that we had stumbled into the Jesus family tomb.

In the end I gave the Jesus family tomb theory one-and-a-half thumbs down. It had too many problems. The historical evidence that Jesus had a son is precisely zilch. Likewise, Matya is not a known relative of Jesus, and the link between Mariamene and the Magdalene is a stretch. Mark Goodacre's blog offered a great analogy:

> If in 2,000 years a tomb was discovered in Liverpool that featured the names John, Paul and George, we would not immediately conclude that we had found the tomb of the Beatles. But if we also found so distinctive a name as Ringo, then we would be interested. Jacobovici claims that the "Ringo" in this tomb is Mariamene, whom he interprets as Mary Magdalene and as Jesus's wife. . . . What we actually have is the equivalent of a tomb with the names John, Paul, George, Martin, Alan and Ziggy. . . . A cluster of names is only impressive when it is a cluster that is uncontaminated by non-matches and contradictory evidence.[30]

I tried again to get Mitch's attention.

"So you do think the body was moved. Just not to Talpiot."

Mitch continued to ignore me, but Creedy was hooked.

"So where *did* they take the body, Mitch?"

"I'd prefer not to discuss that *here*," Mitch replied in a low voice. "Let's just say I am working with several professionals who are extremely eager to answer that very question."

"Professional *archaeologists*?" I blurted.

Silence.

"Or unlicensed tomb robbers?"

One of Guilder's more memorable classroom rants was a scathing rebuke of antiquities collectors who buy from grave robbers and loot traders. Mitch finally took my bait.

"Every hill in this land is an archaeological gold mine! Thousands of tombs wait to be discovered! These treasures don't belong to the state of Israel. They belong to the world!"

"So on the world's behalf you trade in illegal artifacts." I was pushing my luck.

"I shop the antiquities market," Mitch replied coolly.

"Don't you mean the *black* market?" I said.

"Did you bring me to Israel to finance your addiction?" Creedy broke in. "You haven't changed a bit, have you?"

Mitch paused, jaw harder than unexcavated stone, and turned. His eyes blazed. Finally I got a good look at his face.

"The plan was to discuss our project this evening, Mr. Creedy," he said, still glaring at me. Then, guiding Creedy toward the door, "I believe we're finished here."

Alone again in the Syrian chapel, I noticed a sooty icon framed in fire-blackened boards. The blurred and battered image testified to the messy, sometimes impossible task of historical restoration. A small sandbox nearby held three votive candles that cast a trinity of flickering shadows on to the graffiti on the wall. Part of me wanted to track this tomb raider into the underworld of stolen antiquities. Avoiding detection would be tricky, but I had things going for me. For one, Creedy's shiny tote bag bore the American Colony Hotel insignia. For another, I already had an incriminating picture of Mitch. He was the very one I'd seen trespassing at the Dominus Flevit cemetery. And third, I knew who "Mitch" was. He was Mitchell Stevens, the man Guilder knew was up to something. If Guilder heard that his old friend was striking shady deals and buying up pilfered loot in some unholy quest for the "real" tomb of Jesus, he'd be only too eager to help me out.

To my surprise, a larger part of me wanted nothing to do with Tomb Raider and his sidekick. The only tomb I wanted to enter was the curious edifice known as the Edicule—the place millions of Christians revere because it once held the body of their Lord. I hesitated at this crossroads.

On the Loose

Impatient during my deliberations, I found my feet marching me back to where pilgrims waited to enter the small chamber. I took my place at the end of the line, opting for lowly veneration over high adventure. The air around the Edicule hung thick with the chemical fumes of floor cleaner, but I was thinking of Nicodemus's myrrh, brought to honor Jesus's body and hide the stench of decay (John 19:39). A dark-robed priest policed the crowds, but I was picturing the white-robed figure who showed the women where Jesus's

"Is not this the carpenter, the son of <u>Mary</u> and brother of James and <u>Joses</u> and <u>Judas</u> and Simon, and are not his sisters here with us?"

Mark 6:3 RSV

body had lain (Mark 16:5–6). Tourists chattered in tongues Italian, Korean, and Arabic, but I was imagining ancient pilgrims and immigrants hearing Peter's voice at Pentecost (Acts 2:31).

With the line barely moving, my thoughts turned to Jesus's burial, and whether the lateness of the hour demanded a temporary arrangement, and whether distraught disciples mistook emptiness for resurrection.

Mark 15:42–47; 16:1–2	Luke 23:50–56; 24:1	John 19:38–42
When evening had come, and since it was the day of Preparation, that is, the day before the sabbath,	Now . . .	After these things,
Joseph of Arimathea, a respected member of the council . . .	Joseph . . .	Joseph of Arimathea . . .
went boldly to Pilate and asked for the body of Jesus.	went to Pilate and asked for the body of Jesus.	asked Pilate to let him take away the body of Jesus.
Then Pilate . . . granted the body to Joseph.	Then he took it down,	Pilate gave him permission; so he came and removed his body. Nicodemus . . . also came, bringing a mixture of myrrh and aloes, weighing about a hundred pounds.
Then Joseph bought a linen cloth, and taking down the body, wrapped it in the linen cloth, and laid it in a tomb that had been hewn out of the rock.	wrapped it in a linen cloth, and laid it in a rock-hewn tomb where no one had ever been laid.	They took the body of Jesus and wrapped it with the spices in linen cloths, according to the burial custom of the Jews. Now there was a garden in the place where he was crucified, and in the garden there was a new tomb in which no one had ever been laid.

Mark 15:42–47; 16:1–2	Luke 23:50–56; 24:1	John 19:38–42
	It was the day of Preparation, and the sabbath was beginning.	And so, because it was the Jewish day of Preparation, and the tomb was nearby, they laid Jesus there.
When the sabbath was over, Mary Magdalene, and Mary the mother of James, and Salome bought spices, so that they might go and anoint him.	The women who had come with him from Galilee followed, and they saw the tomb and how his body was laid. Then they returned, and prepared spices and ointments. On the sabbath they rested according to the commandment.	
And very early on the first day of the week, when the sun had risen, they went to the tomb.	But on the first day of the week, at early dawn, they came to the tomb, taking the spices that they had prepared.	Early on the first day of the week, while it was still dark, Mary Magdalene came to the tomb and saw that the stone had been removed from the tomb. So she ran and went to Simon Peter and the other disciple, the one whom Jesus loved, and said to them, "They have taken the Lord out of the tomb, and we do not know where they have laid him."

John says the burial site was chosen "because it was the Jewish day of Preparation, and the tomb was nearby," though he also assures us there was time enough for Joseph and Nicodemus to wrap the body in large quantities of spices (19:40). When Mary Magdalene discovers the tomb empty, she decides it could mean only one thing: reburial elsewhere (20:2, 13, 15). Subsequent events in John's narrative, however, conspire to undermine this hypothesis. In Mark, Joseph retrieves Jesus's body from the cross and buries it before Sabbath, but Salome and the two

Marys wait until early Sunday to bring spices (16:1–2). Like John's Magdalene, Mark's women arrive fully expecting to find Jesus's corpse where they know it was laid. Luke more or less follows Mark but explicitly states that the women saw where and how the body was laid (23:55). So whether we follow John or Mark/Luke, the tradition points consistently to a hurried burial, not a temporary one.

The larger problem for the temporary-burial theory is that it cannot explain the early, widespread, and consistent belief in the bodily resurrection of Jesus. Those closest to Jesus were not expecting him to come back to life. On the contrary, the women who visited the tomb on Sunday morning assumed that other corpses would soon be lying alongside Jesus's body, hence the need for aromatic spices. Nor did the empty tomb, by itself, do more than cause alarm. The "young man" in Mark's story (in Matthew, an angel) does not point to the empty tomb *as evidence of* the resurrection. Quite the opposite: he announces that this surprising development was required by another one. The empty tomb does not prove resurrection; resurrection demands an empty tomb.[31] Only when the risen Jesus starts showing up in the flesh can the curious case of the disappearing corpse be solved.

I finally arrived at the front of the line. Past giant candlesticks, beneath oil lamps and icons, through a narrow door, I entered the Chapel of the Angel. Resting on a pedestal here was a cube of white stone that, according to tradition, is all that remains of the stone that blocked the tomb's entrance. For skeptics and agnostics, it's a piece of rock; for believers, an angel's seat. That day I saw both. Beside me a young nun reverently kissed the altar as an older one lit a candle.

According to the Gospels the behavior of the risen Jesus was at once familiar and foreign. We see the familiar when a fully embodied Jesus leaves footprints along the shore, fries fish over a fire, displays wounds, breaks bread, makes physical contact with friends. But this Jesus is also foreign to us. He appears suddenly in locked rooms. He hides or discloses his identity. He ascends to heaven. The resurrection accounts give us both normal and paranormal, both physical and "transphysical," as if the evangelists themselves didn't know how to organize the testimonies they had collected.[32]

Through a smaller door I proceeded into the tiny Chapel of the Holy Sepulchre, the tomb of Christ. I had entered Christendom's holiest space. My first thought was that nothing around me could possibly date back to the first century. However likely it was that I was standing in Jesus's burial chamber, the room was full not of burial niches but of candles and lampstands. In place of ossuaries there were icons. Instead of a folded linen shroud, a gilded banner. Everywhere I looked, tradition. Nowhere, history.

Maybe old Bultmann was right and the "historical Jesus" really *is* hidden from view, like the burial bench beneath this marble slab. Or maybe not. The line between history and tradition is never easily drawn. Tradition is rooted in historical memory. Even the most assured events of the past come to us only through later interpretation. Remembrance and imagination are not enemies but coconspirators. The Gospels weave together testimony, artistry, and commentary so seamlessly that not even Bultmann could tug them apart.

I rested my hand on the cool marble of the burial bench, hoping for a moment of transcendence, a sacred encounter. I heard no voice. Saw no vision. What I got instead were fellow pilgrims whispering and waiting in the doorway. I said a prayer, withdrew my hand, retraced my steps, and was soon shuffling along Christian Quarter Road.

I was certainly not the first person to leave the tomb unsatisfied. The women in Mark's Gospel fled in fearful silence, under orders to seek Jesus elsewhere (16:7–8). Only in John does the risen Jesus show up at the tomb. Not until Mary Magdalene turns her back on the cave, however, does she see before her the risen Jesus (20:14–17).

The four Gospels conclude as they began, very differently, but they agree on one thing:

> Jesus cannot be confined by the tomb any more than by the hopes of his followers or the designs of his enemies. The grave clothes have been shed; Jesus is out of the tomb, on the loose.[33]

If Jesus is to be found anywhere, they insist, it is on this side of the door.

The call from Mom came the next day. Her voice sounded distant, fearful. The test results were not good, she said. Cancer was back, and spreading. It was time for me to be home. Within minutes I was packed and out the door to catch a *sherut*, returning to Tel Aviv the same way I arrived. My soul, like Ben Gurion Airport, was cloaked in gray. How long had Mom protected me from the news? Would my presence at home have made her stronger? Had her worries on my behalf weakened her body's resistance? Beside my mom's battle for life, my intellectual safari seemed a self-indulgent romp.

I purchased a standby ticket, cleared security, and found a quiet corner. Over several hours I read all seven volumes of my journal. Some pages made me smile. A few brought tears. As I advanced through the stack I watched my need for certitude diminish and sensed a growing resolve to linger with the questions. If Jesus was on the loose, I'd learned, the academy's efforts to bind him—with historical criteria, critical axioms, dogmatic categories—were sure to fail. Likewise, any parish that hoped to domesticate him, to Westernize him, to market him, would gain predictability at the expense of authenticity.

Even my modest quest to situate Jesus in his natural habitat had known only limited success. I'd rejected certain caricatures of Jesus—revolutionary zealot;

secular sage—and found that other profiles better accounted for what we knew about him: his ties to the Baptist, his Galilean support base, his subversive stories, his heart for the poor, his apocalyptic expectations, his enemies' response. But even my best work left many questions unresolved, not least of which concerned Jesus's understanding of himself, his death, and things to come. If Jesus is indeed on this side of the tomb, so too are the persistent questions and lingering uncertainties—not unlike, perhaps, those Jesus himself endured in the hours before his death.

If the Jesus of history will not be pegged, pinned, the Jesus of Scripture is almost as elusive. Mark scribes a cryptic healer who announces abruptly, now here, now there, the arrival of God's rule. Matthew's portrait seems more royal: a Davidic Messiah whose rhetorical authority matches his radical demands. Luke paints an oxlike Jesus whose determination to get to Jerusalem is restrained only by his prophetic sense of timing and his compassion to help the needy along the way. In John we encounter a heavenly messenger who descends, eaglelike, to show us the Father's love. These portraits are not contradictory, but their dissimilarities are intriguing.

This, I'd come to realize, is how it must be. The Man who traversed the land and the One who strides the Gospels has many faces. He is preacher and prophet, poet and peasant, seer and sage. He lurks at society's margins and lingers in its marketplaces. His was a suspicious birth, an obscure childhood, and an unlikely public launch in the shadow of a desert holy man. His tales of the kingdom, spun from the common fibers of the underclass, clarified but also mystified. His miracles impressed some and offended others. And his sense of mission drove him to confront not only the minions of hell but also the gatekeepers of the temple. Very little about Jesus was straightforward and self-interpreting. Almost no story pointed in only one direction. If Jesus was often difficult to track, he was always impossible to tame.

Perhaps what surprised me most from rereading my journals was how many people had left their mark on my story. I pictured each encounter. Again I rode with the insurgent Jordanian cab driver. Again I debated on the rooftop with Bernie, the British atheist. I drew again on a water pipe in Deheisheh camp with Max, the filmmaker, and danced again at that Palestinian wedding with Marc, the Frenchman. Through tears I watched the little ones resting by the Tabgha pool. I ascended to Jerusalem with Levy the kibutznik, circled the Temple Mount with Rabbi Feldman, watched an orthodox Jew immerse himself in Siloam pool, and shared fruit with Salah, the Arab tour guide. I even bantered with the Italians on the bus that never made it into Hebron. Each encounter jostled for attention. Strangers paced side by side in the cage of memory.

Moving among them all, I saw four saints—my four evangelists. Sister Yustina from St. Mark's was praying in Aramaic and telling miracle stories. Elias Chacour was raising his voice against resentment and working the wonder of reconciliation. Anna, the volunteer, was quietly caring for the disabled along Galilee's shore. And Father Dan was distributing bread in the Upper Room and refusing to put down his harmonica. If Jesus lives on this side of the tomb, he lives in them. Here where history meets hope, here where seekers of knowledge must settle for narrative, here where faith accompanies uncertainty but does not replace it. Perhaps here that is more than enough.

Notes

Author's Preface

1. Apparently it was the French poet Paul Valéry who said, "A poem is never finished, only abandoned."

2. Wright, *Challenge of Jesus*, 14, 30–32.

3. Hays, *Echoes of Scripture*, 191.

Chapter 1 Between Heaven and Earth

1. In his *Jesus and the Word* (1926), Bultmann offers a nice summary of his perspective: "I do indeed think that we can now know almost nothing concerning the life and personality of Jesus, since the early Christian sources show no interest in either." And, "What the sources offer us is first of all the message of the early Christian community, which for the most part the church freely attributed to Jesus. This naturally gives no proof that all the words which are put into his mouth were actually spoken by him. As can be easily proved, many sayings originated in the church itself; others were modified by the church."

2. Newbigin (*Foolishness to the Greeks*, 49) puts it nicely: Bultmann could "cheerfully accept the dissolution of most of the historical material in the Gospels in the powerful acids of scientific criticism and yet find in the New Testament that which summons them to faith understood as authentic existence."

3. Thielicke, *Little Exercise for Young Theologians*, 12.

4. The Vesuvius excerpts are from book 6, letter 16.

5. The Younger Pliny was a model Roman: loyal, honest, pious, devoted to the public good. At seventeen he inherited his uncle's estate. He specialized in law and diplomacy but liked to troubleshoot water supplies and sewers. In 111 CE, Trajan tasked him to solve problems in Bithynia and Pontus. We have 121 of his official letters to or from Trajan, plus 247 personal letters!

6. Dio Cassius, *Roman History* 52.36.2 (from the early third century).

7. On why and how early Christians got in trouble, see "The Early Persecutions and Roman Law" in appendix 5 of Sherwin-White, *Letters of Pliny: Commentary*, 772–87. Full-blown Roman persecution would not kick in for more than a century, with the purges of 250, 257, and 303 CE. Prior to that, Roman law generally protected Christians from harassment and mob violence. Many Christians experienced benign neglect rather than official opposition.

8. The request for a fire brigade and the emperor's denial appear in letters 42 and 43.

9. Cyprian's writings from the third century (e.g., *On the Lapsed* 7–9 and *Letters* 11:1; 55:11; 65:1; 67:6) describe Christian communities and leaders buckling under state pressure and offering sacrifices to Roman gods (e.g., in Carthage during the anti-Christian campaign in the year 250).

10. Think of the shared meal described in 1 Cor. 11:17–34, but also 14:26 and Acts 2:46–47, and of texts that might contain early Christian hymns, such as Phil. 2:6–11; Col. 1:15–20; 1 Tim. 3:16.

11. Here's Trajan's reply: "You have followed the right course of procedure, my dear Pliny, in your examination of the cases of persons charged with being Christians, for it is impossible to lay down a general rule to a fixed formula. These people must not be hunted out; if they are brought before you and the charge against them is proved, they must be punished, but in the case of anyone who denies that he is a Christian, and makes it clear that he is not by offering prayers to our gods, he is to be pardoned as a result of his repentance however suspect his past conduct may be. But pamphlets circulated anonymously must play no part in any accusation. They create the worst sort of precedent and are quite out of keeping with the spirit of our age." Trajan to Pliny, letter 97, in Pliny the Younger, *Letters*. Trajan's don't-ask-don't-tell policy shows the absence of an empire-wide, official policy against Christianity in the early second century.

Chapter 2 Ghosts at the River

1. Grahame, *Wind in the Willows*, 113.

2. Chesterton, *Orthodoxy*, 5.

3. Lewis, *Screwtape Letters*, letter 23, p. 124.

4. The pecking order is clear from Matt. 3:14.

5. For the details see Crossan, *Historical Jesus*, 232–34; Meier, *Marginal Jew*, 2:5, 7; Sanders, *Historical Figure of Jesus*, 93–94; Dunn, *Jesus Remembered*, 350; Funk, *Acts of Jesus*, 54. Not all scholars agree that John baptized Jesus. See, e.g., DeMaris, "Baptism of Jesus," 137–57.

6. Here again, Guilder is in good company. See, e.g., Dunn, *Jesus Remembered*, 350–52; Sanders, *Jesus and Judaism*, 91. For all the angles, see Meier, *Marginal Jew*, 2:116–30.

7. Guilder had in mind verses like John 1:8, 15, 19–34; 3:26–30; 10:40–42.

8. Guilder was not alone in thinking that John's "Coming One" (Mark 1:7; Matt. 3:11; Luke 3:16) was God, not Jesus. Mason (*Josephus and the New Testament*, 219) asks "whether it is more likely that Josephus has taken a figure who was a herald for Jesus and, erasing his Christian connection, made him into a famous Jewish preacher, or whether the early Christian tradition has co-opted a famous Jewish preacher as an ally and subordinate of Jesus." Crossan (*Historical Jesus*, 234–35) thinks he knows the answer: "John's message was an announcement of imminent apocalyptic intervention by God and not at all about Jesus. . . . John's message about the advent of God has been deftly and smoothly changed into a witness about the advent of Jesus." Cf. idem, *Jesus: A Revolutionary Biography*, 38; Funk, *Acts of Jesus*, 53; Theissen and Merz, *Historical Jesus*, 205.

9. After I read Matt. 3:11–12; Mark 1:7–8; Luke 3:15–17; John 1:26–27.

10. Mason (*Josephus and the New Testament*, 291–93) thinks Luke knew the *Jewish Antiquities* of Josephus. Most scholars, I think, aren't convinced.

11. In all but one Gospel John appears in chapter 1. Matthew, the exception, waits until chapter 3.

12. The École librarian kindly translated for me Puech and Zias's article "Le Tombeau."

13. The story probably goes back to the second or third century and survives in *The Protoevangelium of James* 23:1–3. Someone may have confused John's father with Zacharias, son of Baris, whose murdered corpse the Zealots lobbed into the Kidron Valley during the Jewish War (cf. Josephus, *Jewish War* 4.334–344). A further possibility is that they confused Zechariah with the chap of the same name who was murdered in 2 Chron. 24:20–21 and mentioned in Luke 11:51 (and Matt. 23:35).

14. This is argued by Webb, *John the Baptizer and Prophet*, 371–72.

15. Wright (*New Testament and the People of God*, 378–84) shows how Samuel's story is close to the heart of Luke's message.

16. See Betz, "Was John the Baptist an Essene?" 205–14.

17. Josephus, *Jewish War* 2.120. Apparently they had to adopt because they abstained from sex. Josephus (*Jewish War* 2.161–162) knew of one Essene group that allowed for marriage, but solely to propagate.

18. You can read about sectarian water rituals in *Manual of Discipline* 3.3–5, 9; 5.13–14.

19. Ibid., 8.13–16; 9.19–20.

20. Josephus (*Jewish War* 2.137–139) refers to a three-year probationary period. The *Manual of Discipline* scroll (1QS 6.13–23) seems to require only (!) two years.

21. Scholars who see John's offer of forgiveness to be, one way or another, countertemple, or at least an alternative to temple ritual, include Crossan, *Historical Jesus*, 231; Wright, *Jesus and the Victory of God*, 160–61; Dunn, *Jesus Remembered*, 359; Webb, *John the Baptizer and Prophet*, 203–5, 370–72; idem, "John the Baptist," 197.

22. See Hos. 6:6; Ps. 51:16–17; 1 Sam. 15:22; Prov. 15:8. Then read Taylor, *Immerser*, 106–11.

23. See Matt. 3:7–10, but note that the Pharisees and Sadducees don't escape John's criticism. Interestingly, in Matt. 21:23–27 the temple priests and elders refuse to come down for or against on John's baptism.

24. John 3:23 says John also baptized at "Aenon near Salim," but we don't know where that is. Some say it's in the small part of the Decapolis on the west side of the Jordan, which would be beyond Herod Antipas's reach. See also Meier, *Marginal Jew*, 2:45; Taylor, *Immerser*, 42–48.

25. For a description of traditional sites west of the Jordan, see Gibson, *Cave of John*, 220–32. Most pilgrims seeking baptism, however, head north. Just below the Sea of Galilee, where both sides of the Jordan belong to Israel, is an alternative site. Unlike the natural setting at the Orthodox site (until recently), the northern site has concrete ramps, hand railings, souvenirs, bus fumes, and everything.

26. Jordan planted about two hundred fifty thousand land mines in the Jordan Valley along its border with Israel.

27. Most manuscripts of John 1:28 indicate John was baptizing "in Bethany beyond the Jordan." Some replace *Bethany* with *Bethabara*.

28. This is close to what Meier says in *Marginal Jew*, 2:60–61.

29. The way Taylor (*Immerser*, 231) sees it, Josephus was trapped. If he declared John a true prophet, he'd have to explain why John's apocalyptic scenario hadn't panned out. Call him a false prophet and he can no longer point to him as a righteous man whose death God might want to avenge.

30. On Josephus's hope for Jewish restoration (at Rome's expense), see Sanders, *Judaism*, 288–89. Josephus believed God had sided with the Romans during the war but that God had plans for the Jews as well.

31. Yes, according to Crossan (*Historical Jesus*, 232): "People cross over into the desert and are baptized in the Jordan as they return to the Promised Land."

32. The "embarrassment" criterion offers reason to think that later followers of Jesus would not invent the idea. The trickier question is whether any Jews *before* Jesus expected Elijah to prepare the way *for the Messiah*, as the disciples' question in Mark 9:11/Matt. 17:10 implies. For a resounding *No*, see Robinson, "Elijah, John and Jesus." Robinson thinks John expected Elijah, and that Jesus accepted that mantle until his sense of mission shifted and he handed it back to John.

33. All this can be thoroughly confusing for Christians who tend to "messianize" everything about Jesus, as Croatto complained recently in "Jesus, Prophet like Elijah," 451, 465.

34. In 72 CE. This is history repeating itself. The Hasmonean king Alexander Jannaeus (103–76 BCE) first established Machaerus, but Rome's General Pompey destroyed it in 63 BCE.

35. See 1 Pet. 1:10–12. For the idea that John was intentionally vague and unclear about the one to come, see Dunn, *Jesus Remembered*, 371; Meier, *Marginal Jew*, 2:34–35, 132–33.

36. This wonderfully antique phrase comes from the King James Version of 1 Cor. 13:12. Note that in this context, Paul is talking about the partial and temporary nature of spiritual gifts like *prophecy*.

37. You'll find a similar proposal in Meier, *Marginal Jew*, 2:130–37; Mason, *Josephus*, 221–22.

38. I'm intrigued by the idea (Taylor, *Immerser*, 221–22) that "John's message could be taken, although couched in the language of repentance and morality, as seriously anti-Roman, for imperial rule was one of the things that would be shaken off in the coming day of judgment." Cf. Webb, *John the Baptizer and Prophet*, 366–70.

39. Cf. Matt. 14:3–12; Luke 3:19–20.

40. This might explain Josephus's silence about John's ties to Jesus: to mention those ties would do nothing to clarify his point.

41. Meier, *Marginal Jew*, 2:172. For a good defense of the *Herod a.k.a. Philip* hypothesis, see Hoehner, *Herod Antipas*, 133–36.

42. Bultmann, *History of the Synoptic Tradition*, 301–2.

43. See Theissen, *Shadow of the Galilean*, 47, 201. Alfred Rawlinson, cited by Davies and Allison, *Matthew*, 2:466, called Mark's an account of "what was being darkly whispered in the bazaars or market-places of Palestine." I particularly like the "darkly whispered" part.

44. Holofernes loses his *own* head, whereas Antipas loses someone else's, but the parallel stands.

Chapter 3 Room at the Inn

1. A *synopsis* places Gospel episodes in parallel columns. If you haven't worked through a synopsis line by line using colored pencils to show parallels and differences, you probably shouldn't be speculating about how the Gospels relate to one another. I recommend Aland, ed., *Synopsis of the Four Gospels* and Throckmorton, ed., *Gospel Parallels*.

2. E.g., Mark 1:9, 23; Luke 4:16, 34; John 1:45–46.

3. See Ehrman, *New Testament: A Historical Introduction*, 128.

4. Lewis, *Last Battle*, 161.

5. See Murphy-O'Connor, "Cenacle," 303–22.

6. In Matthew's first two chapters see 1:22; 2:5, 15, 17, 23.

7. See Allison, *New Moses*.

8. For Josephus's version of the Moses birth story, see *Jewish Antiquities* 2.210–216 (chap. 9, par. 3, online at http://www.ccel.org/j/josephus/works/ant-2.htm, but the translation in *The Apostolic Fathers* in the Loeb Classical Library [see bibliography] is better).

9. On Jesus as a "prophet like Moses," see Deut. 18:15–19; John 1:21; 6:14; 7:40; Acts 3:20–23; 7:37.

10. King, "I've Been to the Mountaintop."

11. King, "Where Do We Go from Here?"

12. Crossan argues for "prophecy historicized" in several places, including *The Cross That Spoke*; *Who Killed Jesus?*; *Birth of Christianity*, 520–22. Cf. Borg and Wright, *Meaning of Jesus*, 85, 182. For "history scripturized," see Goodacre, "Scripturalization in Mark's Crucifixion Narrative"; "Prophecy Historicized or History Scripturized?"

13. If Jupiter is the star of kings and Saturn is the star of Saturday (the Jewish Sabbath), a conjunction might lead someone to combine the two. They were certainly never close enough to appear as a single star.

14. You'll find concise treatments in Sanders's *Historical Figure of Jesus*, 85–87, and Mason's *Josephus and the New Testament*, 273–77. For more detail, see R. Brown, *Birth of the Messiah*, 546–56.

15. See Carlson's blog online at http://hypotyposeis.org.

Chapter 4 Mist and Mystery

1. Hopkins, *World Full of Gods*, 296. See also Eliade, *Sacred and the Profane*.

2. A contemporary demythologizer, Crossan (*Jesus: A Revolutionary Biography*, 82) says Jesus healed the leper's illness (not his disease) "by refusing to accept the disease's ritual uncleanness and social ostra-cization." Mack (*Who Wrote the New Testament?* 64) simply calls Mark's miracle stories "preposterous."

3. I'm not convinced that miracles were ever common. I think the Gospels and Acts included miracle stories because they were considered uncommon. As for those who boast (often on stage or TV) miracles on demand, don't get me started.

4. Smith, *Jesus the Magician*, 8.

5. For more, see Fee, "On the Inauthenticity of John 5:3b–4," in *To What End Exegesis?* 17–28.

6. This explains why Jesus could be condemned for healing *on the Sabbath* (cf. Luke 13:14). The charge is not that Jesus used Satan's power but that he tapped into God's power against God's will. See Bryan, "Power in the Pool."

7. And by a line from the famous Copper Scroll (3Q15 11.11–13). Robin Lane Fox counters, how-ever: "A few correct details of setting can also occur in historical novels." *The Unauthorized Version*, 246.

8. Recall C. S. Lewis's *Magician's Nephew*, in which The Wood lies between our world and others. Compare the hallway in *Matrix Reloaded* and Monstropolis in *Monsters, Inc.*

9. Hezekiah reigned in the eighth century BCE. For the spring and tunnel, see 1 Kings 1:33, 38, 45; 2 Kings 20:20; 2 Chron. 32:30. Apparently it was long forgotten in the first century.

10. See, for example, Spivey and Smith, *Anatomy of the New Testament*, 185. Meier, *Marginal Jew*, 2:696, thinks verses 1, 6, and 7 preserve the historical kernel.

11. Martyn (*History and Theology in the Fourth Gospel*, 37, 129–30) persuaded many that John 9 is a two-level drama that tells us as much about John's church in the late first century as it does about Jesus's encounters in Jerusalem decades earlier—or more. Skeptical is Bauckham, *Gospels for All Christians*, 23n26.

12. Helpful is Meier, *Marginal Jew*, 2:696–98.

13. The next chronological marker is the Feast of Dedication, or Hanukkah, in John 10:22.

14. The "criterion of embarrassment" could be invoked here. It is striking, given how eager John is to emphasize Jesus's presence in Jerusalem (2:13–25; 5:1–17; 7:1–52; 8:20, 59; 9:1–41; 10:22–39; 11:18, 56; 12:12–19; 13:1; 18:1–3), that he recounts only two miracles in the city. If John were freely inventing miracles, surely he'd have Jesus heal in the temple, the market, the gates. On authenticity, see R. Brown, *John 1–12*, 379; Meier, *Marginal Jew*, 2:694–98; Twelftree, *Jesus the Miracle Worker*, 302–3; Blomberg, *Historical Reliability of John's Gospel*, 150–52.

15. Crossan, *Historical Jesus*, 325.

16. Saliva was used in folk remedies and was thought to have healing properties. See Pliny the Elder, *Natural History*, book 29, and Marcus, *Mark*, 1:473–74. Turns out the ancients were on to something: Achenbach, "Saliva's Saving Graces," describes the "breathtaking potential" of saliva. Disgusting fact: we swallow almost a quart of spit a day.

17. Pindar, *Nemean Odes*, Pythian Ode 3.47–56.

18. Epidaurus inscription, in Klauck, *Religious Context of Early Christianity*, 164.

19. Asclepiades doesn't really belong on the list since, according to Pliny, he interrupted a funeral to revive its corpse even though the man probably wasn't dead. (Recall the *Bring out your dead* scene from *Monty Python and the Holy Grail*.) My chart excludes miracle workers in Acts since Luke declares the apostles' works to be acts *of Jesus* (e.g., 3:6; 4:10; 16:18).

20. Meier, *Marginal Jew*, 2:966. On John's independence from the Synoptics here, see R. Brown, *John 1–12*, 244; Meier, *Marginal Jew*, 2:951, 956.

21. For a better chart see R. Brown, *John 1–12*, 240–43, reproduced in Meier, *Marginal Jew*, 2:952–55.

22. In defense of two distinct events is Gundry, *Mark*, 398–401.

23. For this theme in Mark, see 4:38–41; 5:31; 6:37, 49–52; 7:18; 8:17–21, 32–33; 9:5, 19, 32–34, 38–39; 10:13, 24–26, 37; 11:21; 14:10–11, 29–31, 37, 40, 68–72.

24. See Jer. 16:1–2 and 1 Cor. 7:7, 26–27. At least some Essenes avoided marriage. See Pliny the Elder, *Natural History* 5.73; Josephus, *Jewish War* 2.120, 160–161.

25. In which case he's in good company; the crowd (v. 25) doesn't understand how Jesus made it to Capernaum.

26. More than that, all three accounts (including John) seem to present Jesus in the role of Israel's God, the "I am" (Matt. 14:27; Mark 6:50; John 6:20) who leads his people across the sea in a new exodus (cf. Pss. 77:19–20; 107:23–33). Helpful is R. Brown, *John 1–12*, 255–56.

27. Gundry (*Matthew*, 300) thinks Matthew supplemented Mark's account with a "haggadic midrash on discipleship." Davies and Allison (*Matthew*, 513) think Peter's failure is a "parable about Christian faith in the face of difficulties." Hays (*Moral Vision of the New Testament*, 105–6) calls the story of Peter walking on water an "allegory of Jesus' presence."

28. E.g., Mark 3:27 (cf. Matt. 12:28; Luke 11:20–22). See Bockmuehl, *This Jesus*, 56.

29. We find the same thing in Matthew (4:24; 8:16; 10:1, 8) and Luke (6:17–18; 7:21; 9:1; 13:32; Acts 8:7), sometimes paralleling but independent of Mark.

30. Strecker, "Jesus and the Demoniacs," 122.

31. *Exorcism of Emily Rose*.

32. Crossan and Reed, *Excavating Jesus*.

33. This status as a boundary town may explain the presence of the tax collector whom Jesus recruited as a disciple (Matt. 9:9).

34. Mark 2:1; Matt. 4:13; 9:1. Richardson (*Building Jewish in the Roman East*, 91–107) thinks Cana was perhaps just as important for Jesus as Capernaum, especially in the early going.

35. For these contrasting kingdom visions, see Crossan and Reed, *Excavating Jesus*, 94–97, 125–35.

36. See their report on nineteen (!) years of excavations (1968–86): http://198.62.75.1/www1/ofm/sites/TScpmenu.html. See also Binder, *Into the Temple Courts*, and his website *Second Temple Synagogues*, http://www.pohick.org/sts/.

37. See Reed and Crossan, *Excavating Jesus*, 25–26, 90–91. Similarly doubtful is Kee, "Transformation of the Synagogue after 70 CE," 1–24.

38. Mark 1:21–29; 3:1; John 6:59.

39. See Luke 4:16–30 (cf. Mark 6:1–5; Matt. 13:54–58).

40. Not counting the later one at Capernaum, there are synagogue remains at Masada (on the Dead Sea), Herodium (near Bethlehem), and Gamla (in the Golan Heights). Remains of two others are on the island of Delos and outside Rome, at Ostia. See Richardson, *Building Jewish in the Roman East*, 111–33. At both Masada and Herodium, the rebels adapted rooms that had other uses prior to the revolt.

41. See Sanders, *Judaism*, 198–208; idem, *Jewish Law from Jesus to the Mishnah*, 77–81, 340–43; Dunn, *Jesus Remembered*, 302–6.

42. Matt. 10:5–14, 23; Luke 9:6; 10:1, 17.

43. See John 2:13; 5:1; 7:9–10; Luke 9:51–53; 13:22; 17:11; 18:31; 19:11, 28.

44. This Cana is not Kefr Kenna, the town close to Nazareth generally preferred by Christian tour operators.

45. For Jesus's miracles as "signs" in John, see John 2:11, 23; 3:2; 4:54; 6:2, etc.

46. Matt. 22:1–14; 25:1–13; Mark 2:18–20; Luke 12:36; John 3:29; Eph. 5:25–27; Rev. 19:7–9. Cf. Isa. 25:6–8.

47. For the coming of Jesus's "hour," see John 13:1; 16:32; 17:1.

48. Lindars, *Gospel of John*, 126, calls the story a "submerged parable." I'm not sure what it means but it has a nice ring.

49. See Meier, *Marginal Jew*, 2:1021–22 on why the Dionysus–Jesus connection probably didn't arise until the fourth century.

50. See Chacour's autobiography, *Blood Brothers*, 175–79.

Chapter 5 Time Imagined

1. See Luke 9:51.

2. See Matt. 16:21; Mark 10:33.

3. Bultmann (*History of the Synoptic Tradition*, 300–301) lists heroes (Jewish, Greek, Egyptian, even Buddhist) whose biographers depict them as precocious children.

4. For a sampling, see Matt. 11:20–24; 17:17; 23:37.

5. See Matt. 17:12–13; 23:37.

6. The sort of thing John's Gospel does (e.g., John 3:13–14; 8:28; 12:31–34). See McKnight, *Jesus and His Death*, 236–38.

7. See Wright, *Resurrection of the Son of God*, 409–10.

8. Elijah helped a single mom in Zarephath on the Phoenician coast. Think Lebanon. See 1 Kings 17:8–24.

9. The mountain Elijah climbed was Carmel, on the coast near Haifa. For Elijah's campaign against idolatry, see 1 Kings 18:19–40. We don't know where to locate Jesus's mountaintop transfiguration, where Elijah and Moses appear (Mark 9:2–10; Matt. 17:1–9; Luke 9:28–36), except that it was on a "high" mountain. The top two candidates are Mount Tabor (Galilee) and Mount Hermon. Since this event happens only days after Jesus is in Caesarea Philippi, I'm giving the nod to Mount Hermon.

10. *Jesus* is the Greek equivalent of the Hebrew *Joshua*. To be picky, Mark 7:24 tells us that Jesus journeyed to the region of Tyre, roughly as far north as Caesarea Philippi. Sidon (Matt. 15:21) is yet farther north.

11. On the phrase "gates of Hades," see Davies and Allison, *Matthew*, 2:630–34, and Nickelsburg, "Enoch, Levi, and Peter," 598.

12. See Acts 25:13–26:32 for Paul's encounter with Agrippa II.

13. Makes you think of Matt. 12:42; Luke 11:31, regarding which Wright (*Jesus and the Victory of God*, 535) remarks: "To claim that Jesus is greater than [Solomon, the Temple-builder] is to claim that he is the true Messiah; that he will build the eschatological Temple; that through him the Davidic kingdom will be restored."

14. See Meyer, *Aims of Jesus*, 186. If Jesus *didn't* think along these lines, his followers certainly did (Eph. 2:19–22; 1 Pet. 2:4–10).

15. Josephus, *Jewish War* 1.411.

16. There is something wonderful about an entire nation (okay, much of it) taking its rest at the same time.

17. I should include Mark 14:25 (cf. Luke 22:18). Jesus's harvest language refers to a coming time of final judgment (Mark 4:2–9, 26–29; Matt. 13:24–30; Luke 10:2).

18. See, for example, Allison, *Jesus of Nazareth*, 149.

19. To see what Meier actually says, see *Marginal Jew*, 2:336–44, 348. For early anxieties about Jesus's return, see 1 Thess. 4:13–18; 2 Thess. 2:2; 2 Pet. 3:4.

20. McKnight, *New Vision for Israel*, 136, who follows Wright, *Jesus and the Victory of God*, esp. 510–19.

21. McKnight, *New Vision for Israel*, 138.

22. Similarly, 1 Thess. 4:16–17, where Paul may be indebted to Jesus's teaching, doesn't sound like a metaphor for the fall of Jerusalem. See Allison, *Jesus of Nazareth*, 159–60.

23. Wright, *Jesus and the Victory of God*, 516.

24. See Matt. 16:14.

25. See Beasley-Murray, *Jesus and the Kingdom of God*, 189–90.

26. His 1906 book was originally called *From Reimarus to Wrede*. Would the last century of Jesus scholarship have followed the same course if the English title had been as boring as the German?

27. Schweitzer, *Quest*, 358–59.

28. According to McKnight (*A New Vision for Israel*, 134) "such a time span would permit anything from a few weeks to a few decades, depending on how long it took for them to raise enough hackles to have to flee like mad to escape."

29. Their books lay open beside me as I slept. According to Ehrman (*Jesus: Apocalyptic Prophet*, 18, 162, 244) "Jesus . . . predicted that the God of Israel was about to perform a mighty act of destruction and salvation for his people. And he thought that some of those listening to him would be alive when it happened. . . . For him, there wasn't going to *be* a long haul. . . . If Jesus . . . really meant that the Son of Man was to arrive in the lifetime of his disciples—he was obviously wrong." Allison (*Jesus of Nazareth*, 218) shows more reserve: "Jesus' generation . . . passed away. They all tasted death. And it is not the kingdom of God that has come but the scoffers who ask, Where is the promise of his coming? . . . Jesus the millenarian prophet, like all millenarian prophets, was wrong: reality has taken no notice of his imagination."

30. I was recalling ideas from Dunn, *Jesus Remembered*, 481, 483.

31. Meyer, *Aims of Jesus*, 246.

32. Ibid., 247–48.

33. An almost persuasive defense of this view is Wenham, "'This Generation Will Not Pass . . .'" If Wenham is right, Jesus promised the imminent fall of Jerusalem but did not claim to know the timing of the subsequent "day or hour" when the Son of Man would come (13:32).

34. Malina, "Christ and Time," 14. See also Harvey, *Jesus and the Constraints of History*, 94.

Chapter 6 Wall of Tears

1. Yup, *kettle*. A flock of vultures is a *venue*, but when they circle they're a *kettle*. I promise.

2. Bauckham (*Jesus and the Eyewitnesses*, 195–96) explains the synoptic silence as a kind of early Christian witness protection program. Since Lazarus's life was threatened during the early years (John 12:10), one way to protect him was to keep his story out of the public record. Since John wrote later, he was free to broadcast the story, name and all. Anything Bauckham says should be taken seriously, though the evidence for this proposal seems thin.

3. C. S. Lewis, quoted in Vanauken, *Severe Mercy*, 105–6.

4. Twain, *Innocents Abroad*, 415.

5. For similar outbursts, see Ezek. 4:1–3; 2 Sam. 12:28; Isa. 29:3; Jer. 6:6, 15.

6. I get the same impression of secrecy from Mark 14:12–16, in which Jesus sends two disciples to prepare a room for Passover. For great detective work, see Bauckham, *Jesus and the Eyewitnesses*, 187–89.

7. Reimarus, *Fragments*, 148.

8. Crossan and Borg, *Last Week*, 3–4; see also Crossan and Reed, *Excavating Jesus*, 220.

9. According to Matt. 12:42 and Luke 11:31, Jesus claimed not equality with but superiority over Solomon.

10. Sanders, *Judaism*, 68.

11. Josephus, *Antiquities* 15.413.

12. See Sanders, *Judaism*, 87–88.

13. On the red heifer see Num. 19 and a tractate in the Mishnah called *Parah*.

14. Mark alone includes "for all the nations" (Isa. 56:7).

15. Gorenberg, "The Collaborator."

16. The idea that Judas was a thief comes from John 12:6 (cf. 13:29), in connection with his designation as group treasurer and his complaint that Mary had wasted expensive perfume when she anointed Jesus's feet.

17. In Mel Gibson's *Passion of the Christ* there's a great slow-motion shot of the high priest throwing the bag of thirty coins at Judas, mirroring Matt. 27:5, when Judas, after Jesus has been condemned, despondently throws the blood money at the priests.

18. Lewis, *The Lion, the Witch and the Wardrobe*, 169.

19. For a better list, see R. Brown, *Death of the Messiah*, 1:655.

20. In Jesus's day Passover lambs were apparently slaughtered around dinnertime on the fourteenth of Nisan. After sunset, under a full moon (as the fifteenth of Nisan began), families would gather to eat roast lamb, unleavened bread, and bitter herbs (Exod. 12:8). For Passover logistics, see Sanders, *Judaism*, 132–38. For attempts to correlate the chronology of John with the Synoptics, see R. Brown, *Death of the Messiah*, 2:1356–73, and Meier, *Marginal Jew*, 1:386–401. Without reconciling the conflict, Wright (*Jesus and the Victory of God*, 555) is content to say that Jesus's last meal was *some kind* of Passover meal, whether or not it fell on the official date of Passover. That seems likely to me.

21. King, "I've Been to the Mountaintop."

22. Some, such as Tabor (*Jesus Dynasty*, 198–99) read Mark 14:13 to imply that they gathered in a home near the pool of Siloam in a blue-collar part of town. Any *man* carrying water would have seemed strange, a fact that might suggest Jesus had prearranged things to keep the location secret until the last moment. Bauckham (*Jesus and the Eyewitnesses*, 188–89) thinks Jesus made "clandestine arrangements" because he expected imminent betrayal and didn't want Judas to know the location of the meeting in advance.

23. See also Mark 14:8 (Matt. 26:12; John 12:7); John 12:23–32; 13:33; 14:28; 15:13; 16:28.

24. Some followers seem to have liked the correlation: John 1:29, 36; 1 Cor. 5:7; 1 Pet. 1:19; Rev. 5:6, 12.

25. Heb. 9:13–22 makes this connection.

Chapter 7 This Side of the Tomb

1. Thus Taylor, "Garden of Gethsemane."

2. David regains his throne; the son of David goes to the cross. Is that a parallel or a contrast?

3. A smooth progression from Mark to John is less compelling if Luke 22:43–44 originally included the bit about the angel and the sweat. R. Brown (*Death of the Messiah*, 1:180–86) thinks it did. Ehrman (*Orthodox Corruption*, 187–94 and 247n39) thinks it didn't. I think Ehrman's case is stronger.

4. Only the last of John's parallels comes from the night of Jesus's betrayal.

5. Mark does, however, have Jesus say that "the Son of Man *must* undergo great suffering . . . and rise again" (Mark 8:31) and that his sufferings were foretold in Scripture (Mark 9:12; 14:21). So Mark's Jesus knew that his death was part of a divine plan. Paul, writing earlier, is more explicit than the Gospels about God's role in Jesus's death. See Rom. 3:25; 5:8; 8:32.

6. Since someone will point out that *Jihadi* is improper Arabic, let's call them *Mujahideen for Messiah*. For the disciples' political aspirations, see Matt. 19:27–28; Mark 10:37; Luke 9:54; 22:24, 30, 38, 49–50; John 18:10–11; Acts 1:6.

7. See Zech. 14:4 (cf. Isa. 64:1) and the citation of Zech. 13:7 at the Last Supper (Mark 14:27). Yoder (*Politics of Jesus*, 45–48) thinks Jesus was tempted along these lines.

8. This paraphrases the eminently quotable Crossan, *Historical Jesus*, 389.

9. *Martyrdom of Polycarp* 16.1.

10. See *Martyrdom of Polycarp* 11:2; 13:3; 14:2; 18:3.

11. See also 4 Macc. 5:37; 6:22; 8:15, 28; 11:26; 13:14; 14:4.

12. See also 2 Macc. 6:19, 30; 4 Macc. 9:29; 10:20.

13. See 4 Macc. 9:24; 12:17; 17:20–22. Cf. Josephus, *Jewish War* 1.650.

14. The plural of *shahid*.

15. See Hovey, *To Share the Body*, 81.

16. Wright, *Jesus and the Victory of God*, 439–42, is helpful here. The evidence that Jesus was deemed a false prophet is plentiful: John 7:12, 47; 10:19–20; Luke 23:2, 5, 14; Matt. 27:63–64. According to the Talmud, "Jesus was . . . 'stoned because he practiced sorcery and enticed and led Israel astray'" (bTalmud 43a).

17. See Dunn, *Jesus Remembered*, 633–34; Meyer, *Aims of Jesus*, 179–80. Similar logic may be driving Mark 12:35–37.

18. This isn't Jesus's first reference to the coming Son of Man. See Mark 8:38–9:1 (cf. Matt. 16:27–28; Luke 12:8–9) and Mark 13:26.

19. Cf. Matt. 19:28; Luke 22:30.

20. Crossan (*Historical Jesus*, 238–59) is among those who deem this saying flatly inauthentic. Wright (*Jesus and the Victory of God*, 519–28) and France (*Matthew*, 1027–28) think Jesus used apocalyptic language to describe his vindication at the resurrection or at the temple's destruction.

21. Lewis, *The Lion, the Witch and the Wardrobe*, 80–81.

22. *IDF* is short for *Israel Defense Forces*. On forty years of Jewish settlements in and around Hebron, I recommend chapter 5 of Zertal and Eldar's *Lords of the Land* and bits of chapters 5–7 in Gorenberg's *Accidental Empire*.

23. If it wasn't obvious, I used Jesus's Hebrew name because it sounds like Yehuda.

24. Mark 15:21 mentions Simon's two sons, Alexander and Rufus, evidently known figures in Mark's day.

25. To imagine how the story *could* have been told, compare the grisly, slow-motion deaths of Eglon and Sisera (Judg. 3:21–22; 5:26–27), of the Maccabean martyrs (2 Macc. 7), and of Polycarp (*Martyrdom of Polycarp*).

26. The idea that Jesus was *nailed* to the cross comes from Luke 24:39 and John 20:25–27. Cf. Gospel of Peter 6:21.

27. Mark (15:38) and Luke (23:45) describe the torn temple curtain but say nothing about an earthquake or risen saints.

28. Bunyan, *Pilgrim's Progress*, Part 1, 3rd Stage.

29. Produced by the Discovery Channel, based on Jacobovici and Pellegrino, *Jesus Family Tomb*.

30. Goodacre, ntweblog.blogspot.com/2007/03/statistical-case-for-identity-of-jesus.html.

31. This is especially true for Mark's Gospel. See Wright, *Resurrection of the Son of God*, 628, 688–93. Not even John 20:8 implies that the empty tomb by itself elicited faith. It was the empty tomb *plus* the presence and condition of Jesus's graveclothes.

32. See Wright, *Resurrection of the Son of God*, 604–15; *Surprised by Hope*, 55–56.

33. Juel, *Master of Surprise*, 113.

Bibliography

Achenbach, Joel. "Saliva's Saving Graces." *National Geographic* 209, no. 4 (2006): 31.

Acts of Pilate. Pages 501–36 in *New Testament Apocrypha*, vol. 1. Edited by Wilhelm Schneemelcher. Louisville: Westminster John Knox, 1992.

Aland, Kurt, ed. *Synopsis of the Four Gospels*. First rev. ed. New York: United Bible Societies, 1982.

Allison, Dale C., Jr. *The New Moses: A Matthean Typology*. Minneapolis: Fortress, 1993.

———. *Jesus of Nazareth: Millenarian Prophet*. Minneapolis: Fortress, 1998.

The Apostolic Fathers. Translated by Kirsopp Lake. 2 vols. Loeb Classical Library. Cambridge, MA: Harvard University Press, 1912–13.

Barrett, C. K. *The Gospel according to St. John*. 2nd ed. Philadelphia: Westminster, 1978.

Bauckham, Richard. "The Coin in the Fish's Mouth." Pages 219–52 in *Miracles in the Gospels*. Edited by D. Wenham and C. L. Blomberg. Gospel Perspectives 6. Sheffield: JSOT Press, 1986.

———. *The Gospels for All Christians: Rethinking the Gospel Audiences*. Grand Rapids: Eerdmans, 1998.

———. *Jesus and the Eyewitnesses: The Gospels as Eyewitness Testimony*. Grand Rapids: Eerdmans, 2006.

Beasley-Murray, G. R. *Jesus and the Kingdom of God*. Grand Rapids: Eerdmans, 1986.

Betz, Otto. "Was John the Baptist an Essene?" Pages 205–14 in *Understanding the Dead Sea Scrolls*. Edited by H. Shanks. New York: Random House, 1996.

Binder, Donald D. *Into the Temple Courts: The Place of the Synagogues in the Second Temple Period*. Atlanta: Society of Biblical Literature, 1999.

Blomberg, Craig. *The Historical Reliability of John's Gospel: Issues and Commentary*. Downers Grove, IL: InterVarsity, 2001.

Bockmuehl, Markus. *This Jesus: Martyr, Lord, Messiah*. Edinburgh: T&T Clark, 1994.

Borg, Marcus. *Jesus: A New Vision; Spirit, Culture, and the Life of Discipleship*. San Francisco: Harper & Row, 1987.

Borg, Marcus, and N. T. Wright. *The Meaning of Jesus*. New York: HarperCollins, 2000.

Bornkamm, Günther. *Jesus of Nazareth*. Minneapolis: Fortress, 1995.

Brown, Dan. *The Da Vinci Code*. New York: Anchor, 2003.

Brown, Raymond. *The Gospel according to John 1–12*. New York: Doubleday, 1966.

———. *The Birth of the Messiah*. New York: Doubleday, 1993.

———. *The Death of the Messiah*. Vol. 1. New York: Doubleday, 1994.

———. *The Death of the Messiah*. Vol. 2. New York: Doubleday, 1999.

Bryan, Steven. "Power in the Pool: The Healing of the Man at Bethesda and Jesus' Violation of the Sabbath (John 5:1–18)." *Tyndale Bulletin* 54, no. 2 (2003): 7–22.

Bultmann, Rudolf. *Jesus and the Word*. New York: Macmillan, 1962.

———. *History of the Synoptic Tradition*. Peabody, MA: Hendrickson, 1994.

Bunyan, John. *The Pilgrim's Progress*. New York: P. F. Collier & Son, 1909.

Carlson, Stephen C. Hypotyposeis. Accessed October 28, 2009. http://www.hypotyposeis.org/weblog/2004/12/luke-22-and-census.html.

Cartlidge, David, and David Dungan, eds. *Documents for the Study of the Gospels*. Minneapolis: Fortress, 1980.

Chacour, Elias. *Blood Brothers*. With David Hazard. 2nd ed. Grand Rapids: Baker Books, 2003.

Chapman, Tracy. *New Beginning*. Electra, 1995.

Chesterton, G. K. *Orthodoxy*. San Francisco: Ignatius Press, 1908.

Cicero. *De Senectute, De Amicitia, De Divinatione*. Loeb Classical Library. Cambridge, MA: Harvard University Press, 1946.

Cockburn, Bruce. *Circles in the Stream*. Golden Mountain Music Corp., 1977.

———. *Inner City Front*. Golden Mountain Music Corp., 1981.

———. *Waiting for a Miracle*. Golden Mountain Music Corp., 1986.

———. *Nothing but a Burning Light*. Golden Mountain Music Corp., 1991.

Cohen, Leonard. *The Future*. Columbia, 1992.

Croatto, J. S. "Jesus, Prophet like Elijah, and Prophet-Teacher like Moses in Luke-Acts." *JBL* 124, no. 3 (2005): 451–65.

Crossan, John D. *The Cross That Spoke: The Origins of the Passion Narrative*. San Francisco: Harper & Row, 1988.

———. *The Historical Jesus: The Life of a Mediterranean Jewish Peasant*. New York: HarperCollins, 1992.

———. *Jesus: A Revolutionary Biography*. San Francisco: HarperSanFrancisco, 1994.

———. *Who Killed Jesus? The Roots of Anti-Semitism in the Gospel Story of the Death of Jesus*. San Francisco: HarperSanFrancisco, 1995.

———. *The Birth of Christianity: Discovering What Happened in the Years Immediately after the Execution of Jesus*. Edinburgh: T&T Clark, 1998.

Crossan, John D., and Jonathan L. Reed. *Excavating Jesus: Beneath the Stones, Behind the Texts*. San Francisco: HarperSanFrancisco, 2001.

Crossan, John D., and Marcus Borg. *The Last Week*. San Francisco: HarperSanFrancisco, 2006.

Cyprian. *Letters*. Pages 275–420 in *Ante-Nicene Fathers*. Vol. 5, *Hippolytus, Cyprian, Caius, Novatian, Appendix*. Edited by R. Roberts and J. Donaldson. Edinburgh: T&T Clark; Grand Rapids: Eerdmans, 1994.

———. *On the Lapsed*. Pages 437–47 in *Ante-Nicene Fathers*. Vol. 5, *Hippolytus, Cyprian, Caius, Novatian, Appendix*. Edited by R. Roberts and J. Donaldson. Edinburgh: T&T Clark; Grand Rapids: Eerdmans, 1994.

Davies, W. D., and D. C. Allison. *The Gospel according to Saint Matthew*. 3 vols. International Critical Commentary. Edinburgh: T&T Clark, 1991.

DeMaris, R. E. "The Baptism of Jesus: A Ritual-Critical Approach." Pages 137–57 in *The Social Setting of Jesus and the Gospels*. Edited by W. Stegemann, B. J. Malina, and G. Theissen. Minneapolis: Fortress, 2002.

Dio Cassius. *Roman History*. Translated by Earnest Carty and Herbert B. Foster. 10 vols. Loeb Classical Library. Cambridge, MA: Harvard University Press, 1924.

Dunn, J. D. G. *Jesus Remembered*. Grand Rapids: Eerdmans, 2003.

Dylan, Bob. *Another Side of Bob Dylan*. Columbia, 1964.

———. *The Times They Are A-Changin'*. Columbia, 1964.

Ehrman, Bart. *The Orthodox Corruption of Scripture*. New York: Oxford University Press, 1996.

———. *Jesus: Apocalyptic Prophet of the New Millennium*. New York: Oxford University Press, 2001.

———. *The New Testament: A Historical Introduction to the Early Christian Writings*. New York: Oxford University Press, 2008.

Eliade, Mircea. *The Sacred and the Profane: The Nature of Religion*. Orlando, FL: Harcourt, 1987.

Eliot, T. S. "The Journey of the Magi." Page 69 in *Collected Poems: 1909–1962*. New York: Harcourt, Brace, 1963.

Euripides. *The Bacchae*. Translated by Ian Johnston. Arlington, VA: Richer Resources Publications, 2008.

The Exorcism of Emily Rose. Screenplay by P. H. Boardman and S. Derrickson. Directed by Scott Derrickson. Sony Pictures, 2005.

Fee, Gordon D. *To What End Exegesis?* Grand Rapids: Eerdmans, 2001.

Fox, Robin Lane. *The Unauthorized Version: Truth and Fiction in the Bible*. New York: Knopf, 1992.

France, R. T. *The Gospel of Matthew*. New International Commentary on the New Testament 1. Grand Rapids: Eerdmans, 2007.

Fredriksen, Paula. *Jesus of Nazareth, King of the Jews: A Jewish Life and the Emergence of Christianity*. New York: Knopf, 1999.

Funk, Robert. *The Acts of Jesus: What Did Jesus Really Do?* San Francisco: HarperSanFrancisco, 1998.

Gibson, Shimon. *The Cave of John the Baptist: The Stunning Archaeological Discovery That Has Redefined Christian History*. New York: Doubleday, 2004.

Goodacre, Mark. "Prophecy Historicized or History Scripturized? Reflections on the Origin of the Crucifixion Narrative." Paper presented to the Historical Jesus section, SBL Annual Meeting. Denver, CO, November 2001.

———. "Scripturalization in Mark's Crucifixion Narrative." Pages 33–47 in *The Passion of Mark*. Edited by G. van Oyen and T. Shepherd. Leuven, Belgium: Peeters, 2006.

———. "The Statistical Case for the Identity of the 'Jesus Family Tomb.'" Accessed October 28, 2009. http://ntweblog.blogspot.com/2007/03/statistical-case-for-identity-of-jesus.html.

Gorenberg, Gershom. "The Collaborator." *New York Times*, August 18, 2002. Accessed October 28, 2009. http://www.nytimes.com/2002/08/18/magazine/the-collaborator.html.

———. *The Accidental Empire: Israel and the Birth of the Settlements, 1967–1977*. New York: Times Books, 2006.

———. *The End of Days: Fundamentalism and the Struggle for the Temple Mount*. New York: Oxford University Press, 2006.

Grahame, Kenneth. *The Wind in the Willows*. New York: Aladdin, 1953.

Gundry, Robert. *Matthew: A Commentary on His Literary and Theological Art*. Grand Rapids: Eerdmans, 1982.

———. *Mark: A Commentary on His Apology for the Cross*. Grand Rapids: Eerdmans, 1993.

Harvey, Anthony E. *Jesus and the Constraints of History*. Philadelphia: Westminster, 1982.

Hays, Richard B. *Echoes of Scripture in the Letters of Paul*. New Haven: Yale University Press, 1989.

———. *The Moral Vision of the New Testament*. New York: HarperCollins, 1996.

Hoehner, Harold. *Herod Antipas*. Cambridge: Cambridge University Press, 1972.

Hopkins, Gerard Manley. "As Kingfishers Catch Fire." Page 51 in *Poems and Prose*. London: Penguin, 1952.

Hopkins, Keith. *A World Full of Gods: The Strange Triumph of Christianity*. New York: Plume, 1999.

Hovey, Craig. *To Share the Body: A Theology of Martyrdom for Today's Church*. Grand Rapids: Brazos, 2008.

Jacobovici, Simcha, and Charles Pellegrino. *The Jesus Family Tomb: The Discovery, the Investigation, and the Evidence That Could Change History*. San Francisco: HarperSanFrancisco, 2007.

Jerome. *Epistle 58*. Pages 531–32 in *Corpus Scriptorum Ecclesiasticorum Latinorum*. Vol. 54. Edited by I. Hilberg. Vienna: VÖAW, 1996.

Jesus Christ, Superstar. Lyrics by Tim Rice. Music by Andrew Lloyd Webber. Decca/MCA/Decca Broadway, 1970.

Johnson, Luke Timothy. *The Real Jesus: The Misguided Quest for the Historical Jesus and the Truth of the Traditional Gospels*. New York: HarperOne, 1997.

Josephus. Translated by H. St. J. Thackeray et al. 10 vols. Loeb Classical Library. Cambridge, MA: Harvard University Press, 1926–1965.

Juel, Donald. *A Master of Surprise: Mark Interpreted*. Minneapolis: Augsburg Fortress, 1994.

Justin Martyr. *Dialogue of Justin, Philosopher and Martyr, with Trypho, a Jew*. Pages 184–270 in *Ante-Nicene Fathers*. Vol. 1, *The Apostolic Fathers with Justin Martyr and Irenaeus*. Edited by R. Roberts and J. Donaldson. Edinburgh: T&T Clark; Grand Rapids: Eerdmans, 1988.

Kee, Howard Clark. "The Transformation of the Synagogue after 70 CE." *New Testament Studies* 36, no. 1 (1990): 1–24.

King, Martin Luther, Jr. "Where Do We Go from Here?" August 16, 1967. Available at http://MKLOnline.net.

———. "I've Been to the Mountaintop." April 3, 1968. Available at http://MKLOnline.net.

Klauck, Hans-Josef. *The Religious Context of Early Christianity: A Guide to Graeco-Roman Religions*. New York: T&T Clark, 2000.

Lahaye, Tim, and Jerry B. Jenkins. *Left Behind: A Novel of the Earth's Last Days*. Carol Stream, IL: Tyndale, 1995.

Lamott, Anne. *Plan B: Further Thoughts on Faith*. New York: Riverhead, 2005.

The Last Temptation of Christ. Screenplay by Nikos Kazantzakis. Directed by Martin Scorsese. Cineplex-Odeon Films, 1988.

Lewis, C. S. *The Last Battle*. New York: HarperCollins, 2000.

———. *The Screwtape Letters*. New York: HarperCollins, 2001.

———. *The Lion, the Witch and the Wardrobe*. New York: HarperCollins, 2005.

Lindars, Barnabas. *The Gospel of John*. The New Century Bible Commentary. Grand Rapids: Eerdmans, 1982.

The Lost Tomb of Jesus? Screenplay by Graeme Ball and Simcha Jacobovici. Directed and produced by Simcha Jacobovici. AP Tomb Productions Ltd., 2007.

Mack, Burton. *Who Wrote the New Testament?* San Francisco: HarperSanFrancisco, 1995.

Malina, Bruce. "Christ and Time: Swiss or Mediterranean?" *Catholic Biblical Quarterly* 51 (1989): 1–31.

Marcus, Joel. *Mark: A New Translation with Introduction and Commentary*. 2 vols. Anchor Yale Bible 27. New York: Doubleday, 2000, 2009.

Marley, Bob. *Exodus*. Island, 1977.

Martinez, Florentino Garcia, ed. *The Dead Sea Scrolls Translated: The Qumran Texts in English*. 2nd ed. Grand Rapids: Eerdmans, 1996.

Martyn, J. Louis. *History and Theology in the Fourth Gospel*. Louisville: Westminster John Knox, 1968.

The Martyrdom of Polycarp. Pages 312–45 in *The Apostolic Fathers*, vol. 2. Translated by Kirsopp Lake. Loeb Classical Library. Cambridge, MA: Harvard University Press, 1912–1913.

Mason, Steve. *Josephus and the New Testament*. 2nd ed. Peabody, MA: Hendrickson, 2003.

McHugh, John. "'In Him Was Life': John's Gospel and the Parting of the Ways." Pages 123–58 in *Jews and Christians: The Parting of the Ways, A.D. 70 to 135*. Edited by James D. G. Dunn. Grand Rapids: Eerdmans, 1992.

McKnight, Scot. *A New Vision for Israel: The Teachings of Jesus in National Context*. Grand Rapids: Eerdmans, 1999.

———. *Jesus and His Death*. Waco: Baylor University Press, 2005.

Meier, John Paul. *A Marginal Jew: Rethinking the Historical Jesus*. Vol. 1, *The Roots of the Problems and the Person*. New York: Doubleday, 1991.

————. *A Marginal Jew: Rethinking the Historical Jesus.* Vol. 2, *Mentor, Message, and Miracles.* New York: Doubleday, 1994.

————. *A Marginal Jew: Rethinking the Historical Jesus.* Vol. 3, *Companions and Competitors.* New York: Doubleday, 2001.

Meyer, Ben F. *The Aims of Jesus.* Eugene, OR: Pickwick Publications, 1979.

Mishnah, The. Translated by Herbert Danby. London: Oxford University Press, 1933.

Mitchell, Stephen. *The Gospel according to Jesus.* New York: HarperCollins, 1991.

Monty Python's Life of Brian. Screenplay by Graham Chapman, John Cleese, et al. Directed by Terry Jones. HandMade Films, 1979.

Murphy-O'Connor, Jerome. "John the Baptist and Jesus: History and Hypotheses." *New Testament Studies* 36 (1990): 359–74.

————. "The Cenacle—Topographical Setting for Acts 2:44–45." Pages 303–22 in *The Book of Acts in Its Palestinian Setting.* Vol. 1 of *The Book of Acts in Its First Century Setting.* Edited by Richard Bauckham. Grand Rapids: Eerdmans, 1995.

Newbigin, Lesslie. *Foolishness to the Greeks: The Gospel and Western Culture.* Grand Rapids: Eerdmans, 1986.

Nickel Creek. *Why Should the Fire Die?* Sugarhill, 2005.

Nickelsburg, George. "Enoch, Levi, and Peter: Recipients of Revelation in Upper Galilee." *Journal of Biblical Literature* 100, no. 4 (1981): 575–600.

Origen. *Against Celsus.* Pages 395–669 in *Ante-Nicene Fathers.* Vol. 4, *Fathers of the Third Century.* Edited by R. Roberts and J. Donaldson. Edinburgh: T&T Clark; Grand Rapids: Eerdmans, 1994.

Perrin, Norman. *Rediscovering the Teaching of Jesus.* New York: HarperCollins, 1967.

Philo. *Every Good Man Is Free.* Pages 2–101 in *Philo,* vol. 9. Translated by F. H. Colson. Loeb Classical Library 363. Cambridge, MA: Harvard University Press, 1994.

Pindar. *Nemean Odes, Isthmian Odes, Fragments.* Translated by William H. Race. Leob Classical Library 485. Cambridge, MA: Harvard University Press, 1997.

Pliny the Elder. *Natural History.* Translated by John F. Healey. London: Penguin, 1991.

Pliny the Younger. *The Letters of the Younger Pliny.* Translated by Betty Radice. Baltimore: Penguin, 1963.

Puech, Émile, and Joe Zias. "Le Tombeau de Zacharie et Siméon au monument funéraire dit d'Absalom dans la vallée de Josaphat." *Revue Biblique* 110, no. 3 (2003): 321–35.

Quintilian. *The Lesser Declamations*. Translated by D. R. Shackleton Bailey. 2 vols. Loeb Classical Library. Cambridge, MA: Harvard University Press, 2006.

Reimarus, Hermann Samuel. *Fragments*. Edited by C. Talbert. Translated by R. Fraser. Minneapolis: Fortress, 1970.

Richardson, Peter. *Building Jewish in the Roman East*. Waco: Baylor University Press, 2004.

Robinson, J. A. T. "Elijah, John and Jesus: An Essay in Detection." *New Testament Studies* 4 (1958): 263–81.

Sanders, E. P. *Jesus and Judaism*. Minneapolis: Fortress, 1985.

———. *Jewish Law from Jesus to the Mishnah*. Philadelphia: Trinity, 1990.

———. *Judaism: Practice & Belief, 63 BCE–66 CE*. Harrisburg, PA: Trinity Press International, 1992.

———. *The Historical Figure of Jesus*. London: Penguin, 1993.

Sanders, E. P., and M. Davies. *Studying the Synoptic Gospels*. London: SCM Press, 1989.

Schweitzer, Albert. *The Quest of the Historical Jesus*. New York: Collier, 1968.

Sherwin-White, A. N. *The Letters of Pliny: A Historical and Social Commentary*. Oxford: Clarendon, 1985.

Smith, Morton. *Jesus the Magician: Charlatan or Son of God?* Berkeley: Ulysses Press, 1998.

Spivey, Robert A., and D. Moody Smith. *Anatomy of the New Testament*. 5th ed. Upper Saddle River, NJ: Prentice Hall, 1995.

Stanton, G. *The Gospels and Jesus*. 2nd ed. Oxford: Oxford University Press, 2002.

Strecker, Christian. "Jesus and the Demoniacs." Pages 117–33 in *The Social Setting of Jesus and the Gospels*. Edited by W. Stegemann, B. Malina, and G. Theissen. Minneapolis: Fortress, 2002.

Tabor, James. *The Jesus Dynasty: The Hidden History of Jesus, His Royal Family, and the Birth of Christianity*. New York: Simon & Schuster, 2006.

Tacitus. *The Annals of Imperial Rome*. Translated by M. Grant. Rev. ed. New York: Penguin, 1971.

Taylor, Joan E. "The Garden of Gethsemane: Not the Place of Jesus' Arrest." *Biblical Archaeology Review* 21, no. 4 (1995): 26–35, 62.

———. *The Immerser: John the Baptist within Second Temple Judaism*. Grand Rapids: Eerdmans, 1997.

Theissen, Gerd. *The Shadow of the Galilean*. Minneapolis: Fortress, 1987.

Theissen, Gerd, and A. Merz. *The Historical Jesus*. Minneapolis: Fortress, 1996.

Thielicke, Helmut. *A Little Exercise for Young Theologians.* Grand Rapids: Eerdmans, 1962.

Throckmorton, Burton H. *Gospel Parallels: A Comparison of the Synoptic Gospels, NRSV Edition.* 5th ed. Nashville: Thomas Nelson, 1992.

Twain, Mark. *The Innocents Abroad.* Signet Classics. New York: Penguin Putnam, 1966.

Twelftree, Graham H. *Jesus the Miracle Worker: A Historical & Theological Study.* Downers Grove, IL: InterVarsity, 1999.

Vanauken, Sheldon. *A Severe Mercy.* New York: Harper & Row, 1977.

Webb, R. L. *John the Baptizer and Prophet: A Sociohistorical Study.* Sheffield: JSOT Press, 1991.

———. "John the Baptist and His Relationship to Jesus." Pages 179–230 in *Studying the Historical Jesus: Evaluations of the State of Current Research.* Edited by Bruce Chilton and Craig Evans. Leiden: Brill, 1994.

Wenham, David. "'This Generation Will Not Pass . . .': A Study of Jesus' Future Expectation in Mark 13." Pages 127–50 in *Christ the Lord.* Edited by H. Rowdon. Downers Grove, IL: InterVarsity, 1982.

Wilcox, David. *Airstream.* What Are Records? 2008.

Wilson, Steven G. *Related Strangers: Jews and Christians, 70–170 CE.* Minneapolis: Augsburg Fortress, 1995.

Wright, N. T. *The New Testament and the People of God.* Minneapolis: Fortress, 1992.

———. *Jesus and the Victory of God.* Minneapolis: Fortress, 1996.

———. *The Challenge of Jesus: Rediscovering Who Jesus Was and Is.* Downers Grove, IL: InterVarsity, 1999.

———. *The Resurrection of the Son of God.* Minneapolis: Fortress, 2003.

———. *Surprised by Hope: Rethinking Heaven, the Resurrection, and the Mission of the Church.* New York: HarperCollins, 2008.

Yeats, William Butler. "The Second Coming." Page 19 in *Michael Robartes and the Dancer.* Churchtown, Dundrum, Australia: Cuala Press, 1920.

Yoder, John Howard. *The Politics of Jesus.* Grand Rapids: Eerdmans, 1972.

Zertal, Idith, and Akiva Eldar. *Lords of the Land: The War over Israel's Settlements in the Occupied Territories, 1967–2007.* New York: Nation Books, 2007.